Richard Grenville and
the Lost Colony of Roanoke

D0613429

Richard Grenville and the Lost Colony of Roanoke

ANDREW GABRIEL-POWELL

McFarland & Company, Inc., Publishers

Jefferson, North Carolina

LIBRARY OF CONGRESS CATALOGUING-IN-PUBLICATION DATA

Names: Gabriel-Powell, Andrew, author.
Title: Richard Grenville and the Lost Colony of Roanoke / Andrew
  Gabriel-Powell.
Description: Jefferson, North Carolina : McFarland & Company,
  Inc., 2016. | Includes bibliographical references and index.
Identifiers: LCCN 2016039317 | ISBN 9781476665719 (softcover :
  acid free paper) ∞
Subjects: LCSH: Roanoke Colony. | Roanoke Island (N.C.)—His-
  tory—16th century. | Grenville, Richard, Sir, 1541?-1591. | Ship
  captains—Great Britain—Biography.
Classification: LCC F229 .G13 2016 | DDC 975.6/175—dc23
LC record available at https://lccn.loc.gov/2016039317

BRITISH LIBRARY CATALOGUING DATA ARE AVAILABLE

ISBN (print) 978-1-4766-6571-9
ISBN (ebook) 978-1-4766-2668-0

Front cover: Sir Richard Grenville, unknown artist, oil on canvas,
1571, 41¾" × 28⅞" (1060 mm × 733 mm) (National Portrait
Gallery, London); *background* Map of Roanoke, North Carolina
coast (Library of Congress)

Printed in the United States of America

McFarland & Company, Inc., Publishers
  Box 611, Jefferson, North Carolina 28640
    www.mcfarlandpub.com

For
Jennifer Lynn Gabriel-Powell
Sunrise: July 23, 1979–Sunset: March 30, 2014

Moonbeam,
Thank you for the 147 days we spent apart,
but never lost for each other,
and for the 527 days we spent together,
always lost in each other…

Our time will come again
your Celt

"Historians desiring to write the actions of men, ought to set down the simple truth...."
—Sir Walter Raleigh

Table of Contents

Acknowledgments

I give my biggest thanks to Sir Richard Grenville for providing the inspiration and determination never to give up, even under the most trying circumstances.

Further acknowledgments go to the Lost Colony Research Group (LCRG) of whose principals I thank: Roberta Estes for her considerable help on the subject of DNA, Anne Poole for her wisdom and assistance in sourcing documents, and the honorable George Ray for his benevolence and constant support. Mentions too for Dawn Taylor (thanks for the biscuits); Baylus Brooks, (for the debates); and fellow digging companions Alex Davis and Sharon Broward (for the "Wooderferds").

I also thank Professor Mark Horton of the University of Bristol (England) for undertaking the role of Archaeologist on the LCRG Hatteras Island excavations that were to prove significant in our understanding of the lost colony story. A special mention however, must go to the Continental Airline pilots whose skill during some of the worst tornadoes and thunderstorms the eastern United States of America has ever seen, got me home safely in April 2011.

For the LCRG's 2012 archaeological excavation, I thank Principal Investigator Professor "Charlie" Ewen of East Carolina University. On a personal note, I also thank him for his fateful choice of Project Archaeologist that year because it introduced me to the woman who was to become my gorgeous wife, Jennifer Gabriel-Powell, a woman I later lost in the most tragic of circumstances, and to whose memory this book is dedicated.

Back in England, thanks must go to David Carter of Nimrod Research for his work on the history of the Grenville manor houses in Bideford, and period re-enactor Peter Hood for his superior knowledge of early English weapons and social commentary. I also thank Martin Horler, Liveryman at the Worshipful Company of Painters and Stainers, for his assistance in searching the Guild's records for references to John White, Painter, and Governor of the lost colony of Roanoke. In addition to the above, I must thank Dr. Kim Sloan, Curator of the Department of prints and drawings at the British Museum, and Clive Cheesman, Richmond Herald of the Royal College of Arms, for sharing their correspondence, and answering my many questions.

Finally, I give thanks to my proofreaders and favorite critics: Yasmin Olins-Dixon and Jennifer Gabriel-Powell; and "Grenvillers" Carolyn Hinton (for the GRAFTAs), "Queen Elizabeth" Natalie Curtis, Bideford Town Cryer Jim Weeks, Videographer Tony Koorlander, and everyone else who supported our cause.

Preface

In 2006, a visitor from Manteo, the town situated near the site of the lost colonists' foothold on Roanoke Island, North Carolina, arrived unannounced at the Town Hall of Bideford, England. His mission, to present the town with a gift marking more than twenty years of friendship between the two towns, an association Manteo had instigated following their research into Bideford's founding role in the story of the lost colony of Roanoke. Rather embarrassingly, the Town Council could find no record of this "Twinning," as we English call such arrangements. This was of course, food for the international media, who quickly labelled Bideford as "the town that forgot it was twinned," and, more unkindly, entitled the moment under the headline: "What a clock up," in reference to the clock that represented the gift. Bideford's embarrassment reputedly gave Manteo's economy a significant tourism boost that year.

It was not until a small group of the more cognitive of Bideford's Commissioners visited Manteo on a fact-finding mission that the significance of the American interest was finally realized. It turned out that Bideford's prodigal son, and Lord of the Manor, Sir Richard Grenville, had been intrinsically involved in an attempt to establish an English colony on Roanoke Island some thirty-three years before the *Mayflower* had set sail for America in 1620. Incredible as it may seem, the story of the attempt, like Sir Richard, had simply become forgotten history back in England.

Fired up by the visit to Manteo, and now elected as Mayor of Bideford, I attempted to raise the profile of the lost colony story by galvanizing the search for their ancestors and descendants in England. Despite the quest making headlines in the national press, the response was perplexingly poor. I decided therefore to turn my attentions towards studying the historical evidence, principally with the intention of reaching a greater understanding of what actually took place more than 425 years ago.

During my search for this evidence, a private collector of antiquarian books kindly gave me access to his collection. Among this collection were two first editions of Richard Hakluyt's *The Principall Navigations, Voiages, and Discoveries of the English Nation*, one from 1589, and the other from 1600. Given such a rare opportunity, and with the collector's generous but anonymous permission, I found myself compelled to transcribe the sections that related to the Roanoke voyages.

Further research over the next seven years led me to uncover additional evidence, both in this private collection, and in a variety of national and academic resources. While some of these sources are undoubtedly secondary in nature, many of them contained information from original documents whose whereabouts today remains either unknown, or have simply proved inaccessible to the author.

At some point in all this research, I became aware of two important factors that stood to influence the direction of my research:

1. The pivotal research of David Beers Quinn, and;

2. the realization that although the Charter to settle America was in Sir Walter Raleigh's name, there had been a rather more substantial involvement, perhaps an almost obsessive one, by his cousin, Sir Richard Grenville.

In consideration of the first factor, having started my research with Hakluyt and essentially allowing that to lead me to other sources, I had, by the time I discovered the work of Beers Quinn, already accumulated more than four years research from my own endeavors. These endeavors also included first-hand knowledge gained through taking part in a number of archaeological excavations focused on searching for evidence of the lost colony. I had also enjoyed privileged access to a number of newly discovered documents in England. I elected therefore, to continue my own path of discovery, knowing that by doing so, rightly or wrongly, I was eliminating the potential for influence by Beers Quinn, but perhaps also by more current works, works that, I might add, commonly drew their foundation from his research. With nothing but respect intended towards my peers and Beers Quinn, this book has therefore evolved to become an entirely fresh, unsponsored study of the lost colony story, and one of the very few to give the work of Beers Quinn only passing mention.

Regarding the second factor, it became clear very early on in my research that Raleigh's direct involvement with the colony's fortunes had been relatively minor, while Grenville, a man much maligned by history, had evidently worked tirelessly to ensure its success. Indeed, I note it is sad to record that until the publication of this book, Grenville's singular and lasting moment of fame has remained his death, when, in life, he had clearly done so much more. Given his extraordinary efforts on behalf of Raleigh and the other investors, it seems fitting to expand upon his involvement through the pages of this book, and in doing so, provide the foundation for his overdue credit.

At this point, I wish to raise the subject of why the Hakluyt texts appear in this book, albeit in their earliest form. I believe it a worthwhile exercise; I say this because I am convinced they should be more widely accessible than their current preserve of academic halls and obscure internet resources, not least because they represent a truly remarkable record of one of the most extraordinary events in English history.

Portrait of Sir Richard Grenville (author's photograph, courtesy of Bideford Town Council, England).

To assist in their modern interpretation, I examined a range of English dictionaries and thesauri. Principal among these was the *Oxford English Dictionary*, referenced in the notes to chapters as "Source: OED," and an excellent website on the works of Shakespeare, www.shakespeareswords.com. I also spent a considerable amount of time peering over a plethora of maps of the North Carolina coast, ranging from John White's map of 1585, through to the latest LIDAR and GPR surveys. Coupled with some excellent geological and other specialized surveys, they proved invaluable in identifying the modern day location of many of the villages, inlets, and other geographical references contained within the Hakluyt texts.

My final note on the texts relates to the spelling of personal names, islands, and villages. They are inconsistent. This is because, in Elizabethan England, the phonetics of the spoken word often determined their written interpretation.

I have no doubt that some of the new discoveries I have made, and the resulting conclusions drawn from them, will challenge established beliefs and hypotheses. However, while it is not an academic qualification, this work does represent the first time anyone from the town where much of the history surrounding the colony evolved has stepped forward to give their interpretation of the story. In any consideration, it is almost certainly the first work in perhaps sixty years to return purely to the earliest known references in an attempt to re-examine and perhaps re-evaluate the story of Sir Richard Grenville and his involvement in the mystery of the lost colony of Roanoke.

ONE

Prologue

For the benefit of those who are unfamiliar with the story of England's attempts to colonize America, it all began when Italian explorer Giovanni Caboto. John Cabot, as the English knew him, set sail from Bristol, England, and become the first European since the Vikings to make land-fall in what is now Newfoundland, a province of Canada. He arrived there on June 24, 1497. Yet, it was another sixty years before anyone in England took much notice of this new land, and only then because they thought it might offer a short cut to the Spice Islands, India and China.

It was Martin Frobisher who finally convinced a consortium of merchantmen to finance his voyage in search of the Northwest Passage to India. He set sail with just thirty-five men and three tiny ships weighing between ten and twenty-five tons each. Despite venturing twice more over the following years and with ever-increasing flotillas of ships and supplies, Frobisher never once sailed south along the coast towards America, his almost obsessive focus being the elusive Northwest Passage.

While Frobisher's voyages were grabbing all the attention, English financiers were becoming aware that Spain in particular was accruing enormous wealth from lands much further south. Indeed, Spain already dominated the Caribbean and southern regions of the continent, with Mexico City becoming a metropolitan center of trade, politics and culture, and San Agustin a major port.

To the north, France had also attempted to establish missionary and trading posts in what is now Canada; Tadoussac had become a small but vital French outpost on the St. Lawrence River. Both nations therefore had established colonies on the Atlantic coast of the Americas while England, with all its aspirations of expansion, had yet to arrive.

It was Sir Humphrey Gilbert, half-brother to Sir Walter Raleigh, a cousin of Sir Richard Grenville, who finally received at the tender age of forty, Letters Patent authorizing him to plant an English colony in America. He assembled a fleet, which sailed from Dartmouth on September 26, 1578. However, storms forced the ships to seek refuge in Plymouth, just a few miles down the coast, until November 19. With winter closing in, Gilbert abandoned the attempt, but his efforts were enough to encourage his brothers, Walter and Carew Raleigh, to join him in the exploration of America.

It took Gilbert over five years to muster a second attempt, this time sailing from Plymouth on June 11, 1583. The voyage did not start well. One ship, the *Barke Ralegh*, owned by his half-brother Sir Walter Raleigh, turned back almost immediately because of illness. Nevertheless, Gilbert and the other ships arrived at St. John's, Newfoundland, on August 3, the same year, and took possession of the land for Queen Elizabeth and England two days later. His act was, in effect, the first overseas territory of what became the British Empire.

Because it was small and could therefore navigate the harbors and creeks, Gilbert chose to explore the land he had claimed, in the *Squirrel*, a ship of a mere 10 tons, rather than the *Delight*, his own 120-ton flagship. On August 29, the *Delight* ran aground with the loss of 100 lives and many of Gilbert's records. Perhaps because of this, Gilbert chose to remain aboard the *Squirrel* rather than transfer to a much larger ship, the *Golden Hinde*, despite the pleas of his men, for the arduous voyage back to England. On the evening of Monday September 9, 1583, and in heavy swell, the *Squirrel*, along with Sir Humphrey, disappeared.

Gilbert's death must have deeply moved his half-brother, Sir Walter Raleigh. The latter had voyaged with Sir Humphrey in the expedition of 1578 and had fitted out a ship intended to participate in the great voyage of 1583 to Newfoundland. Thus, when Gilbert's Patent was due to expire, Raleigh, being in high favor with Queen Elizabeth at the time, obtained a Charter which conferred to him the powers formerly enjoyed by Sir Humphrey Gilbert.

Much of the impetus to explore and settle America at this time had come from writers and academics. Men like George Peckham and Richard Hakluyt wrote long promotional pieces, advertisements if you wish, urging the Queen and the wealthy of England to support exploration and colonization. Peckham's work was not exclusively about exploration, for, as he inferred in his subtitle, he would "Briefly set down her highness's lawful title thereunto, and the great and manifold commodities, that is likely to grow thereby...." He concluded the title with the enticing words: "Together with the easiness and shortness of the voyage."[1] An obvious encouragement to persuade a reluctant Queen that England should expand its horizons and its coffers, before France, and in particular, Spain, had carved up the new world between them. Academic Richard Hakluyt chose to write a more practical thesis on the subject of exploration and settlement of America. His promotional piece, written in 1584, entitled *A Particular Discourse Concerning the Great Necessity and Manifold Commodities that are Like to Grow to this Realm of England by the Western Discoveries Lately Attempted*,[2] urged Queen Elizabeth to support English colonies and convince rich businessmen to invest in them. Hakluyt's work, later known simply as *A Discourse Concerning Western Planting*, is particularly fascinating as it includes his list of what he considered the necessary personnel and supplies for a colony to succeed, something no doubt not lost on Raleigh's aspirations.

Raleigh, with his Charter now duly extended to permit him to explore and colonize farther south towards the Spanish colonies in Florida, and with the Queen and numerous financial backers in tow, the scene was now set for the English attempt to settle America. In so doing, Raleigh was to involve his cousin Sir Richard Grenville, over a hundred military men, numerous landed gentry, at least two dozen ships and their crews, several Native American tribes and at least 119 civilian men, women and children.

Two

An Introduction to
Sir Richard Grenville

Sir Richard Grenville was born the son of Sir Roger Grenville and Thomasine Cole, daughter of the same Cole family we can now also connect to John White, Painter and Governor of Virginia.[1]

Sir Richard's date of birth has been widely quoted as occurring anywhere between 1540 and 1543. Yet his year of birth, at least, is obvious to anyone who has seen and understood the Latin inscription on his portrait.[2] The inscription on the painting reads "AN. DNI. 1571. AETATIS SUAE. 29" and translates as "1571 A.D. in his age 29," meaning Grenville was twenty-nine years old in 1571, and therefore born in 1542. Yet we can go further by determining his birthday from the final line of his grandfather's elaborate six-page will, written and proved in 1550/51. It concludes "…et XV die junii ultimo predictus idem Richardus GREYNFELD sunt etato otto annorum et non amplius" (…on the 15th June last [1550] the aforesaid same Richard GREYNFELD was aged eight years and no more). Sir Richard Grenville was therefore born on June 15, 1542.[3]

As to where Grenville was born, this appears to have been resolved in 2013 when David Carter, with assistance from the author, published a research document concluding he could only have been born in the original family manor house, in the town of Bideford.[4]

Grenville was one of three brothers. Brother John died in infancy, but his place of burial is unknown, while Charles appears in the Register of Burials at Buckland Monachorum Parish Church on August 28, 1544.

In 1545, less than a year after losing the last of his brothers, Richard's father drowned while serving as Captain on board King Henry VIII's ill-fated flagship, the *Mary Rose*. The ship sank in extraordinary circumstances, just outside the entrance to Portsmouth harbor.

These family tragedies meant that at just three years of age, all Richard Grenville had left to call family was his mother Thomasine.

The site of the original thirteenth-century manor house of the Grenville family in Bideford. Although the building that stands there today dates largely from the seventeenth to nineteenth century, it contains significant evidence of its earlier origins (photograph by David Carter, Docton Court Gallery, Appledore, Devon, England).

For the following fourteen years of his life, Grenville disappears into obscurity. We do know that his mother re-married, to Thomas Arundell and the family moved to Clifton, on the Cornish side of the river Tamar near the village of St. Germans. The Arundells went on to have nine children, the first of whom was eight years younger than Grenville, as a consequence of which, he probably led a relatively isolated childhood before finally resurfacing in 1559 to be admitted to the Inner Temple of London to study law at the tender age of seventeen.

In 1562, at the age of twenty, we have the first inkling of a possibly volatile temper when we find Grenville involved in an "Act of Affray" on November 19, which resulted in the death of his antagonist, Roger Bannester. The incident took place near St. Clement Dane church in the Strand, London. What the argument was about we do not know, but there were several witnesses on both sides. Thomas Allen, a yeoman of the deceased, reported that Grenville had killed his antagonist by, quote, "running him throughe wit his sworde."[5] Even back in the brutal days of Elizabethan England such actions could readily have resulted in the death penalty; yet, whether by having the right connections or simply perhaps for being highly regarded in his studies, Grenville obtained a pardon for his rash actions, albeit after a discreet period in hiding.

The following year Grenville became a Member of Parliament for Dunheved, Launceston. He remained in office, serving various constituencies in Cornwall, in all three Parliaments called before his death in 1591.[6]

Early in 1565, Grenville married Mary St. Leger, the daughter of John St. Leger of Annery, Weare Giffard, a house and family long disappeared from our heritage. Although we do not know where or when the ceremony took place, the Parish Church for Annery was in nearby Monkleigh, a few miles south of Bideford, therefore, this would have been the most likely setting. It was evidently a happy marriage, for the Grenvilles were to go on to have at least eight children. Although incomplete, it is perhaps worth recording a little of their fate.

The Grenville's first child, Roger, born sometime late in 1565, must have died in infancy. A possible record of his death may be a reference in the Kilkhampton parish records for December 10, that year. Happier news came in the form of their second child, Mary. Born in 1567 she went on to marry Arthur Tremayne of Collacombe, at Kilkhampton on June 2, 1586. The marriage produced a prolific twenty-one children. The first two, Edmund, born 1587, and Digory, born 1588, appear in the baptismal records of St. Mary's Parish Church, Bideford. Mary died in June 1608 and lies buried at Lamerton church, in Devon. Bernard, Sir Richard's heir, was also born in 1567, but whether he was a twin brother to Mary is unknown. In 1570, Catherine arrived. She married Justinian Abbot of Hartland Abbey, and had one daughter, Mary, who died young. Catherine reputedly died in 1603, but according to her mother's will of 1619, she was in fact still alive at that time.

Son John, born 1571, was very much in the mould of his father who made him Captain of one of his ships at the early age of just 18. He died, probably from some form of sickness, in 1595 while captaining a ship on Sir Walter Raleigh's ill-fated voyage to Guyana. In 1573, another daughter, Bridget, was born to the Grenville family. She married John Weekes, one time rector of Shirwell parish who later became the Bishop of Bristol Cathedral. Her husband erected a monument to her, which still stands in the cathedral today. She died on February 14, 1627.

Rebecca the seventh child of the Grenvilles arrived in 1577 but died aged twelve, on June 9, 1589, possibly from an outbreak of influenza. She appears in the Burial register of St. Mary's Parish Church, Bideford. As an aside, whatever she died from, probably also claimed the life of the Grenville's indentured black servant, Lawrence.

The eighth and last child born to the Grenville family was Ursula, in 1581. She was born at a time when her mother was aged around forty and died unmarried in 1643, an unusual circumstance for someone of noble birth. Further investigation of the circumstances surrounding her spinsterhood revealed that in her mother's will of 1619, she is referred to with the following, somewhat astonishing commentary:

> Item: My will and desire is that my daughter Ursula shall after my decease remaine and be under the government and tuition of my daughters Katherine ABBOTT and Bridgett GRENVILE and they to have and receave her yeerly rent or annuytie of theretie pounds from her brother (Bernard) for her maintenance.[7]

Ursula must therefore have had a debilitating condition. Given the age of her mother at the time of her birth, and the use of the words "government and tuition" at a time when Ursula was already 38 years of age, it is conceivable that Ursula may be one of the first recorded Down's syndrome children in English history.

A family man Grenville may have been, but in 1566, he left his pregnant wife to join other Englishmen travelling to fight the Ottoman Empire. He returned to England in 1568 and began to focus on attempts to colonize the province of Munster in Ireland. In 1569, he duly took up joint ownership of the Kerrycurrihy estate with his father-in-law. It was the first of numerous acquisitions Grenville was to make in Munster over the remainder of his life. There can be no doubt that Grenville's experience of colonizing Ireland would have been of value to Raleigh in his later attempts to settle America.

It was not long after Grenville began his adventures in settling Ireland that he and his family found themselves besieged at Cork by an Irish uprising. It is at this point we realize Mary must have been an equal match for Grenville, for she and their young family managed to avoid capture while he slipped away to England in search of reinforcements.

For all his exploits in Ireland, Grenville's interests in his home town of Bideford were never far from his mind. The area had become rundown; the market and associated fair largely having ceased to take place. If Bideford was to be the home of the Grenville family, then, as Lords of the Manor, this was clearly an unacceptable state of affairs. In 1572, three hundred years after his ancestors secured the first Charter, Grenville applied for a new Charter for the town. Whether this was a deliberate tercentennial act of celebration, we do not know. What is certain though is that the new Charter, officially granted December 16, 1573, whilst making great play on the structure of the towns governing body of Aldermen and Burghers, their powers, and the resurrection of the market and fair also established Bideford as a revenue earning port. Grenville evidently had a clear vision for the future of Bideford, not least for the potential revenue he and the town might gain from its proximity to the Irish estates both he, Raleigh, and numerous other landed gentry, were developing in the Province of Munster, a mere 140 nautical miles from Bideford.[8]

To get such sweeping powers for the new governing body for the town, Grenville had to obtain consent from the local landowners and merchants. To do this, he was obliged to ensure their businesses remained profitable. Grenville therefore, promptly chose John Salterne (a Merchant Venturer), as his Mayor, and other town nobles Thomas Leach, Aldred Stockombe and Anthony Honey to join him as Aldermen; while Richard Burgin "Gent," John Suzan "Gent," George Stafford "Gent," William Davie, John Short, Thomas Meager and Raimond Anthony served as his seven Burgesses. Perhaps his only concession being to allow the newly elected Mayor to choose Richard Willott "Gent" as the private Alderman to his Mayoral Chamber, in effect Willott became Bideford's first Town Clerk. The council sat for the first time on December 10, 1574.

Grenville was not finished with the fine tuning of his Charter and secured a further covenant, dated September 4, 1575, which granted his family the revenues and profits within the Manor of Bideford "excepting fee-farm rent of 10s 6d per annum and the office of Port Reeve."[9] As an aside, one wonders when the office of the Port Reeve was dissolved for it does not exist today. Nevertheless, in return for this grant, Grenville gave the town various rights including the "use of the chapel standing at the west end of the bridge and ground whereof certain limekilns sometime stood, and where a quay, or wharf, is now lately builded."[10]

On March 22, 1574, Grenville presented a petition to the Court of Queen Elizabeth to seek approval for what amounted to a round-the-world voyage. Grenville had already purchased a ship, the *Castle of Comfort*, at Plymouth four years earlier, specifically for the purpose. Grenville stated that the voyage's primary intention was to find a shorter trading route to the Spice Islands of the East Indies via what the Elizabethans called the "South Sea," today the Pacific Ocean. With hindsight, it might have served his purpose better if he had not mentioned that the petition would provide an opportunity to attack Spanish settlements and shipping found along the coast of South America and that these acts would most likely finance the voyage. Ultimately, the combination of his choice of ship, one noted in the State Papers as "never once found in peaceful trade,"[11] and the belief that a delicate but workable relationship still existed with Spain probably amounted to a simple case of bad timing on the part of Grenville. The petition failed.

It is a contentious claim to make, but, in considering what Sir Francis Drake subsequently conducted three years later, the similarities between Drake's voyage and Grenville's petition are startling. Small comfort for Grenville but at least his application is endorsed "Mr. Grynfolds (Grenville) voyadge/discoverie of a ... passage to Cathay and ye E. Indies"[12] and signed in Lord Burghley's own hand, thus confirming his was the first round the world voyage planned by the English.

With the funds built up in preparation for his South Sea venture now obsolete of purpose, Grenville set about expanding his property portfolio. Two purchases enlarged his holdings at Bideford. They included the neighboring Manor of Lancras, known today as Landcross, and the hamlet of Upcott Snarland, known today simply as Upcott. His purchase of Lancras was subject to bitter legal dispute, which Grenville eventually won.

In 1577, Grenville became High Sheriff of Cornwall. At about this time he also took possession of Lundy Island from his father-in-law John St. Leger, which he at once began to fortify in the expectation that a fight with the Spanish was inevitable. Lundy's strategic importance had obviously not been lost on Grenville, sitting as it does at the mouth of the Bristol Channel and commanding the approach to England's heart.

Grenville was often in London on parliamentary or court duties, and probably made social calls on his cousin Raleigh among others. Exactly where he lived while in London, like so much of his life, has remained something of a mystery, however, documents in the State Papers make it clear he resided at the St. Leger's family home near St. Olave's in Southwark. The house was formerly owned by the abbot of St. Augustine's, Canterbury and according to John Stow's Survey of London, 1598, described as "Sentlegar: The Bridge house...." It was adjacent to "a large plot of ground, on the banke of the riuer Thames: containing diuers large buildings, for stowage of things necessary towards reparation of the said bridge."[13] It is no longer there.

Of the other Grenville family homes, what was once termed "Old Place House"[14] in the town of Bideford was the original manor house of the family which Grenville appears to have last used sometime after completing his new home, referred to as "Place House," on the nearby quayside in 1585.[15] The family also owned a manor house at Stowe, near Kilkhampton in Cornwall.

The one other house few recognize as having belonged to the family is Buckland Abbey, a location so intrinsically linked with Sir Francis Drake, yet a house the Grenville family owned for nearly forty years prior. Grenville's grandfather, in fact, acquired the abbey towards the end of 1541. He and his grandson were to spend a substantial amount of money rebuilding and remodeling the abbey. Quite how long he and his family spent there though is debatable; given the number of Grenville children and their regular addition to the family, it is surprising that only Bridget's christening is noted at Buckland on November 1, 1578. Quite why Grenville finally sold the Abbey in 1580 after spending so much money on it is also open to conjecture. Its proximity to Plymouth and Sir Francis Drake, someone whom, although related, Grenville had every reason to despise, was probably enough. He sold Buckland Abbey to Christopher Harris for £3,400 in 1580, who in turn sold it to Sir Francis Drake barely six months later. One wonders whether Harris was merely acting as intermediary between Grenville and Drake.

Over the next few years, Grenville busied himself with his estates in Ireland, serving his country as a regular investigator into piracy, and in curtailing the practicing of the Roman Catholic faith. The latter conducted with particular vengeance, most notably at Launceston in Cornwall where he presided over the hanging of at least one unfortunate priest. Thus, by the time his cousin Sir Walter Raleigh had secured his Charter for the New World, Grenville had become a wealthy and respected member of the landed gentry, and one who was already highly regarded by Queen Elizabeth.

THREE

The Voyage of Amadas and Barlowe, 1584

With his Charter secured and extended, Raleigh set about planning his first expedition to America. His choice of Captains for the journey probably extended from his connections with the west of England since both Arthur Barlowe (Plymouth) and Philip Amadas (Launceston) hail from there. It is perhaps worth noting that the rather obscure Amadas family of Launceston also provided Joan Amadas who became matriarch to the noted Hawkins dynasty. This latter point could lead one to conclude that Philip Amadas may have received his maritime apprenticeship from the Hawkins. Nevertheless, it fell to Captain Arthur Barlowe to record the voyage:

The 27. day of April in the yeere of our redemption, 1584 we departed the west of England[1] with two barkes, well furnished with men and victuals, having recevued our last and perfect directions by your letters, confirming the former instructions, and commandements delivered by your selfe at our leaving the river of Thames.[2] And I thinke it a matter both unnecessarie, for the manifest discoverie of the country, as also for tediousnes sake, to remember unto you the diurnall[3] of our course, sailing thither, and returning: only I have presumed to present unto you this briefe discourse, by which you may judge how profitable this land is likely to succeede, as well to your selfe (by whose direction and charge, and by whose servants this our discoverie hath bene performed) as also to her highnes, and the common wealth, in which we hope your wisdome will be satisfied, considering, that as much by us hath bene brought to light, as by those small meanes, and number of men we had, could any way have been expected, or hoped for.[4]

The tenth of May, we arrived at the Canaries, and the tenth of June in this present yeere, we were fallen with the islands of the West Indies, keeping a more south easterly course then was needefull, because we doubted that the current of the baye of Mexico, disbagging[5] betwene the Cape of Florida, and the Havana, had bene of greater force then afterwards we found it to be.

At which islands we found the aire very unwholsome, and our men grewe for the most part ill disposed: so that having refreshed our selves with sweete water, and fresh victuall, we departed the twelfth daye after our arrivall there. These islands, with the rest adjoining, are so well known to your selfe, and to many others, as I will not trouble you, with the remembrance of them.

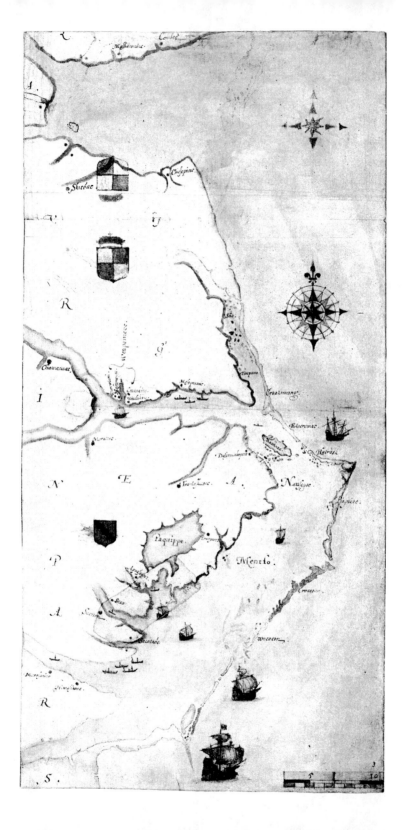

The second of July, we found shole water, which smelt so sweetely, and was so strong a smell, as if we had bene in the midst of some delicate garden, abounding with all kinde of odouferous flowers, by which we were assured, that the land could not be farre distant: and keeping good watch, and bearing but slacke saile, the fourth of the same moneth, we arrived upon the coast, which we supposed to be a continent, and firme land,[6] and wee sailed along the same, a hundred and twentie English miles, before we could finde any entrance, or river, issuing into the sea.[7]

The first that appeared unto us, we entired, though not without some difficultie, and cast anker about three harquebushot[8] within the havens mouth, on the left hande of the same: and after thankes given to God for our safe arrivall thither, we manned our boates and went to viewe the land next adjoining[9] and to take possession of the same, in the right of the Queenes most excellent majestie, as rightfull Queene and Princesse of the same, and after delivered the same over to your use, according to her majesties grant, and letters patents, under her highnes great seale.[10]

Which being performed, according to the ceremonies used in such enterprises, wee viewed the land about us, being whereas the first landed, very sandie, and lowe towards the water, but so full of grapes, as the very beating, and surge of the sea overflowed them, of which we founde such plentie, as well there, as in all places else, both on the sande, and on the greene soile on the hils, as in the plaines, as well on every little shrubbe, as also climbing towards the toppes of the high Cedars, that I thinke in all the world the like abundance is not to be found: and myselfe having seene those partes of Europe that most abound, find such difference, as were incredible to be written.[11]

We passed from the seaside, towardes the toppes of those hils next adjoining, being but of meane height, and from thence we behelde the sea on both sides to the North, and to the South, finding no ende any of both waies. This lande laye stretching itselfe to the West, which after we founde to be but an island of twentie leagues long,[12] and not above five miles broade. Under the banke or hill, whereon we stoode, we beheld the vallies replenished with goodly Cedar trees, and having discharged our harquebushot, such a flock of Cranes (the most part white) arose under us, with such a crye redoubled by many ecchoes, as if an armie had showted alltogether.[13]

This Island had many goodly woods, and full of Deere, Conies, Hares, and Fowle, even in the middest of summer, in incredible abundance.[14] The woods are not such as you finde in Bohemia, Moscovia,[15] or Hyrcania,[16] barren and fruitlesse, but the highest and reddest Cedars of the world, farre bettering the Cedars of the Acores,[17] of the India's or of Lybanus,[18] Pines, Cypress, Sassafras, the Lentisk or the tree that beareth the Masticke,[19] the tree that beareth the rinde of Black Sinamon, of which Master Winter brought from the streights of Magellane, and many other of excellent smell, and qualitie.

We remained by the side of this Island two whole daies, before we sawe any people of the countrey: the third daye we escried one small boate rowing towards us, having in it three persons: this boate came to the landes side, foure harquebushot from our shippes, and there two of the people remaining, the thirde came along the shoare side towards us, and we being then all within board, he walked up and downe upon the point of the lande next unto us: then the Master and the Pilot of the Admirall, Simon Ferdinando, and the Captaine Philip Amadas, myselfe,[20] and others, rowed to the lande whose comming this fellowe attended, never making any shewe of feare, or doubt.

Opposite: **"Virginia Pars." John White's 1585 map of the area of the Outer Banks of North Carolina, the detail of which remains accurate more than 400 years later (© The Trustees of the British Museum).**

And after he had spoken of many things not understoode by us, we brought him with his owne good liking, aboard the shippes, and gave him a shirt, a hatte, and some other things, and made him taste of our wine, and our meate, which he liked very well: and after having viewed both barkes, he departed, and went to his owne boate againe, which he had left in a little Cove, or Creek adjoining: as soone as he was two boweshoote[21] into the water, hee fell to fishing, and in lesse than halfe an houre, he had laden his boate as deepe, as it could swimme, with which he came againe to the point of the lande, and there he divided his fishe into two partes, pointing one part to the shippe, and the other to the Pinesse: which after he had (as much as he might,) requited the former benefits received, he departed out of our sight.

The next day there came unto us divers boates and in one of them the King's brother, accompanied with fortie or fiftie men, very handsome, and goodly people, and in their behaviour as mannerly, and civil, as any of Europe. His name was Granganimeo, and the King is called Wingina, the countrey Wingandacoa, (and nowe by her majestie, Virginia,)[22] the manner of his coming was in this sorte: he left his boates altogether, as the first man did a little from the shippes by the shoare, and came along to the place over against the shippes, followed with fortie men.

When hee came to the place, his servants spread a long matte upon the grounde, on which he sate downe, and at the other ende of the matte, foure others of his companie did the like: the rest of his men stoode round about him, somewhat a farre off: when wee came to the shoare to him with our weapons, he never mooved from his place, nor any of the other foure, nor never mistrusted any harme to be offered from us, but sitting still, he beckoned us to come and sitte by him, which wee performed: and beeing sette, hee makes all signes of joy, and welcome, striking on his head, and his breast, and afterwardes on ours, to shewe we were all one, smiling, and making shewe the best hee could, of all love, and familiaritie.

After hee had made a long speech unto us, wee presented him with divers thinges, which hee receaved very joyfully and thankefully. None of his companie durst to speake one worde all the tyme: onely the foure which were at the other ende, spake one in anothers eare very softly.

The king is greatly obeyed, and his brothers, and children reverenced: the king himselfe in person was at our beeing there sore wounded, in a fight which he had with the King of the next countrey, called Wingina, and was shotte in two places through the bodye, and once cleane thorough the thigh, but yet he recovered: by reason whereof, and for that hee lay at the chiefe Town of the Countrey, beeing five dayes journeye off, wee sawe him not at all.

After wee had presented this his brother, with such things as we thought he liked, we likewise gave somewhat to the other that sate with him on the matte: but presently he arose, and tooke all from them, and put it into his owne basket, making signes and tokens, that all things ought to be delivered unto him, and the rest were but his servants, and followers.

A day or two after this, we fell to trading with them, exchanging some thinges we had for Chammoys, Buffe, and Deere skinnes: when we shewed him all our packet of merchandize, of all things that he saw, a bright tinne dishe most please him, which he presently tooke up, and clapt it before his breast, and after made a hole in the brimme thereof, and hung it about his necke, making signes, that it would defende him against his enemies arrowes: for those people maintaine a deadlie and terrible warre, with the people and king adjoining. We exchanged our tinne dishe for twentie skinnes, worth twentie crownes, or twentie nobles: and a copper kettle for fiftie skinnes, worth fiftie crownes. They offered us very good exchange for our hatchets, and axes, and for knives, and would have given anything for swordes: but we would not depart with any. After two or three daies, the kings brother came aboord the shippes, and dranke wine, and ate of our meate, and of our bread, and liked exceedingly thereof: and after a few daies overpassed, he brought his wife with him to the shippes, his daughter, and two or three little children: his wife was very well favoured, of meane stature, and very bashfull: she had on her backe a long cloke of leather, with the furre side next to her bodie, and before her a peece of the same: about her forehead, she had a broad bande of white Corall,[23] and so had her husband many times: in her eares she had bracelets of pearles, hanging downe to her middle, (whereof we delivered your Worship a little bracelet)[24] and those were of the bigness[25] of good pease.

The rest of her women of the better sorte, had pendants of copper, hanging in every eare: and some of the children of the Kings brother, and other Noblemen, have five or six in every eare: he himselfe had upon his head, a broad plate of golde or copper, for being unpolished, we knew not what metall it should be, neither would he by any meanes suffer us to take it off his head, but feeling it, it would bowe very easily. His apparell was as his wives, onely the women weare their haire long on both sides, and the men but on one. They are of colour yellowish, and their haire blacke for the most, and yet we sawe children that had very fine aburne[26] and chestnut colour haire.

After that these women had bene there, there came downe from all parts great store of people, bringing with them leather, corall, divers kindes of dies very excellent, and exchanged with us: but when Granganimeo, the Kings brother was present, none durst[27] to trade but himselfe, except such as weare redde peeces of copper on their heades, like himselfe: for that is the difference betweene the Noble men, and Governours of Countries, and the meaner sort. And we both noted there, and you have understood since by these men, which we brought home[28] that no people in the worlde carry more respect to their king, Nobilitie, and Governours, than these doe.

The king's brothers wife, when she came to us, as she did many times, she was followed with fortie of fiftie women alwaies: and when she came into the shippe, she left them all on lande, saving her two daughters, her nurse, and one or two more. The Kings brother alwaies kept this order, as many boates as he would come withall to the shippes, so many fires would he make on the shore a farre off, to the ende wee might understand with what strength, and companie he approached. Their boates are made of one tree, either of Pine, or of Pitch trees: a wood not commonly knowen to our people, nor found growing in England.

They have no edge tooles to make them withall: if they have any, they are very fewe, and those it seemes they had twentie yeeres since, which as those two men declared,[29] was out of a wrecke which happened upon their coast of some Christian ship being beaten that way by some storme, and outragious weather, whereof none of the people were saved, but onely the shippe, or some part of her, being cast upon the lande, out of whose sides they drewe the nailes and spikes, and with those they made their best instruments.[30] Their manner of making their boates is this: they burne downe some great tree, or take such as are winde fallen, and putting myrrhe, and rosen upon one side thereof, they sette fire into it, and, when it hath burnt it hollowe, they cutte out the coale with their shels, and everiwhere they would burne it deeper or wider, they laye on their gummes, which burneth away the timber, and by this meanes they fashion very fine boates, and such as will transport twentie men. Their oares are like scoopes, and many times they sette with long poles, as the depth serveth.

The kings brother had great liking of our armour, a sworde and divers other things, which we had: and offered to laye a great bore of pearles in gage[31] for them: but wee refused it for this time, because we would not make them knowe, that wee esteemed thereof, untill wee had understoode in what places of the countrey the pearle grewe: which nowe your Worshippe doth very well understand.

He was very just of his promise: for many times wee delivered him merchandize uppon his worde, but ever he came within the daye, and performed his promise. Hee sent us every daye a brace or two of fatte Buckes, Conies, Hares, Fishe, the best of the worlde, hee sent us divers kindes of fruites, Melons, Walnuts, Cucumbers, Gourdes, Pease, and diverse rootes, and fruites very excellent good, and of their Countrey corne, which is very white, faire, and well tasted, and groweth three times in five moneths: in Maye they sowe, in July they reape: in June they sowe, in August they reape: in July they sowe, in September they reape: onely they cast the corne into the ground, breaking a little of the soft turfe with a woodden mattocke, or pickeaxe: our selves prooved the soile, and put some of our pease into the ground, and in tenne daies they were of fourteene inches high: they have also Beanes very faire, of divers colours, and wonderfull plentie: some growing naturally, and some in their gardens, and so have they both wheat and oates.

The soile is the most plentifull, sweete, fruitfull, and wholsome of all the world: there are about fourteene severall sweete smelling timber trees, and the most part of their underwoods[32] are Bayes, and such like: they have those Okes that we have, but farre greater, and better.

After they had bene divers times aboord our shippes, my selfe, with seven more, went twentie mile into the River, that runneth toward the Citie of Skicoake, which River they call Occam[33]: and the evening following, we came to an Island, which they call Roanoak, distant from the harbour by which we entired, seven leagues,[34] and at the North ende thereof, was a village of nine houses built of Cedar, and fortified round about with sharpe trees, to keepe out their enemies, and the entrance into it made like a turne pike very artificially: when we came towards it, standing neere unto the waters side,[35] the wife of Granganimeo the Kings brother, came running out to meete us very cheerefully and friendly, her husband was not then in the village: some of her people she commanded to drawe our boate on the shoare, for the beating of the billoe[36]: others shee appointed to carry us on their backes to the dry ground, and others to bring our oares into the house for feare of stealing.

When we were come into the outher roome, having five roomes in her house, she caused us to sitte down by a great fire, and after tooke off our clothes, and washed them, and dried them againe: some of the women pulled off our stockings, and washed them, some washed our feete in warme water, and shee her self took great paines to see all thinges ordered to the best manner shee coulde, making great haste to dresse some meate for us to eate.

After we had thus dried our selves, she brought us into the inner roome, where shee set out the boord standing along the house, some wheate like ferment, sodden venison, and roasted, fishe sodden, boyled, and roasted, Melons rawe, and sodden, rootes of divers kindes, and divers fruites: their drinke is commonly water, but while the grape lasteth, they drinke wine[37] and for want of caskes to keepe it all the yeere after, they drinke water, but it is sodden with Ginger in it, and blacke sinamon, and sometimes sassaphras, and divers other wholesome, and medicinable hearbes and trees.

We were entertained with all love, and kindnes, and with as much bountie, after their manner, as they could possibly devise.

We found the people most gentle, loving, and faithfull, void of all guile, and treason, and such as lived after the manner of the golden age. The Earth bringeth foorth all things in abundance, as in the first creation, without toile or labour.

The people onely care to defend themselves from the cold, in their short winter, and to feede themselves with such meate as the soile affoordeth: their meate is very well sodden, and they make broth very sweete, and savourie: their vessels are earthen pots, very large, white, and sweete[38]: their dishes are wooden platters of sweet timber: within the place where they feede, was their lodging, and within that their Idoll, which they worship, of which they speake incredible things. While we were at meate, there came in at the gates, two or three men with their bowes and arrowes, from hunting, whome when we espied, we beganne to looke one towardes another, and offered to reach our weapons: but as soone as she espied our mistrust, she was very much mooved, and caused some of her men to runne out, and take away their bowes, and arrowes, and breake them, and withall beate the poore fellowes out of the gate againe.

When we departed in the evening, and would not tarry all night, she was very sorrie, and gave us into our boate our supper halfe dressed, pots, and all, and brought us to our boates side, in which wee laye all night, remooving the same a prettie distance from the shoore: shee perceiving our jealousie, was much grieved, and sent divers men, and thirtie women, to sitte all night on the bankes side by us, and sent us into our boates fine mattes to cover us from the rayne, using very many wordes to intreate us to rest in their houses: but because wee were fewe men, and if wee had miscarried, the voyage had bene in very great daunger, wee durst not adventure any thing, although there was no cause of doubt: for a more kinde, and loving people, there can not be found in the world, and farre as we have hitherto had triall.

Beyonde this Island, there is the maine lande, and over against this Island falleth into this spatious water, the great river called Occam, by the inhabitants, on which standeth a Towne called Pemeoke,[39] and five daies journey further upon the same is situate their greatest citie called Schycoake, which this people affirme to be very great: but the Savages were never at it, onely they speake of it, by the report of their fathers, and other men, whome they have heard affirme it, to be above one daies journey about.[40]

Into this river falleth another great river called Cipo, in which there is found great store of the Muscels, in which there are pearles: like wise there descendeth into this Occam, another river, called Nomopana,[41] on the one side whereof standeth a great towne, called Chowanoake, and the Lord of that Towne and Countrey is called Pooneno: this Pooneno is not subject to the King of Wingandancoa, but is a free Lord. Beyond this countrey, there is another King, whom they call Menatoan, and these three Kinges are in league with each other.

Towards the sunneset, foure daies journey, is situate a Town called Sequotan, which is the Westermost Town of Wingandacoa, neere unto which, five and twenty yeeres past, there was a shippe cast away, whereof some of the people were saved, and those were white people, whom the Countrey people preserved.

And after ten daies, remaining in an out Island unhabited, called Wococan, they with the helpe of some of the dwellers of Sequotan, fastened two boates of the Countrey together, and made mastes unto them, and sailes of their shirtes, and having taken into them such victuals as the Countrey yeelded, they departed after they had remained in this out Island three weekes: but shortly after, it seemed they were cast away, for the boates were found uppon the coast, cast aland in another Island adjoining[42]: other than these, there was never any people apparelled, or white of colour, either seene, or heard of amongst these people, and these aforesayde were seene onely of the inhabitants of Sequotan: which appeared to be very true, for they wondred marvellously when we were amongest them, at the whitenes of our skinnes, ever coveting to touch our breastes, and to vie the same: besides they had our shippes in marvellous admiration, and all things els was so strange unto them, as it appeared that none of them had ever seene the like.

When we discharged any peece, were it but a harquebush, they would tremble thereat for very feare, and for the strangeness of the same: for the weapons which themselves use, are bowes and arrowes: the arrowes are but of small canes, headed with a sharpe shell, or tooth of a fishe[43] sufficient enough to kill a naked man. Their swordes are of wood hardened: likewise they use wooddeen breastplates for their defence. They have besides a kinde of clubbe, in the ende whereof they fasten the sharpe hornes of a stagge, or other beast. When they goe to warres, they carry with them their Idoll, of whom they ask counsell, as the Romanes were woont of the Oracle of Apollo. They sing songs as they march towards the battell, in steede of drummes, and trumpets: their warres are very cruell, and bloodie, by reason whereof, and of their civill dissentions, which have happened of late yeeres amongest them, the people are marvellously wasted,[44] and in some places, the Countrey left desolate.

Adjoining unto this Towne aforesaide, called Sequotan, beginneth a Countrey called Ponouike, belonging to another King, whome they call Piemacum, and this King is in league with the next King, adjoining towardes the setting of the Sunne, and the Country Neiosioke, situate uppon the side of a goodly River, called Neus[45]: these Kings have mortall warre with Wingina, King of Wingandacoa, but about two yeeres past, there was a peace made between the King Piemacum, and the Lorde of Sequotan, as these men which we have brought with us into England, have made us understande: but there remaineth a mortall malice in the Sequotanes, for many injuries and slaughters done upon them by this Piemacum. They invited divers men, and thirtie women, of the best of his Countrey, to their Towne to a feast: and when they were altogether merrie, and praying before their Idoll, which is nothing else, but a mere illusion of the Devill: the Captaine or Lorde of the Towne came suddenly upon them, and slewe them every one, reserving the women, and children: and these two have oftentimes since persuaded us to surprise Piemacum his Towne, having promised, and assured us, that there will be founde in it great store of commodities. But whether their persuasion be to the ende they may be revenged of their enemies, or for the love they beare to us, we leave that to the triall hereafter.[46]

Beyonde this Island called Croonoake,[47] are many Islands, very plentiful of fruites, and other naturall increases, together with many Townes, and villages, along the side of the continent, some bounding the Islands, and some stretching up further into the land.

When we first had sight of this Countrey, some thought the first lande we sawe, to be the continent: but after we entired into the Haven, wee sawe before us another mightie long Sea: for there lieth along the coast a tracte of Islands, two hundreth miles in length, adjoining to the Ocean Sea, and betweene the Islands, two or three entrances: when you are entred betweene them (these Islands being very narrowe, for the most part, as in most places five miles broad, in some places lesse, in fewe more,) then there appeareth another great Sea, containing in bredth in some places, fortie, and in some fiftie, in some twentie miles over, before you come unto the continent: and in this inclosed Sea, there are about a hundreth Islands, of divers bignesses, whereof one is fifteene miles long, at which we were, finding it to be a most pleasant, and fertile ground, replenished with goodly Cedars, and divers other sweete woods, full of Currans, of flaxe, and many other notable commodities, which we at that time had no leasure to view. Besides this Island, there are many, as I have saide, some of two, of three, of foure, of five miles, some more, some lesse, most beautifull, and pleasant to behold, replenished with Deer, Conies, Hares, and divers beastes, and about them the goodliest and best fishe in the world, and in greatest abundance.

Thus Sir, we have acquainted you with the particulars of our discoverie, made this present voyage, as farre foorth as the shortnes of the time we there continued, would affoord us to take viewe of: and so contenting our selves with this service at this time, which we hope hereafter to inlarge, as occasion and assistance shall be given, we resolved to leave the Countrey, and to apply our selves to returne for England, which we did accordingly, and arrived safely in the West of England about the middlest of September.

And whereas we have above certified you of the Countrey, taken in possession by us, to her Majesties use, and so to yours, by her Majesties grant, wee thought good for the better assurance thereof to recorde some of the particular Gentlemen, and men of accomp, who then were present, as witnesses of the same, that thereby all occasion of cavill to the title of the Countrey, in her Majesties behalfe, may be presented, which otherwise, such as like not the action may use, and pretend,[48] whose names are:

Of the Companie: William Grenville,[49] John Wood, James Browewich, Henrie Greene, Benjamin Wood, Simon Ferdinando,[50] Nicholas Petman, John Hewes.[51]

The 1600 edition closes with the following additional statement: "We brought home also two of the Savages being lustie men, whose names were Wanchese and Manteo."

FOUR

The First Voyage of Sir Richard Grenville, 1585

Amadas and Barlowe arrived back in Plymouth in mid–September. Sometime between then and the middle of March 1585, Raleigh must have held several discussions with Thomas Harriot and others to debate his next steps in establishing a foothold on American soil. It is likely that Grenville would have been privy to some of these discussions; his knowledge of colonizing the Irish province of Munster, coupled with his military skill would have been invaluable. It is also difficult to believe that Raleigh's choice of Grenville to lead the critical next voyage was inappropriate as has been suggested by others.[1]

Grenville was a prudent man and almost certainly took the lead in determining who would sail with him. He surrounded himself therefore with an able pilot, and a number of seasoned Captains and friends he felt he could trust and respect. For example, John Arundell was a close relative of Grenville while "Master Stukeley" was essentially his next-door neighbor back in Devon. Given his previous experience of planning long voyages at sea, we can also be sure that this venture received the same meticulous attention. Nor were the risks of such a venture lost on Grenville, for on March 16, 1585, he signed an Indenture, to all intents and purposes a last will and testament, giving clear instructions as to what was to happen to his estates if he did not return from Roanoke. This remarkable document was thought lost until contact received from a Gentleman in November 2015 confirmed that it was hanging on the wall of the restroom at his private residence in England! Further examination of the document established it as being entirely genuine. Of note is that not only does it contain the signature of Sir Richard Grenville, but importantly, confirms the role of Sir Walter Raleigh as one of the executors of his estates.

Sometime shortly after this signing, Grenville must have departed from Bideford with his ships, the *Tyger* and the *Roebuck*, bound for Ply-

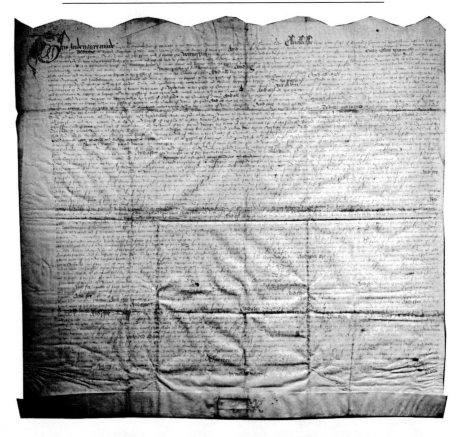

Above: Sir Richard Grenville's indenture of March 16, 1585, recently discovered hanging on the wall of the restroom in a private house (courtesy of the owner; photograph by David Carter, Docton Court Gallery, Appledore, Devon, England). *Below:* Detail of Sir Richard Grenville's signature on his indenture. He signs himself "Greynvile R," the "R" written through the underscore (courtesy the owner, photograph by David Carter, Docton Court Gallery, Appledore, Devon, England).

mouth, where he took charge of the fleet bound for Roanoke. The record of the voyage follows:

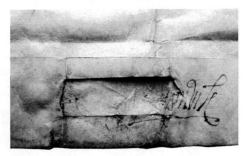

The 19. day of Maye,[2] in the yeere above saide, wee departed from Plymmouth, our fleete consisting of the number of seven sailes, to wit, the *Tyger*, of the burden of seven score tunnes: a flie-boat called the *Roe Bucke*, of the like burden: the *Lyon* of

a hundred tunnes, or thereabouts: the *Elizabeth*, of fifty tunnes, and the *Dorothie*, a small barke, whereunto were also adjoined for speedie services, small pinnesses. The principall Gentlemen of our companie were, Master Ralfe Lane, Master Thomas Candishe,[3] Master John Arundell, Master Raimund, Master Stukeley, Master Bremige, Master Vincent, and Master John Clarke, and divers others, whereof some were Captaines, and other some Assistants for Counsell, and good directions in the Voyage.

The 14. day of Aprill, we fell with Lancacota,[4] and Forte Ventura,[5] Isle of the Canaries, and from thence we continued our course for Dominica, one of the Antilles of the West India, wherewith we fell the 7. day of Maye, and the 10. day following,[6] we came to an anker at Cotesa, a little Iland situate near to the Iland of St John,[7] where wee landed, and refreshed our selves all that day.

The 15.[8] day of Maye, we came to an anker, in the Baye of Muskito,[9] in the Iland of St John, within a Fawlcon shot[10] of the shoare: where our Generall Sir Richard Greenvill,[11] and the most part of our companie landed, and began to fortifie, very neere to the sea side: the river ranne by the one side of our forte, and the other two sides were environed with woods.

The 13. day we began to builde a new pinnesse within the Fort, with the timber that we then felled in the countrey, some part whereof we fet[12] three myles up in the land, and brought it to our fort upon trucks, the Spanyards not daring to make or offer resistance.

The 16. day, there appeared unto us out of the woods 8. horsemen of the Spanyards, about a quarter of a myle from our Fort, staying about halfe an hower in viewing our forces: but as soone as they saw 10 of our shot marching towards them, they presently retyred into the woodes.

The 19. day, Master Candish, who had bene separated from our fleete in a storme in the Bay of Portingal arrived at Cotesa, within the sight of the *Tyger*[13]: we thinking him a farre off to have bene either a Spaniard or French man of warre thought it good to waigh ankers, and to goe roome with him, which the *Tyger* did, and discerned him at last to be one of our Consorts, for joy of whose comming, our ships discharged their ordinance, and saluted him, according to the manner of the Seas.

The 22. day, 20 other Spanish horsemen shewed them selves to us upon the other side of the river: who being seene, our General dispatched 20. footmen towards them, and two horsemen of ours, mounted upon Spanish horses, which wee before had taken in the time of our being on the Island: they shewed to our men a flagge of truce, and made signes to have a parle with us: whereupon two of our men went halfe of the way upon the sands, and two of theirs came and met them: the two Spaniards offred very great salutations to our men, but began according to their Spanish proud humors, to expostulate with them, about their arrival and fortifying in their countrie, who not withstanding by our men's discrete answers were so cooled, that wheras they were told, that our principal intention was onely to furnish our selves with water, and victuals, and other necessaries whereof we stood in neede, which we craved might be yelded us with faire, and friendly means, otherwise our resolution was to practice force, and to releeve our selves by the sworde: the Spanyards in conclusion, seeing our men so resolute, yelded to our requestes with large promises of all courtesie, and great favor, and so our men and theirs departed.[14]

The 23. day our pinnesse was finished, and lanched, which being done, our Generall with his Captaines, and Gentlemen, marched up into the countrey about the space of 4. myles where in a plaine marsh, they stayed expecting the comming of the Spanyardes according to their promise, to furnish us with victuals: who keeping their old custome for perjurie and breache of promise came not, whereupon our General fired the woods thereabouts, and so retired to our Fort, which the same day was fired also, and each man came aboord to be ready to set saile the next morning.[15]

The 29.[16] day we set saile from St Johns, being many of us stoong before upon shoare with the moskitoes: but the same night, we tooke a Spanish Frigate, which was forsaken by the Spanyardes upon the sight of us, and the next day in the morning very early, wee took another frigat, with good and rich fraight, and divers Spanyardes of accomp in her, which afterwards we ransomed for good round summes, and landed them in Saint Johns.

The 26. day our Lieutenant Master Ralfe Lane, went in one of the Frigates which we had taken, to Roxo bay[17] upon the Southwest side of Saint Johns, to fetch salt, being thither conducted by a Spanish pilot: as soone as he arrived there, he landed with his men, to the number of 20, and intrenched him self upon the sandes immediatly, compassing one of their salt hils within the trench: who being seene of the Spanyardes, there came downe towards him two or three troopes of horsemen, and footemen, who gave him the looking, and gazing on, but durst not come neere him to offer any resistance, so that Master Lane mauger[18] their troopes, caried their salt aboord and laded his frigate, and so returned againe to our fleete the 29. day, which road at Saint Germans Bay. The same day we all departed, and the next day arrived in the Island of Hispaniola.

June
The 1. day of June we ankered at Isabella, in the North side of Hispaniola

The 3. day of June, the Governor of Isabella, and Captaine of the Port de Plata, beeing certyfied by the reports of sundry Spanyardes, who had bene wel intertained aboord our shippes by our Generall, that in our fleete were many brave, and gallant Gentlemen, who greatly desired to see the Governor aforesaid, he thereupon sent gentle commendations to our Generall, promising within few daies to come to him in person, which he performed accordingly.

The 5. day the foresaid governor, accompanied with a lusty frier, and 20. other Spaniards, with their servants and Negroes, came downe to the sea side, where our ships road at anker, who being seene, our Generall manned immediately the most part of his boats with chiefe men of our fleete, every man appointed, and furnished in the best sort: at the landing of our Generall, the Spanishe Governor received him very curteously, and the Spanish Gentlemen saluted our English Gentlemen, and their inferior sort did also salute our Souldiers and Seamen, liking our men, and likewise their qualities, although at the first, they seemed to stand in feare of us, and of so many of our boats, whereof they desired that all might not land their men, yet in the end, the curtesies that passed on both sides were so great, that all feare and mistrust on the Spanyardes part was abandoned.

In the meanetime while our English Generall and the Spanish Governor discoursed betwixt them of divers matters, as of the state of the Country, the multitude of the Townes and people, and the commodities of the iland, our men provided two banquetting houses covered with green boughs, the one for the Gentlemen, the other for the servants, and a sumptuous banquet was brought in served by us all in Plate,[19] with the sound of trumpets, and consort of musick wherewith the Spanyards were more than delighted. Which banquet being ended, the Spanyardes in recompense of our courtesie, caused a great heerd of white buls, and kyne,[20] to be brought together from the Mountaines, and appointed for every Gentlemen and Captaine that woulde ride, a horse ready sadyled, and then singled out three of the best of them to be hunted by horsemen after their manner, so that the pastime grew very plesant, for the space of three houres, wherein all three of the beasts were killed, whereof one tooke the sea, and there was slaine with a musket. After this sport, many rare presents and gifts were given and bestowed on both partes, and the next day we plaied the Marchants in bargaining with them by way of trucke and exchange for divers of their commodities, as horses,[21] mares, kyne, buls, goates, swine, sheepe, bul hides, sugar, ginger, pearle, tabacco, and such like commodities of the Iland.[22]

The 7. day we departed with great good will from the Spanyardes from the Island of Hispaniola: but the wiser sort do impute this greate shew of friendship, and courtesie used towardes us by the Spanyards rather to the force that we were of, and the vigilance, and watchfulnes that was amongst us, than to any harty good will, or sure friendly intertainment: for doubtlesse if they had been stronger than wee, we might have looked for no better courtesie at their handes, than Master John Hawkins received at Saint John de Ullua,[23] or John Oxnam neere the streights of Dariene,[24] and divers others of our Countrymen in other places.

The 8. day we ankered at a small Iland to take seales which in that place wee understood to have bene in great quantitie, where the Generall and certaine others with him in the Pinnesse, were in very great danger to have bene cast away, but by the helpe of God they escaped the hazard, and returned aboord the Admirall in safetie.

The 9. day we arrived and landed in the Isle of Caycos, in which Islande we searched for salt pondes, upon the advertisement and information of a Portingall: who indeede abused our General and us, deserving a halter for his hire,[25] if it had so pleased us.

The 12. day we anchored at Guanema,[26] and landed.

The 15. and 16. we ankered and landed at Sygateo.[27]

The 20. we fell with the mayne of Florida.

The 23. we were in great danger of a Wrecke on a breache called the Cape of Feare.

The 24. we came to anker in a harbor where we caught in one tyde so much fishe as woulde have yelded us 20 pounds in London: this was our first landing in Florida.

The 26. we came to anker at Wocokon.

The 29. wee waighed anker to bring the *Tyger* into the harbour, where through the unskillfulnesse of the Master whose name was Fernando, the Admirall stroke on grounde, and sunke.[28]

July

The 3. we sent word of our arriving at Wococon, to Wingino at Roanoke.

The 6. Master John Arundell was sent to the mayne, and Manteo with him: and Captaine Aubry, and Captaine Boniten the same day were sent to Croatoan, where they found two of our men left there, with 30 other by Captaine Reymond, some 20 dayes before.[29]

The 8. Captain Aubry, and Captain Boniten returned with two of our men found by them to us at Wococon.

The 11. day the Generall accompanied in his Tilt boate with Master John Arundell, Master Stukelye, and divers other Gentlemen, Master Lane, Master Candish, Master Harriot, and 20 others in the new pinnesse, Captaine Amadas, Captaine Clarke, with tenne others in a ship boate, Francis Brooke, and John White in another ship boate passed over the water from Ococon to the mayne land victualled for eight dayes, in which voyage we first discovered the townes at Pomioke, Aquascogoc, and Secota, and also the great lake called by the Savages Paquype,[30] with divers other places, and so returned with that discovery to our fleete.

The 12. we came to the Towne of Pomeioke.

The 13. we passed by water to Aquascococke.

The 15. we came to Secotan and were well intertayned there of the Savages.

The 16. we returned thence, and one of our boates with the Admirall was sent to Aquascococke to demand a silver cup which one of the savages had stolen from us, and not receiving it according to his promise, we burnt, and spoyled their corne, and Towne, all the people beeing fledde.[31]

The 18. we returned from the discovery of Secotan, and the same day came aboord our fleete ryding at Wocokon.

The 21. our fleet ankering at Wokocon, we wayed anker for Hatoraske.

The 27. our fleete ankered at Hatoraske, and there we rested.

The 29. Grangino, brother to King Wingino, came aboord the Admirall, and Manteo with him.[32]

August

The 2. The Admirall was sent to Weapemeoke.

The 5. Master John Arundell was sent for England.

The 25. our Generall wayed anker, and set saile for England.

About the 31. he took a Spanish ship of 300 tunne richly loaden, boording her with a boate made with boards of chests, which fell asunder, and sunke at the shippes side, as soone as ever hee and his men were out of it.[33]

September

The 10. of September, by foule weather the Generall then shipped in the prize lost sight of the *Tyger.*

October

The First the *Tyger* fell with the landes ende,[34] and the same day came to anker at Falmouth.[35]

The 18. the Generall came with the prize to Plymmouth, and was courteously received by diverse of his worshipfull friends.[36]

The names of all those as well Gentlemen as others, that remained one whole yeere in Virginia, under the Government of Master Ralfe Lane.

Master Philip Amades, Admirall of the countrie

Master Snelling, Master Thomas Harvie, Master Hariot, Master Anthony Russe, Master Acton, Master Allyne, Master Edward Stafford, Master Michel Polyson, Thomas Luddington, John Cage, Master Marvyn, Thomas Parre, Master Gardiner, William Randes, Captain Vaughan, Geffery Churchman, Master Kendall, William Farthowe, Master Prideox, John Taylor, Robert Holecroft, Phillipe Robyns, Rise Courtney, Thomas Phillippes, Master Hugh Rogers, Valentine Beale, Thomas Foxe, James Skinner, Edward Nugen, George Eseven, Darby Glande, John Chaundeler, Edward Kelle, Philip Blunt, John Gostigo, Richard Poore, Erasinus Clefs[37]

Robert Yong, Edward Ketcheman, Marmaduke Constable, John Linsey, Thomas Hesket, Thomas Rottenbury, William Wasse, Roger Deane, John Fever, John Harris, Daniel,[38] Frauncis Norris, Thomas Taylor, Matthewe Lyne, Richard Humfrey, Edward Kettell, John Wright, Thomas Wisse, Gabriell North, Robert Biscombe, Bennet Chappell, William Backhouse, Richard Sare, William White, James Lacie, Henry Potkin, Smolkin,[39] Dennis Barnes, Thomas Smart, Joseph Borges, Robert,[40] Doughan Gannes,[41] John Evans, William Tenche, Roger Large, Randall Latham, Humfrey Garden, Thomas Hulme, Frauncis Whitton, Walter Myll, Rowland Griffyn, Richard Gilbert, William Millard, Steven Pomarie, John Twyt, John Brocke, Edward Seklemore, Bennet Harrye, John Anwike, James Stevenson, Christopher Marshall, Charles Stevenson, David Williams, Christopher Lowde, Nicholas Swabber, Jeremy Man, Edward Chipping, James Mason, Sylvester Beching, David Salter, Vincent Cheyne, Richard Ireland, Haunce Walters,[42]

Thomas Bookener, Edward Barecombe, William Phillippes, Thomas Skevelabs,[43] Randall Mayne, William Walters.[44]

On August 12 1585, Ralph Lane wrote the following letters:

Aug. 12 1585: Port Ferdinando Virginia. Ralph Lane to Sec. Walsingham.

The Generals return to England cuts him off from reporting upon the peculiarities of the country. Although they arrived there late in the year, wholly through the fault of him who intends to accuse others, they have nevertheless discovered so many rare and singular commodities in the Queen's new kingdom of Virginia, as by the universal opinion of all the apothecaries and merchants there, no state in Christendom doth yield better or more plentiful. Leaves the particulars to the General's report; the ship's freight will prevent all suspicion of fraud. They have not yet found one stinking weed growing in the land. Describes the vast and huge territory, its natural fortifications, and the climate very healthy: There are only three entries and ports; these they have named, Trinity, Scarborough, and Ococan,[45] where their fleet struck aground, and the *Tyger* was nearly lost: The best port discovered by Simon Ferdinando, the master and pilot major of the fleet, after whom it is named, and which, if fortified by a sconce, could not be entered by the whole force of Spain. Account of their soundings. Has undertaken with a good company to remain there, resolute rather to lose their lives than to defer possession of so noble a kingdom to the Queen, their country, and their noble patron Sir Walter Raleigh, through whose and his Honour's most worthy endeavour and infinite charge an honourable entry is made to the conquest of. Is assured they will, by this means, be relieved from the tyranny of Spain, and their enemies, the Papists, will not be suffered by God to triumph at the overthrow either of this most Christian action, or of His poor servants, in their thorough famine or other wants. God will command even the ravens to feed them.

Aug. 12 1585: Port Ferdinando Virginia. Ralph Lane to Walsingham.

Commends to his favour the bearer, Mr. Atkinson, who carried himself so honestly and industriously throughout the voyage. Has also written by Mr. Russell to the like effect, and is persuaded, notwithstanding the general displeasure towards Mr. Atkinson that he will clear himself of every charge or imputation.

Aug. 12 1585: Port Ferdinando Virginia. Lane to Sir Philip Sydney.

Will not omit writing to him, although in the midst of infinite business, having the charge of savages as well as wild men of his own nation, whose unruliness prevents his leaving them. Refers him to his letter to Mr. Secretary for an account of the singularities of Virginia. Has discovered the infinite riches of St. John and Hispaniola by dwelling upon the islands five weeks. Thinks if the Queen should find herself burdened with the King of Spain, that to attempt them would be most honourable, feasible, and profitable. Exhorts him not to refuse the good opportunity of rendering so great a service to the Church of Christ, he only being fit for the chief command of such an expedition. The strength of Spain doth altogether grow from the mines of her treasure.[46]

Ralph Lane wrote a further letter titled "Sept. 8 1585: From the New Fort in Virginia. Lane to Sec. Walsingham." In the letter, he observes:

They have discovered a kind of Gynneye[47] wheat, that yields both corn and sugar, of which their physician bath sent an assay to Sir W. Raleigh. There are fertile and pleasant provinces in the main land, populated only by savages, fit to be civilly and christianly inhabited. Means, with the favour of God, to visit them and pass some part of the winter in their provinces, 140 miles within the main.[48]

Grenville's reward for his efforts at Roanoke was the capture near Bermuda, of the flagship of a Spanish treasure fleet, the *Santa Maria de San Vincente*, during his return voyage to England. It is thanks to the remarkable eyewitness account of an unfortunate passenger on that ship, Enrique Lopez of Fayal, that we know so much more about Grenville and the fate of those subjected to his piratical activities:

Statement made by Enrique Lopez, resident in the city of Lisbon, who arrived in the island of Fayal on November 18th 1585, in search of a vessel in which to continue on his way with certain companions, who, having been robbed, were set ashore on the island of Flores.

He says that he and other merchants embarked as passengers in the ship called *Santa Maria de San Vincente*, Master Alonso Corniele, native of Seville. This vessel left from the harbour of the city of Santo Domingo in La Hispaniola[49] as flagship of seventeen others which set out in its convoy laden with hides and sugars and other merchandise. They were bound for the city of Seville, to which these cargoes were consigned.

He says that the entire fleet came to anchor at Ocoa, which is in that island, from where they made sail on the first day of July of this year on a course for Havana, there to join the Tierra Firma[50] and New Spain[51] fleets in continuance of their voyage. And after thirty days they came to anchor within the port of Havana and four days after they had arrived the Tierra Firma fleet came into that harbour, with General don Antonio Osorio in command.

He says that four days after the Tierra Firma fleet entered they all made sail, being some 33 vessels, on a course for Spain and eight days later disembogued. They had sailed for two days and one night when the sea rose and the wind blew against them in such fashion that they had to strike sail and lie in a cross sea,[52] and so remained all night, supposing that all the rest of the fleet would do the same. When day broke, however, they could discover only six or seven sail, all in one direction, and immediately made sail to follow and over-take the fleet. This they were unable to do, although they tried.

He says that since they could not overtake the fleet they kept on their course after it until they were just about athwart Bermuda. When they reached this position, on September 4, about ten o'clock in the morning, they discovered a sail following in their wake which they thought was some one of the units of the fleet which had lagged, as some usually do, and assuming this, they took in sail and waited for her, that the ships might continue on their voyage together.

And as they lay in this fashion the vessel came up, having the wind, and as she did so they fired a round of artillery to salute her in token of amity. Whereupon the ship opened fire and bore down on them, firing her guns with the intention of disabling them, and so cut up their rigging that they were disabled. Then recognizing that this was a corsair which intended to rob them, they made sail, hoping to get away, for they had neither arms nor artillery with which to defend themselves.[53] One man on board was killed, four or five were injured, and two shots struck near the water line, so that they were sinking. In order not to go down they struck sail and lay in a cross sea. They could do nothing else because their ship was badly damaged.

The corsair then lowered a boat with 30 armed soldiers and a captain whom they called their general, named Richard Grenville. It was said that he left England with 14 ships for the Indies.

They say that as the English general and his men boarded he ordered the master and the rest on board to hand over all the gold and silver and other things they had in the vessel, promising that he would do them no bodily hurt. The passengers gave up the keys to their boxes and he unlocked some and broke open others and removed lots of gold and silver and pearls which were in them. He took possession of the ships register and according to it demanded the gold and silver and pearls entered on it, and it was all delivered to him, nothing missing. The total was over 40,000 ducats.

He says that after he had taken possession of the ship the Englishman ordered twenty of its seamen to be taken to his vessel, which was done. This left only 22 persons, passengers and seamen, on board of theirs.

He says that after he had captured this ship with the aforesaid consignments of gold and silver and pearls and 200 boxes of sugar of 40 arrobas[54] each and 7000 hides and a thousand hundredweight of ginger and other merchandise, to a total value of 120,000 ducats, the Englishman kept his prize with him.[55] The two vessels continued on a course to within 400 leagues of these islands, where, in a storm, the vessels were separated and they never saw the English ship again.

He says that the English general and 36 of his men had remained on the *Santa Maria de San Vincente* and now kept on their course with it alone. All on board suffered great hardship and want because they had almost no supplies, for the corsair had removed most of those they had had to his ship, being in need of them. It came to a point where they had only a few oats a day, cooked in salt water, and so continued until October 12 when they sighted the island of Flores.

He says that as soon as they sighted the land they approached it, that some craft might come out and show them the harbour, in order to anchor in it; and the general ordered that none of the Englishmen should speak or appear, but only the seamen and passengers of the captured vessel; and he asked that a boat with five men should be sent out to him. When these had come alongside he took them on board by force and made them prisoners, and told them he would not release them until he was given the supplies he needed, for which he would pay. Recognizing that he was a corsair, the people of the island did not wish to furnish him supplies. One of the principal passengers in the ship (among those who had been robbed) then landed and begged the people of the island to sell them the supplies they wanted, for if they refused the English would throw him and his companions overboard to drown, and they would so be made to suffer for it. They believed that the general had determined to do this. Therefore, to avoid it, the people of the island sold the English the supplies they needed.

He says that as soon as the corsair had received these supplies on board he set deponent[56] and the other seamen and passengers on shore, in all about 22 persons, and as they left the ship to go to land he stripped them all to see whether they were carrying off anything hidden.[57]

He says that this English corsair's ship was built like a Galliasse,[58] was a swift sailer and carried a good armament and equipment, two tiers of ordnance on each side, and many fireworks. That the pilot was one Simon Fernandez, Portuguese, a native of Terceira.[59]

In talking with some of the private persons who accompanied the said Richard Grenville, they were told that in the Indies the English had been at Puerto Rico, on the north side of the island, where they took two frigates carrying merchandise, and from there with five ships went to Florida, where they nearly wrecked on certain shoals.[60]

There in Florida the general disembarked about 300 men with orders to begin to fortify for a settlement, and he sent a frigate to England with orders to have equipment and munitions ready for him upon his arrival that he might return immediately to where he left these people.[61]

That Richard Grenville seemed to be a man of quality, for he was served elaborately on silver and gold plate, by servants. Many musical instruments were played when he dined, and his appearance was that of an important person.[62]

On October 29, 1585, Grenville wrote to Queen Elizabeth's Principal Secretary, Sir Francis Walsingham from Plymouth. The State Papers Colonial contains the following entry:

Sir Rich. Grenville to Sec. Walsingham. Acquaints him with the success of his voyage. Has performed the action directed, and discovered, taken possession of, and peopled a new country [Virginia], and stored it with cattle, fruits, and plants. The commodities that are found there are such as he was advertised of by his cousin Sir Walter Raleigh. In his way home captured, after some fighting, a Spanish ship, returning from St. Domingo, laden with ginger and sugar. The report that the Spaniards bring great quantities of pearl and gold and silver from St. Domingo is incorrect.[63]

The Pilot of the *Santa Maria de San Vincente* was Pedro Diaz, a Portuguese. The deposition he made to the Spanish authorities, when he finally escaped from Grenville three years later, provides a valuable insight to the Roanoke voyages and to Grenville's plans in Bideford.[64] In it, he states of the capture of the *Santa Maria de San Vincente*:

(The) vessel was seized in the vicinity of Bermuda by a ship of the queen called the *Tyger*, under the command of a principal English Gentleman named Sir Richard Grenville, the same who in that year was in the island of Puerto Rico and at La Isabella, where he obtained cattle, horses and dogs with which he went to establish a settlement in Florida.

After they captured him in the vicinity of Bermuda they carried the informant straight to England by way of the island of Flores. They reached England, port of Plymouth, on November 26, 1585,[65] and the said captain went to London. His home and residence are at Bideford, which is on the bar of Barnstaple.[66]

Detail of John White's map ("Virginia Pars"), showing what appears to be Sir Richard Grenville's ship the *Tyger*, as deduced from the description by Enrique Lopez, and supported by the image of the galliass *Swallowe* from the Anthony Rolls, British Library Additional MS 22047 (© The Trustees of the British Museum).

Grenville sailed the *Santa Maria de San Vincente* back to Bideford. The contemporary diary of Philip Wyot, Town Clerk of nearby Barnstaple, acknowledges the arrival of the ship, where he writes, "In december this year Sir Richard Greynfild came home bringing a prise with him, laden with sugar, ginger & hyds."[67]

Although its fate is unknown, it seems plausible Grenville converted it into an English man of war. A ship with no prior history emerged from Bideford as the *Virgin God Save Her* in 1588 as part of Bideford's fleet sent to fight the Spanish Armada. In 1895 a number of Spanish cannons discovered below the quayside at Bideford pre-date those used by the Armada, and thus perhaps relate to that conversion.

FIVE

The Military Colony, 1585 (Part One)

Following Grenville's departure, Ralph Lane set about establishing his base on Roanoke Island and went on to record his stay and explorations of the Outer Banks area of North Carolina. He provides his record in two parts. This first part details his explorations of the area, the American hinterland, and his early dealings with the Native Indians:

That I may proceed with order in this discourse, I thinke it requisite to divide into two partes. The first shall declare the particularities of such partes of the Country within the mayne, as our weake number, and supply of things necessary did inable us to enter into the discovery thereof.

The second part, shall set downe the reasons generally moving us to resolve on our departure at the instant with the General Sir Francis Drake, and our common request for passage with him, when the barkes, pinnesses, and boates with the Masters and Mariners ment by him to be lefte in the Countrie for the supply of such, as for a further time ment to have stayed there were caried away with tempest, and foule weather: In the beginning whereof shal be declared the conspiracy of Pemisapan,[1] with the Savages of the mayne to have cutt us off at.

The first part declaring the particularities of the countrey of Virginia:

First therefore touching the particularities of the Countrey, you shall understand our discovery of the same hath bene extended from the Island of Roanoak, (the same having been the place of our settlement or inhabitation) into the South, into the North, into the Northwest, and into the West.

The uttermost place to the Southward of any discoverie was Secotan, being by estimation foure score miles distant from Roanoak.[2] The passage from thence was thorowe[3] a broad sound within the mayne, the same being without kenning of land,[4] and yet full of flats and shoales: we had but our boate with foure oares to passe through the same, which boat could not carry above fifteene men with their furniture,[5] baggage, and victuall for seven dayes at the most: and as for our Pinnesse, besides that she drewe too deep water for that shalow sound, she would not stirre for an oare: for these and other reasons (winter also being at hand) we thought good wholy to leave the discovery of those partes untill our stronger supplie.[6]

To the Northwarde our furthest discoverie was to the Chesepians, distant from Roanoak about 130 miles, the passage to it was very shalow and most dangerous, by

35

reason of the breadth of the sound, and the litle succour that upon any flawe was there to be had.[7]

But the territorie and the soyle of the Chesepians (being distant fifteene miles from the shoare) was for pleasantnes of seate, for temperature of Climate, for fertilitie of soyle, and for the commoditie of the Sea, besides multitude of beares (being an excellent good victuall, with great woods of Sassafras and Wallnut trees) is not to be excelled by any other whatsoever.[8]

There be sundry Kings, whom they call Weroances, and Countries of great fertilitie adjoining to the same, as the Mandoages, Tripanicks, and Opossians, which all came to visit the Colonie of the English, which I had for a time appointed to be resident there.[9]

To the Northwest the farthest place of our discoverie was to Choanoke distant from Roanoak about 130 miles. Our passage thither lyeth through a broad sound, but all fresh water, and the chanell of great depth, navigable for good shipping, but out of the chanell full of shoales.[10] The townes about the water side situated by the way, are these following: Pysshokonnok, The womans Towne, Chipanum, Weopomiok, Muscamunge, and Mattaquen: all these being under the jurisdiction of the King of Weopemiok, called Okisco: from Muscamunge we enter into the River, and jurisdiction of Choanoke: There the River beginneth to straighten untill it come to Choanoke, and then groweth to be as narrowe as the Thames between Westminster and Lambeth.[11]

Between Muscamunge and Choanoke upon the left hand as we passe thither, is a goodly high land, and there is a Towne which we called the blinde Towne, but the Savages called it Ooanoke, and hath a very goodly cornefield belonging unto it: it is a subject to Choanoke.[12] Choanoke itselfe is the greatest Province and Seigniorie lying upon that River, and the very Towne itself is able to put 700 fighting men into the fielde, besides the forces of the Province itselfe.

The King of the said Province is called Menatonon, a man impotent in his lims,[13] but otherwise for a Savage, a very grave and wise man, and of very singular good discourse in matters concerning the state, not onely of his own Countrey, and the disposition of his owne men, but also of his neighbours round about him as wel farre as neere, and of the commodities that each Countrey yeeldeth. When I had him prisoner with me, for two dayes that we were together, he gave me more understanding and light of the Countrey than I had received by all the searches and savages that before I or any of my companie had had conference with: it was in March last past 1586. Amongst other things he tolde me, that going three dayes journey in a canoa by his River of Choanoke, and then descending to the land, you are within foure dayes journey to passe over land Northeast to a certaine Kings countrey, whose Province lyeth upon the sea, but his place of greatest strength is an Iland situate as he described unto me in a Bay, the water round about the Iland very deep.[14]

Out of this Bay he signified to mee, that this King had so great a quantitie of Pearle, and doeth so ordinarily take the same, as that not onely his owne skins that he weareth, and the better sort of his Gentlemen and followers, are full set with the said Pearle, but also his beds, and houses are garnished with them, and that he hath such quantitie of them, that it is a wonder to see.

He shewed me that the sayd King was with him at Choanoak two yeeres before, and brought him certaine Pearle, but the same of the worst sort, yet was hee feign to buy them of him for copper at a dere rate as he thought: He gave me a rope of the same Pearle, but they were blacke and naught, yet many of them were very great, and a fewe amongst a number very orient and round, all which I lost with other things of mine, comming aborde Sir Francis Drake his Fleet: yet he tolde me that the sayd King had great store of Pearle that were white, great, and round, and that his blacke Pearle his men did take out of shalowe water, but the white Pearle his men fished for in very deepe water.

It seemed to mee by his speech, that the sayd King had trafficke with white men that had clothes as we have for these white Pearle,[15] and that was the reason that he would not depart with other than with blacke Pearles, to those of the same Country.

The King of Choanoak promised to give me guides to go over land into that Kings Countrey whensoever I would: but he advised me to take good store of men with mee, and good store of victual, for he sayd, that King would be loth to suffer any strangers to enter into his Countrey, and especially to meddle with the fishing for any Pearle there, and that he was able to make a great many of men into the fielde, which he sayd would fight very well.

Hereupon I resolved with my self, that if your supplie had come before the end of April, and that you had sent any store of boats, or men, to have had them made in any reasonable time, with a sufficient number of men, and victuals to have found us untill the new corne were come in, I woulde have sent a small Barke with two Pinesses about by Sea to the Northwarde to have found out the Bay he spoke of, and to have sounded the barre if there were any, which shoulde have ridden there in the sayd Bay about that Iland, while I with all the small Boats I could make, and with two hundredth men would have gone up to the head of the River of Choanoak, with the guides that Menatonon would have given, which I would have bene assured should have bene of his best men, (for I had his best beloved sonne prisoner with me) who also should have kept me companie in an handlocke with the rest foote by foote all the voyage over land.

My meaning was further at the head of the River in the place of my descent where I would have left my boates to have raysed a sconse[16] with a small trench, and a palisado upon the top of it, in the which, and in the garde of my boates I would have left five and twentie, or thirtie men, with the rest would I have marched with as much victuall as every man could have carried, with their furniture, mattocks, spades, and axes, two days journey.

In the ende of my marche upon some convenient plot would I have raysed another sconse according to the former, where I would have left 15 or 20. And if it woulde have fallen out conveniently, in the way I woulde have raised my sayd sconse upon some corne field that my companie might have lived upon it.

And so I would have holden this course of insconsing every two dayes march, untill I had bene arrived at the Bay or Porte he spake of: which finding to be worth the possession, I would there have raised a mayne fort, both for the defence of the harboroughs,[17] and our shipping also, and would have reduced our whole habitation from Roanoak and from the harborough and port there (which by proofe is very naught) unto this other before mentioned, from whence, in the foure dayes marche before specified could I at all times returne with my companie backe unto my boats ryding under my sconse, very neere whereunto directly from the West runneth a most notable River, and in all those parts most famous, called the River of Morotico.[18] This River openneth into the broad sound of Weopomiok: And whereas the River of Choanoak, and all the other sounds, and Bayes, salt and fresh, shewe no currant in the world in calme weather, but are mooved altogether with the winde: This River of Morotico hath so violent a currant from the West and Southwest, that it made me almost of opinion that with oares it would scarse be navigable: it passeth with many creeks and turnings, and for the space of thirtie miles rowing and more, it is as broad as the Thames betwixt Greenwich, and the Ile of Dogges,[19] in some places more, and in some lesse: the currant runneth as strong being entred so high into the River, as at London Bridge upon a bale water.[20]

And for that not onely Menatonon, but also the Savages of Morotico themselves doe report strange things of the head of that River, and that from Morotico itselfe, which is a principall Towne upon that River, it is thirtie dayes as some of them say, and some say fortie dayes voyage to the head thereof, which head they say springeth out of a main rocke in that abundance, that forthwith it maketh a most violent streame: and further, that this huge rock standeth neare unto a Sea, that many times in stormes (the winde comming outwardly from the Sea) the waves thereof are beaten into the said fresh streame, so that the fresh water for a certaine space, groweth salt and brackish[21]: I took a resolution with my selfe, having dismissed Menatonon upon a ransome agreed for, and sent his sonne into the Pinnesse to Roanoak, to enter presently so farre into that River with two double whirries, and fortie persons one or other, as I could have victuall to carrie us, untill we could meete with more either of the Moratiks, or of the Mangoaks which is another kinde of Savages, dwelling more to the Westwarde of the sayd River: but the hope of recovering more victual from the Savages made me and my company as narrowly to escape starving in that discoverie before our returne, as ever men did that missed the same.

For Pemisapan, who had changed his name of Wingina upon the death of his brother Granganimeo, had given both the Choanists and Mangoaks word of my purpose touching them, I having been inforced to make him privie to the same, to be served by him of a guide to the Mangoaks, and yet he did never rest to solicite continually my going upon them, certifying me of a generall assembly even at that time made by Menatonon at Choanoak of all his Weroances, and allyes to the number of 3,000 bowes preparing to come upon us at Roanoak and that the Mangoaks also were joined in the same confederacie, who were able of themselves to bring as many more to the enterprise: And true it was, that at this time the assembly was holden at Choanoak about us, as I found at my comming thither, which being unlooked for did so dismay them, as it made us have the better hand at them. But this confederacie against us of the Choanists and Mangoaks was altogether and wholly procured by Pemisapan himselfe, as Menatonon confessed unto me, who sent them continuall worde that our purpose was fully bent to destroy them: on the other side he tolde me that they had the like meaning towards us.

Hee in like sort having sent worde to the Mangoaks of mine intention to passe up into their River, and to kill them (as he sayd) both they and the Moratiks, with whom before we were entred into a league, and they had ever dealt kindly with us, abandoned their Townes along the River, and retyred themselves with their Crenepoes,[22] and their corne within the mayne: Insomuch as having passed three dayes voyage up the River, we could not meete a man, nor finde a grain of corne in their Townes: whereupon considering with my selfe, that wee had but two dayes victuall left, and that wee were then 160 miles from home, besides casualtie of contrarie windes or stormes, and suspecting treason of our owne Savages in the discoverie of our voyage intended, though we had no intention to be hurtfull to any of them, otherwise them for our copper to have had corn of them: I at night upon the Corps of Garde, before the putting foorth of centinels, advertised the whole companie of the case wee stoode in for victualls, and of mine opinion that we were betrayed by our owne Savages, and of purpose drawen foorth by them, upon vaine hope to be in the ende starved, seeing all the fledde before us, and therefore while we had those two dayes victuall left, I thought it good for us to make our returne homewarde, and that it were necessarie for us to get the other side of the sound of Weopomiok in time, where we might be relieved upon the weirs[23] of Chypanum, and the womans Towne, although the people were fled.

Thus much I signified unto them, as the safest way: neverthelesse, I did referre it to the greatest number of voyces, whether we should adventure the spending of our whole victuall in some further viewe of that most goodly River in hope to meete some better hap, or otherwise to retyre ourselves backe againe: And for that they might be the better advised, I willed them to deliberate all night upon the matter, and in the morning at our going aborde to set our course according to the desires of the greatest part. Their resolution fully and wholly was (and not three found to be of the contrary opinion) that whiles there was left one halfs pints of corns for a man, that we should not leave the search of that River, and that there were in the companie two mastives,[24] upon the pottage of which with sassafras leaves (if the worst fell out) the companie would make shift to live two dayes, which time would bring them downe the currant to the mouth of the River, and to the entrie of the sound, and in two days more at the farthest they hoped to crosse the sounde and to be relieved by the wares, which two dayes they would fast rather than be drawen back a foote till they had seene the Mangoaks, either as friends or foes. This resolution of theirs did not a little please mee, since it came of them selves, although for mistrust of that which afterwards did happen, I pretended to have bene rather of the contrary opinion.

And that which made me most desirous to have some doings with the Mangoaks either in friendship or otherwise to have had one or two of them prisoners, was, for yet is it a thing most notorious to all the countrey, that there is a Province to the which sayd Mangoaks have recourse and traffike up that River of Moratico, which hath a marvellous and most strange Minerall. This Mine is so notorious amongst them, as not onely to the Savages dwelling up by the sayd river, and also to the Savages of Choanoke, and all them to the westward, but also to all them of the mayne: the countries name is of same, and is called Chaunis Temoatan.

The mineral they say is Wassador, which is copper, but they call by the name of Wassador every metall whatsoever: they say it is of the couler of our copper, but our copper is better than theirs: and the reason is for that it is redder and harder, whereas that of Chaunis Temoatan is very soft, and pale: they say that they take the sayd metall out of a river that falleth very swift from hie rocks, and hils, and they take it in shallowe water: the manner is this. They take a great bowle by their description as great as one of our targets, and wrap a skinne over the hollowe part thereof, leaving one part open to receive in the minerall: that done, they watch the comming down of the currant, and the change of the couler of the water, and then suddenly chop downe the sayd bowl with the skin, and receive into the same as much oare as will come in, which is ever as much as their bowle will hold, which presently they cast into a fire, and forthwith it melteth, and doeth yeelde in 5. partes, at the first melting, two parts of metall for three partes of oare.[25] Of this metal the Mangoaks have so great a store, by report of all the Savages adjoining, that they beautifie their houses with great plates of the same: and this to be true, I received by report of all the country, and particularly by yong Skiko, the King of Choanokes sonne of my prisoner, who also himselfe had been prisoner with the Mangoaks, and set down all the particularities to mee before mentioned: but hee had not bene at Chawnis Temoatan himselfe: for he sayd, it was twentie dayes journey overlande from the Mangoaks, to the said minerall country, and that they passed through certaine other territories between them and the Mangoaks, before they came to the said country.

Upon report of the premisses, which I was very inquisitive in all places where I came to take very particular information of, by all the savages that dwell towards those parts, and especially of Menatonon himselfe, who in every thing did very particularly informe mee, and promised mee guides of his owne men, who shoulde passe over with mee, even to the sayde country of Chaunis Temoatan, (for over lande from Choanoak to the Mangoaks is but one dayes journey from sunne rising to sunne setting, whereas by water it is 7 daies with the soonest:) These things I say, made me verie desirous by all meanes possible to recover the Mangoaks, and to get some of their copper for an assay, and therefore I willingly yeelded to their resolution: But it fell out very contrarie to all expectation, and likelyhood: for after two dayes travell, and our whole victual spent, lying on shoare all night, wee could never see man, only fires we might perceive made alongst the shoare where we were to passe, and up into the countrie untill the very last day. In the evening whereof, about three of the clocke we heard certain savages call as we thought, Manteo, who was also at that time with mee in boate, whereof we all being very glad, hoping of some friendly conference with them, and making him to answere them, they presently began a song, as we thought in token of our welcome to them: but Manteo presently betooke him to his peece, and tolde mee that they meant to fight with us: which word was not so soone spoken by him, and the light horsemen ready to put to shoare, but there lighted a vollie of their arrowes amongst them in the boate, but did no hurt God be thanked to any man. Immediately, the other boate lying ready with their shot to skeure[26] the place for our hand weapons to land upon, which was presently done, although the lande was very high and steepe, the Savages forthwith quitted the shoare, and betooke themselves to flight: we landed, and having fayre and easily followed for a small time after them, who had wooded themselves we know not where: the sunne drawing then towards the setting, and being then assured that the next day, if wee would pursue them, though wee might happen to meete with them, yet we should bee assured to meet with none of their victuall, which we then had good cause to thinke of, therefore choosing for the companie convenient grounde in safetie to lodge in for the night, making a strong Corps of Garde, and putting out good sentinels, I determined the next morning before the rising of the sunne to be going backe againe, if possibly wee might recover the mouth of the river into the broade sounde, which at my first motion I found my whole companie ready to assent unto: for they were nowe come to their dogs poridge, that they had bespoken for themselves, if that befell them which did, and I before did mistrust we should hardly escape. The ende was, we came the next day by night to the rivers mouth within 4 or 5 miles of the same, having rowed in one day downe the currant, as much as in 4 dayes we had done against the same: we lodged upon an Islande, where wee had nothing in the worlde to eate but pottage of sassafras leaves, the like whereof for a meate was never used before as I thinke. The broad sownde wee had to passe, the next day all fresh and fasting: that day the winde blewe so strongly, and the billow so great, that there was no possibilitie of passage without sinking our boates. This was upon Easter eve,[27] which was fasted very trulie. Upon Easter day in the morning the wind comming very calme, wee entred the sownde, and by 4 of the clocke we were at Chipanum, where all the Savages that wee had left there were fled, but their wears did yeelde us some fish, as God was pleased not utterly to suffer us to be lost for some of our companie of the light horsemen were far spent. The next morning we arrived at our home Roanoke.

I have set down this voyage somewhat particularly, to the ende it may appeare unto you, (as true it is) that there wanted no great good will from the most to the least amongst us, to have perfited[28] this discoverie of the mine: for that discovery of a good mine, by the goodnesse of God, or a passage to the South Sea, or someway to it, and nothing els can bring this country in request to be inhabited by our nation. And with the discovery of any of the two above shewed, it wil be the most sweete, and healthfullest climate, and there withall the most fertile soyle, being manured in the world: and then will Sassafras, and many other rootes and gummes there found make good Marchandise and lading for shipping, which otherwise of themselves will not bee worth the fetching.

Provided also, that there be found out a better harborough then yet there is, which must bee to the Northward, if any there be, which was mine intention to have spent this summer in the search of, and of the mine of Chawnis Temoatan: the one I would have done, if the barks that I should have had of Sir Francis Drake, by his honorable coutesie, had not bene driven away by storme: the other if your supply of more men, and some other necessaries had come to us in any convenient sufficiencie. For this river of Moratico promiseth great things, and by the opinion of Master Harriots the heade of it by the description of the country, either riseth from the bay of Mexico, or els from very neere unto the same that openeth out into the South sea.

And touching the Minerall, thus does Master Yougham[29] affirme that though it be but copper, seeing the Savages are able to melt it, it is one of the richest Minerals in the worlde.

Wherefore a good harborough founde to the Northward, as before is sayd, and from thence foure dayes overland, to the river of Choanoak sconses being raysed, from whence againe overlande through the province of Choanoak one dayes voyage to the first towne of the Mangoaks up the river of Moratico by the way, as also upon the sayd river for the defence of our boats like sconses being set, in this course of proceeding you shall cleare your selfe from all those dangers and broad shallowe sowndes before mentioned, and gayne within foure dayes travell into the heart of the mayne 200 myles at the least, and to passe your discoverie into that most notable, and to the likeliest parts of the mayne, with farre greater felicitie than otherwise can bee performed.

Thus sir, I have though simply, yet truly set downe unto you, what my labour with the rest of the Gentlemen, and poore men of our company, (not without both payne, and perill which the lorde in his mercy many wayes delivered us from) could yeelde unto you, which might have bene performed in some more perfection, if the lorde had bene pleased that onely that which you had provided for us had at the first bene left with us, or that he had not in his eternall providence now at the last set some other course in these things, then the wisdome of man could looke into, which truly the carrying away, by a most strange, and unlooked for storme all our provision, with barks, master, marryners, and sundrie also of mine owne company, all having bene so courteously supplyed by the Generall Sir Francis Drake, the same having bene most sufficient to have performed the greatest part of the premisses, must ever make me thinke, the hand of God only, for some his good purpose to my selfe yet unknowne, to have bene in the matter.[30]

SIX

The Military Colony, 1585 (Part Two)

The second part of Ralph Lane's account of the military colony's occupation of Roanoke, which covers the complex relationship Lane and his men had with the Native Indian tribes, and their plots and counterplots against the English. It also covers Lane's exodus from Roanoke; something that was much against the instructions he had received from Raleigh and Grenville:

Ensenore a savage father to Pemisapan being the only friend to our nation that we had amongst them, and about the King, died the 20. Aprill 1586, hee alone, had before opposed himselfe in their consultations against al matters proposed against us, which both the King, and all the rest of them after Granganimeo's death, were very willing to have preferred. And he was not onely by the meere providence of God during his life, a meane to save us from hurt, as poisonings and such like, but also to doe us very great good, and singulerly in this.

The King was advised and of himselfe disposed, as a ready meane to have assuredly brought us to ruine in the moneth of March 1586 himselfe also with all his Savages to have runne away from us, and to have left his ground in the Iland unsowed, which if he had done, there had bene no possibility in common reason, (but by the immediate hand of God) that we could have bene preserved from starving out of hand. For at that time wee had no weares for fishe, neither could our men skill of the making of them, neither had wee one grane of corne for feede to put into the ground.

In mine absence on my voyage that I had against the Choanists, and Mangoaks,[1] they had raised a bruite[2] among themselves, that I and my company were part slayne, and part starved by the Choanists, and Mangoaks. One part of this tale was too true, that I and mine were like to be starved, but the other false.

Neverthelesse until my return, it tooke such effect in Pemisapan's breast, and those against us, that they grew not onely into contempt of us, but also (contrary to their former reverend opinion in shew, of the almightie God of heaven, and Jesus Christ, whome wee serve and worship, whome before they woulde acknowledge and confesse the onely God:) nowe they began to blaspheme, and flatly to say, that our Lord God was not God, since hee suffered us to sustaine much hunger, and also to be killed of the Renapoaks, for so they call by that generall name, all the inhabitants of the whole mayne, of what province so ever. Insomuch as olde Ensenore, neither any of his fellowes, coulde for his sake have no more credite for us: and it came so farre that the King was resolved to have presently gone away as is aforesaid.

"The village of Secoton" by John White (© The Trustees of the British Museum).

But even in the beginning of this bruite I returned, which when hee saw contrarie to his expectation, and the advertisement that he had received: that not only my selfe, and my company were al safe, but also by report of his owne 3. Savages, which had bene with mee besides Manteo in that voyage, that is to say, Tetepano, his sisters husband Eracano, and Cossine, that the Choanists, and Mangoaks, (whose name, and multitude besides their valour is terrible to al the rest of the provinces) durst not for the most part of them abide us, and that those that did abide us were killed, and that we had taken Menatonon prisoner, and brought his sonne that he best loved to Roanoak with me, it did not a little asswage all devices against us: on the other side, it made Ensenors opinions to be received againe with greater respects.

For hee had often before tolde them, and then renewed those his former speeches, both to the King and the rest, that wee were the servants of God, and that wee were not subject to be destroyed by them: but contrariwise, that they amongst them that fought our destruction, should finde their owne, and not be able to worke ours, and that we being dead men were able to doe them more hurt, then now we coulde do being alive: an opinion very confidently at this day holden by the wisest amongst them, and of their olde men, as also, that they have bene in the night, being 100 myles from any of us in the ayre shot at, and stroken by some men of ours, that by sicknesse had dyed among them[3]: and many of them holde opinion, that wee be dead men returned into the worlde againe, and that we doe not remayne dead but for a certain time, and that then we returne againe. All these speeches then againe grew in ful credite with them, the King and all touching us, when hee saw the small troupe returned againe, and in that sort from those whose very names were terrible unto them: but that which made up the matter on our side for that time, was an accident, yea rather, (as all the rest was) the good providence of the Almightie for the saving of us, which was this.

Within certain days after my return from the said journey, Menatonon sent a messenger to visite his sonne the prisoner with me, and sent me certaine pearle for a present, or rather as Pemisapan told me, for the ransome of his sonne, and therefore I refused them: but the greatest cause of his sending then, was to signifie unto me, that hee had commanded Okisko King of Weopomiok, to yeelde himselfe servant, and homager, to the great Weroanza of England,[4] and after her to Sir Walter Ralegh: to performe which commandement received from Menatonon, the sayd Okisko jointly with this Menatonone messenger, sent foure and twentie of his principall men to Roanoak to Pemisapan, to signifie that they were readie to performe the same, and so had sent those his men to let me knowe, that from that time forwarde hee, and his successors were to acknowledge her Majestie their only Soveraigne, and next unto her, as is aforesaide.

All which being done, and acknowledged by them all, in the presence of Pemisapan his father, and all his Savages in counsel then with him, it did for the time, thorowly (as it seemed) change him in disposition toward us: Insomuch as forthwith Ensenore wan this resolution of him, that out of hand he should goe about and withall, to cause his men to set up weares forthwith for us: both which he, at that present went in hand withal and did so labour the expedition of it, that in the end of April, he had sowed a good quantitie of ground, so much as had bene sufficient, to have fed our whole company (God blessing the growth) and that by the belly for a whole yere: besides that he gave us a certaine plot of grounde for ourselves to sowe. All which put us in marvellous comfort, if we could passe from Aprill, until the beginning of July, (which was to have bene the beginning of their harvest,) that then a newe supplie out of England or else our own store would well enough maintayne us: All our feare was of the two moneths betwixt, in which meane space, if the Savages should not helpe us with Cassada,[5] and Chyna,[6] and that our weares should fayle us, (as often as they did,) wee might very well starve, notwithstanding the growing corne, like the starving horse in the stable, with the grow-ing grasse as the proverbe is, which we very hardlye had escaped but onely by the hand of God, as it pleased him to try us. For within few days after, as before is sayd Ensenore our friende dyed, who was no sooner dead, but certaine our great enemies about Pemis-apan, as Osocan a Weroance, Tanaquiny and Wanchese most principally, were in hand again to put their old practices in use against us, which we readily imbraced, and all their former devices against us renewed, and new brought in question.

But that of starving us, by their forbearing to sowe, was broken by Ensenore in his life, by having made the King all at one instant to sowe his grounde not onely in the Islande but also at Addesinocopeio in the mayne, within two leagues over against us. Neverthelesse there wanted no store of mischevous practices among them, and of all they resolved principally of this following.

First that Okisko, king of Weopomiok, with the Mandoages, should bee moved, and with great quantitie of copper intertayned to the number of seven, or 800 bowes to the interprise the matter thus to be ordred. They of Weopomiok should be invited to a cer-taine kind of moneths minde[7] which they do use to solemnise in their Savage maner for any great personage dead, and should have bene for Ensenore. At this instant also should the Mangoaks, who were a great people with the Chesepians, and their friends to the number 700 of them to be armed at a day appoynted to the mayne of Addesinocopeio, and there lying close at the signe of fyres, which should interchangeably be made on both sides, where Pemisapan with his troup above named should have exe-cuted me, and some of our Weroances (as they called all our principall officers,) the mayne forces of the rest should have come over into the Iland where they ment to have dispatched the rest of the company, whome they did imagine to finde both dismayed and dispersed abroade in the Island seeking of crabs, and fish to live withall. The manner of their enterprise was this.

Tarraquine and Andacon two principall men about Pemisapan, and very lustie fel-lowes with twentie more appointed to them had the charge of my person to see an order taken for the same, which they ment should in this fort have bene executed. In the dead time of the night they would have beset my house, and put fire in the reedes, that the same was covered with: meaning (as it was likelye) that my self would have come running out of a sudden amazed in my shirt without armes, upon the instant whereof they would have knocked out my brayns.

The same order was given to certaine of his fellowes, for Master Harriots: so for all the rest of our better sort, all our houses at one instant being set on fire as afore is sayde, and that as well for them of the forte, as for us at the towne.[8] Now to the end that we might be the fewer in number together, and so be the more easilie dealt withall (for in deed ten of us with our arms prepared, were a terror to a hundred of the best sort of them,) they agreed and did immediately put it in practice, that they should not for any copper, sell us any victuals whatsoever: besides that in the night they should send to have our weares robbed, and also to cause them to be broken and once being broken never to be repayred again by them. By this meanes the King stood assured, that I must bee enforced for lacke of sustenance, there to disband my company into sundry places to live upon shell fysh, for so the Savages themselves doe, going to Ottorasko,[9] Crotoan, and other places fishing and hunting, while their grownds be in sowing, and their corne growing, which fayled not his expectation. For the famine grewe so extreeme among us, our weares fayling us of fish, that I was enforced to send Captaine Stafford with 20 with him to Croatoan my lord Admirals Island[10] to serve two turnes in one, that is to say to feede himselfe and his company, and also to keepe watch, if any shipping came upon the coast to warn us of the same, I sent Master Prideox with the Pynnesse to

Otterasco, and ten with him, with the Provost Marshall to live there, and also to wayte for shipping: also I sent every weeke 16 or 20 of the rest of the companie to the mayne over against us, to live off Cassava, and Oysters.

In the meane while Pemisapan went of purpose to Addesinocopeio for 3 causes, the one to see his grounds there broken up, and sowed for a second croppe: the other to withdrawe himselfe from my daily sending to him for supply of victuall for my company, for hee was afrayd to denye me anything, neither durst he in my presence but by colour, and with excuses, which I was content to accept for the time, meaning in the ende as I had reason, to give him the jumpe once for all: but in the meane whiles, as I had ever done before, I and mine bare all wrongs, and accepted of all excuses.

My purpose was to have relyed my selfe with Menatonon, and the Choanists, who in truth as they are more valiant people and in greater number then the rest, so are they more faithful in their promises, and since my late being there, had given many tokens of earnest desire they had to joyne in perfect league with us, and therefore were greatly offended with Pemisapan and Weopomiok for making him beleeve such tales of us.

The third cause of his going to Addesinocopeio was to dispatch his messengers to Weopomiok, and to the Mandoages, as aforesaid, all which he did with great impresse of copper in hand, making large promises to them of greater spoyle.

The answere within few days after, came from Weopomiok, which was divided into two parts. First for the King Okisko, who denyed to be of any partie for him selfe, or any of his especial followers, and therefore did immediatly retyre himselfe with his force into the mayne: the other was concerning the rest of the sayd province who accepted of it: and in like sort the Mandoags received the imprest.[11]

The day of their assembly aforesayd at Roanoke, was appoynted the 10 of July: all which the premises were discovered by Skyco, the King Menatonon his sonne my prisoner, who having once attempted to run away, I laid him in the bylboes,[12] threatyning to cut off his head, whome I remitted at Pemisapans request: whereupon he being perswaded that he was our enemie to the death, he did not only feede him with himselfe, but also made him acquainted with all his practices.

On the other side, the yong man finding himself as well used at my hand, as I had meanes to shew, and that all my companie made much of him, he flatly discovered al unto me, which also afterwards was revealed unto me by one of Pemisapans own men, the night before he was slaine.

These mischiefes being al instantly upon mee, and my companie to be put in execution, stood mee in hand to study how to prevent them, and also to save all others, which were at that time as aforesaid so farre from me: whereupon I sent to Pemisapan to put suspicion out of his heade, that I ment presently to goe to Crotoan, for that I had heard of the arival of our fleete, (though I in trueth had neither heard nor hoped for so good adventure,) and that I meant to come by him, to borrow of his men to fish for my company, and to hunt for me at Crotoan, as also to buy some foure dayes provision to serve for my voyage.

He sent mee word that he would himselfe come over to Roanoak, but from day to day hee deferred, only to bring the Weopomioks with him, and the Mandoags, whose time appoynted was within 8 dayes after. It was the last of May 1586 when all his owne Savages began to make their assembly at Roanoak, at his commandement sent abroad unto them, and I resolved not to stay longer upon his comming over, since he ment to come with so good company, but thought good to go, and visite him with such as I had, which I resolved to do the next day: but that night I ment by the way to give them in the Island a Canuisado,[13] and at the instant to seise upon all the Canoas[14] about the Island to keepe him from advertisements.

But the towne took the allarum,[15] before I ment it to them. The occasion was this. I had sent the Master of the light horsemen with a few with him, to gather up all the Canoas in the setting of the sunne, and to take as many as were going from us to Adessinocopeio, but to suffer any that came from thence to land: he met with a Canoa, going from the shoare, and overthrew the Canoa, and cut off 2 Savages heads: this was not done so secretly but hee was discovered from the shoare, whereupon the cry arose: for in trueth they, privie to their owne villainous purposes against us, held as good espial upon us, both day and night, as we did upon them.

The allarum given, they took themselves to their bowes, and we to our armes: some three or foure of them at the first were slayne with our shot, the rest fled into the woods: The next morning with the light horseman, and one Canoa, taking 25. with the Colanel of the Chesepians, and the serjiant major, I went to Adessinocopeio, and being landed sent Pemisapan word by one of his owne Savages that met me at the shore, that I was going to Crotoan, and ment to take him in the way to complaine unto him of Osocon, who the night past was conveying away my prisoner, whom I had there present tied in a Handlocke: hereupon the King did abide my comming to him and finding my selfe amidst 7 or 8 of his principal Weroances, and followers, (not regarding any of the common sort) I gave the watchword agreed upon, (which was Christ our victory,) and immediatly those his chiefe men, and himselfe, had by the mercie of God for our deliverance, that which they had purposed for us. The King himselfe being shot thorow by the Colonell with a pistoll lying on the ground for dead, and I looking as watchfully for the saving of Manteos friends, as others were busie that none of the rest should escape, suddenly he started by and ran away as though he had not bene touched, insomuch as he overran all the companie, being by the way shot thwart the buttocks by mine Frish boy with my Petronell.[16] In the end an Frishman serving me, one Nugent and the deputie provost undertooke him, and following him in the woods overtook him, and I in some doubt least we had lost both the King, and my man by our owne negligence to have bene intercepted by the Savages, we met him returning out of the woods with Pemisapan's head in his hand.[17]

This fell out the first of June 1586, and the 8 of the same came advertisement to me from Captain Stafford, lying at my lord Admiral's Island, that he had discovered a great fleete of 23 sailes: but whether they were friends or foes, he could not yet discerne, he advised me to stand upon as good gard as I could.

The 9 of the said month, he himselfe came unto me, having that night before, and that same day travelled by land 20 miles, and I must truly report of him from the first to the last, he was the Gentleman that never spared labour or perill either by land or water, faire weather or fowle, to performe any service committed unto him.

He brought me a letter from the Generall Sir Francis Drake, with a most bountifull and honourable offer for the supplie of our necessities to the performance of the action, we were entered into, and that not onely of victuals, munitions and clothing, but also of barkes, pinnaces and boates, they also by him to be victualled, manned, and furnished to my contentation.[18]

The 10 day hee[19] arrived in the road of our bad harborough, and comming there to an anker, the 11 day I came to him, whom I found in deeds most honourably to performe that which in writing and message he had most curteously offered, he having aforehand propounded the matter to all the captains of his fleete, and got their liking and consent thereto.

With such thanks unto him and his captaines for his care of us and of our action, not as the matter deserved, but as I could both for my companie and my self, I (being aforehand) prepared what I would desire, craved at his hands that it would please him to take with him into England a number of weake, and unfit men for my good action, which I would deliver to him, and in place of them to supply me of his company, with oaresmen, artificers, and others.

That he would leave us so much shipping and victuall, as about August then next followyng, would carry me and all my companie into England, when we had discovered somwhat that for lacke of needfull provision in time left with us as yet remained undone.

That it would please him withall to leave some sufficient masters not onely to carry us into England when time should be, but also to search the coast for some better harborow if there were any, and especially to helpe us to some small boats and oaresmen.

Also for a supplie of Calievers,[20] handweapons, match and lead, tooles, apparell and such like.

He having received these my requests according to his usuall commendable maner of governement (as it was told me) calling his captaines to counsell, the resolution was that I should send such of my officers of my companie, as I used in such matters, with their notes to goe aboord with him, which were the master of the victuals, the keeper of the store, and the Vicetreasurer, to whom he appointed foorthwith for me the *Francis*, being a very proper barke of 70 tunnes, and tooke present order for bringing of victuall aboord her for 100 men for foure moneths withall my other demaunds whatsoever, to the uttermost.

And further appointed for me two fine pinnaces, and 4 small boats, and that which was to performe all his former liberalitie towards us, was that he had gotten the full assents of two of as sufficient experimented[21] master as were any in his fleete, by judgement of them that knewe them, with very sufficient gings[22] to tarry[23] with mee, and to employ themselves most earnestly in the action, as I should appoynt them, until the terme which I promised of our returne into England agayne.[24] The names of one of those masters was Abraham Kendall, the other Griffith Herne.

While these things were in hand, the provision aforesayd being brought, and in bringing aboord, my said masters being also gone aboord, my sayd barkes having accepted of their charge, and mine owne officers with others in like sort of my company with them, all which was dispatched by the said Generall the 12 of the said moneth: the 13 of the same there arose such an unwonted storme, and continued foure dayes that had like to have driven all on shore, if the Lord had not held his holy hand over them, and the generall very providently foreseene the worst himselfe, then about my dispatch putting himselfe aboord: but in the ende having driven sundry of the fleete to put to sea, the *Francis* also with all my provisions, my two masters, and my companie aboord, she was seene to be free from the same, and to put cleare to sea.

This storm having continued from the 13 to the 16 of the moneth, and thus my barke put away as aforesayd, the Generall comming ashore, made a new proffer to me, which was a shippe of 170 tunnes, called the *Barke Bonner*, with a sufficient master and guide to tarrie with mee the time appointed, and victualled sufficiently to carrie mee and my companie into England with all provisions as before: but hee tolde mee that hee would not for any thing undertake to have her brought into our harbour, and therefore hee was to leave her in the roade, and to leave the care of the rest unto my selfe, and advised mee to consider with my companie of our case, and to deliver presently unto him in writing, what I would require him to doe for us: which being within his power, he did assure me as well for his Captaines, as for himselfe should be most willingly performed.

Hereupon calling such Captaines and Gentlemen of my companie as then were at hand, who were all as privie as my selfe to the Generals offer, their whole request was to mee, that considering the case that we stood in, the weaknesse of our companie, the small number of the same, the carrying away of our first appointed barke, with those two especiall masters, with our principall provisions in the same, by the very hand of God as it seemed, stretched out to take us from thence: considering also, that his second offer, though most honourable of his part, yet of ours not to be taken, insomuch as there was no possibilitie for her with any safetie to be brought into the harbour: Seeing furthermore our hope for supplie with Sir Richard Greenvill so undoubtedly promised us before Easter, not yet come, neither then likely to come this yeere considering the doings in England for Flaunders,[25] as also for America, that therefore I would resolve my selfe, with my companie to goe into England in that fleete, and accordingly to make request to the Generall in all our names, that he would bee pleased to give us present passage with him. Which request of ours by my selfe delivered unto him, hee most readily assented unto, and so hee sending immediately his pinnaces unto our Island for the fetching away of fewe that there were left with our baggage, the weather was so boysterous, and the pinnaces so often on ground, that the most of all we had, with all our Cardes, Bookes and writings, were by the Saylers cast overboord, the greater number of the fleete being much aggrieved with their long and dangerous abode in that miserable road.

From whence the Generall in the name of the almightie, waying his ankers (having bestowed us among his fleete) for the reliefe of whom hee had in that storme sustained more perill of wrecke then in all his former most honourable actions against the Spaniards, with praises unto God for all, set saile the 19 June 1586, and arrived in Portsmouth, the 27 of Julie the same yeere.[26]

Captain Walter Bigges, who sailed with Sir Francis Drake, witnessed the relief of Lane's colony. His version of events differs slightly from Lane's, particularly in the number of personnel rescued:

The ninth of June upon sight of one speciall great fire (which are verie ordinary all alongst this coast, even from the Cape Florida hither) the Generall sent his Skiffe to the shore, where they found some of our English countreymen (that had bene sent thither the yeare before by Sir Walter Raleigh) and brought one aboord, by whose direction we proceeded along to the place, which they make their Port. But some of our ships being of great draught unable to enter, we ankered all without the harbour in a wild road at sea, about two miles from shore.

From whence the General wrote letters to Master Ralfe Lane, being Governour of those English in Virginia, and then at his fort about six leagues from the road in an Island, which they call Roanoac, wherein specially he shewed how readie he was to supply his necessities and wants, which he understood of, by those he had first talked withall.

The morrowe after Master Lane him selfe and some of his companie comming unto him, with the consent of his Captaines, he gave them the choise of two offers, that is to say: Either he would leave a ship, a Pinnace, and certaine boates with sufficient Masters and mariners, together furnished with a moneths victuall to stay and make farther discoverie of the country and coastes, and so much victuall likewise that might be sufficient for the bringing of them all (being an hundred and three persons)[27, 28] into England if they thought good after such time, with anie other thing they would desire, and that he might be able to spare.

Or else if they thought they had made sufficient discoverie alreadie, and did desire to return into England, he would give them passage. But they as it seemed, being delirious to stay, accepted verie thankefully, and with great gladnesse that which was offered first. Whereupon the ship being appointed and receaved into charge, by some of their owne companie sent into her by Master Lane, before they had receaved from the rest of the Fleete, the provision appointed them, there arose a great storme (which they sayde was extraordinarie and verie straunge) that lasted three dayes together, and put all our Fleete in great daunger, to be driven from their ankering upon the coast. For we brake manie cables, and lost manie ankers. And some of our Fleete which had lost all (of which number was the ship appointed for Master Lane and his companie) were driven to put to sea in great danger, in avoiding the coast, and could never see us againe untill we met in England. Manie also of our small Pinnaces and boates were lost in this storme.

Notwithstanding after all this, the Generall offered them (with consent of his Captaines) another ship with some provision, although not such a one for their turnes, as might have bene spared them before, this being unable to be brought into their harbour. Or else if they would, to give them passage into England, although he knewe he should performe it with greater difficultie then he might have done before.

But Master Lane with those of the chiefest of his companie he had then with him, considering what should be best for them to doe, made request unto the Generall under their handes, that they might have passage for England: the which being graunted, and the rest sent for out of the countery and shipped, we departed from the coast the eighteenth of June.[29]

Thus, as Ralph Lane left Roanoke Island, England, and Raleigh, effectively abandoned their first attempt to establish an English colony in America.

SEVEN

The Second Voyage of Sir Richard Grenville, 1586

In April 1586, Grenville sailed again for Roanoke from Bideford with his ships, the *Tyger* and the *Roebuck*, his intention being to resupply Ralph Lane's colony. However, things did not go according to plan as Philip Wyot, Town Clerk of Barnstaple observed: "1586, 16 Ap. [April] ... Sir Richard Greynvylle sailed over the barr with his flee boat and friget. but for want of suffic. water on the barr being neare upon neape, he left his ship. This Sir Richard Greynvylle pretended his goinge to Wyngandecora, where he was last year."[1]

We also read from Pedro Diaz that Grenville "equipped six vessels, one of 150 tons and the rest from 100 to 60, and with these and 400 seamen and soldiers and supplies for a year he made sail on May 2, 1586...."[2]

Hakluyt's transcription is somewhat general in nature, but reads:

In the yeere of our Lord, 1586, Sir Walter Raleigh at his owne charge prepared a ship of 100 tunnes, fraighted with all maner of things in most plentiful maner for the supplie and relief of his Colonie then remaining in Virginia: but before they set saile from England, it was after Easter, so that our Colonie half despaired of the comming of any supplie, wherefore every man prepared for himself, determining resolutely to spend the residue of their lifetime in that countrey, and for the better performance of this their determination, they sowed, planted, and set such things as were necessarie for their reliefe in so plentifull a manner, as might have sufficed them two yeeres without any further labor: thus trusting to their owne harvest they passed the summer till the tenth of June, at which time their corne which they had sowed was within one fortnight of reaping, but then it happened, that Sir Francis Drake in his prosperous returne from the sacking of Saint Domingo, Cartagena, and Saint Augustines determined in his way homewarde to visit his countrymen the English Colonie then remaynning in Virginia: so passing along the coastes of Florida, he fell with the partes, where our English Colony inhabited, and having espied some of that company, there he ankered, and went alande where he conferred with them of their state and welfare, and howe thinges had passed with them: they aunswered him that they lived all, but hitherto in some scarcitie, and as yet could hear of no supplye out of England: Therefore they requested him that he would leave with them some two or three shippes, that if in some reasonable time they

"A Cheife Herowans Wyfe of Pomeoc and her daughter of the age of 8," by John White. Note the daughter appears to be carrying an English toy doll (© The Trustees of the British Museum).

heard not out of England, they might then return themselves: which he agreed to: while some were then writing their letters to send into England, and some others making reportes of the accidentes of their travels each to other, some on lande, some on boord, a great storme arose, and drove the most of their fleete from their ankers to Sea, in which shippes, at that instant were the chiefest of the English Colony: the rest on land perceiving this, hasted to those three sayles which were appointed to be left there, and for feare they should be left behinde, left all thinges so confusedly, as if they had bene chased from thence by a mightie armie, and no doubt they were, for the hande of God came upon them for the crueltie, and outrages committed by some of them against the native inhabitantes of that Countrie.[3]

Immediately after the departing of our English Colonie out of this paradise of the worlde, the shippe above mentioned sent, and set forth at the charges of Sir Walter Raleigh, and his direction, arrived at Hatorask, who after some time spent in seeking our Colony up in the Countrie, and not finding them, returned with all the aforesaid provision into England.[4]

About fourteene or fifteene daies after the departure of the aforesayd shippe, Sir Richard Grindfield[5] Generall of Virginia, accompanied with three shippes well appointed for the same voyage arrived there, who not finding the aforesaid ship according to his expectation,[6] nor hearing any newes of our English Colony, there seated, and left by him anno 1585, him selfe travailling up into divers places of the Countrey, as well to see if he could here any newes of the Colony left there by him the yeere before, under the charge of Master Lane his deputy, as also to discover some places of the Countrie[7]: but after some time spent therein not hearing any newes of them, and finding the place which they inhabited desolate, yet unwilling to loose the possession of the Countrie, which Englishmen had so long helde: after good deliberation he determined to leave some men behinde to retaine possession of the Country: whereupon he landed 15 men in the Ile of Roanoke furnished plentifully with all manner of provision for two years, and so departed for England.

Not long after he fell with the Isles of the Azores, on some of which Islands he landed, and spoyled the Townes of all such thinges as were worth carriage, where also he tooke divers Spanyardes: with these, and many other exploits done by him in this voyage, as well outward as homeward, he returned into England.[8]

Written in the margin of the transcript are the words "Grenville's third voyage." However, Grenville only undertook two voyages that we know of, to Roanoke: the 1585 voyage to settle the military colony, and this one of 1586.

Pedro Diaz's account of Grenville's 1586 voyage is far more detailed than Hakluyt's, and quite revealing, for he states that after leaving Bideford, the fleet headed for Finisterre where they "encountered fourteen French and Flemish ships out of San Lucar and Cadiz for France and Flanders, of which he (Grenville) captured two. The rest escaped. With these he took a great quantity of merchandise which he sent to his home in the prizes themselves."[9]

Diaz continues:

Later he met a Flemish flyboat bound for San Lucar with a cargo of merchandise, and kept this vessel with him after removing its cargo to the six ships of his squadron. He armed this flyboat to fight, for it was a good sailer. With these seven ships he came up to Porto Santo, an island close to Madeira, and sent a boat to shore to discover conditions there, and to take water and whatever else they might find to hand. The people there were few but they stood on their defence to prevent the English from landing. They offered to give them a ton of water for each ship, if they would not land. This angered the commander and he attempted to land with the intention of burning and destroying the place and its inhabitants. For this purpose he made ready his boats and ordered his men into them and went to the shore, but the people there prevented him from landing and fought valiantly, in such manner that the Englishman returned to his ships.

Next day he brought his ships close in, to sweep the beach with their artillery. This did the people there little damage because of their defensive works. They held him off until midday, when the Englishman made sail and continued on his course for Florida, where he had left settlers, in latitude 36°.[10]

Beyond Santa Maria Bay the coast runs to the northeast for about 80 leagues to Cape San Juan; from there the coast runs north and south twelve leagues to where this settlement is on an island close to the main. The Island can be crossed on foot. The land produces little to eat. There is only maize and of that little and poor in quality.[11]

And so they found the island deserted; they found an Englishman and an Indian who had been hanged. Of the natives they found only three, and as they were conducting these to their ships two escaped. The other was held prisoner,[12] and of him they learned that Francis Drake had taken away what settlers there were in the island. They have there a timber fort of no great strength, which stands in the water.[13]

There is an abundance of timber. The soil is sandy and wet and swampy. Pedro Diaz does not know the quality of the soil of the main, but it seems fertile and heavily wooded. In this fort the Englishman left eighteen men. He would not permit Pedro Diaz to land or to go into the fort. The captain remained there fourteen days: and in the fort were left four pieces of iron ordnance and supplies for the eighteen men for a year.[14] In command of them he left a Master Coffin, Englishman, and another called Chapman.[15] This done, the captain made sail with his ships and steered for the open sea, with the intention of encountering vessels from the Indies.

He reached the Azores with his men very sick. About 34 died. From there he crossed to Newfoundland and entered San Francisco Bay where the men went on shore to refresh, and they laid in a supply of fish.[16] From there he returned to the Azores again, about 400 leagues sailing, and he had been among the islands about eight days when he took a bark with passengers from San Miguel de la Terceira.

They were humble folk and he carried them along with him and most of them died. A lad told him that a vessel with a cargo of hides was at an island called Villafranca, where they had unloaded the hides to careen the ship because it leaked. The Englishman went there and carried the hides into his ship.

Off San Miguel he sent a ship to La Terceira which came up to another English vessel which was chasing a frigate from Puerto Rico and together they took her. After which he steered for England where he arrived on December 26, 1586.[17]

Pedro Diaz, along with about forty other Spaniards and Portuguese held captive in Bideford almost certainly provided the slave labor for the building of Grenville's new manor house on the quayside there, a project funded by the proceeds of the capture of the *Santa Maria de San Vincente* the previous year. Evidence supporting this, come from a letter dated February 27, 1588, and written by the two Portuguese pilots Grenville held captive, Francisco De Valverde and Pedro Diaz (who signs himself "De Santa Cruz"). They describe themselves as "Prisoners of War in England." The letter, sent to Bernardino De Mendoza, the Spanish Ambassador in France continues:

> ...(We) poor pilots who were captured by Richard Grenville of Cornwall, and are now held prisoners by him. He is a pirate; and brought to England 22 Spaniards whom he treated as slaves, making them carry stones on their backs all day for some building operations of his, and chaining them up all night. Twenty of them have died or escaped...[18]

EIGHT

Preparations for the "Cittie of Ralegh"

When Sir Walter Raleigh finally set out to colonize America, he had a clear idea of the type of people he was going to need. He would have gained this knowledge from the report made for him following the exploratory voyage of Amadas and Barlowe in 1584, and from Richard Hakluyt, whose *Discourse on Western Planting*, however naïve it may be considered to have been, provided a useful checklist of trades and disciplines for the colony. He also received reports from Ralph Lane, and certainly had some assistance from Grenville, whose attendance Pedro Diaz confirms by his deposition which declares that, "The commander (Sir Richard Grenville) then went to London and raised men for that establishment (Raleigh's colony) to the number of 210 persons, men and women...."[1]

Hakluyt's *Discourse* is worth further examination as its lists of required occupations provide some indication towards the likely social structure of the colony. According to his *Discourse*, the colony would need among others: "Millwrights, sawyers and carpenters for buildinges," blacksmiths, salt makers, brick and tile makers and layers and lime makers (for which evidence of this skill might be deduced from the copious volumes of burnt and powdered seashells found on Hatteras Island during the 2011 LCRG Archaeological excavations).

The list continues: thatchers, barbers (surgeons), tailors, cooks, bakers, brewers, butchers, shoemakers, tanners, skinners and dyers, fowlers and sea fishers and freshwater fishers (fishermen).

In addition, and at perhaps a more fascinating level, the need for "Sugar cane, vine and olive planters," hunters "skilfull to kill wilde beasts for vittell" and warreners "to breede conies (rabbits) and to kill vermin." "Mynerall men" (presumably miners, but it could also be inferred to mean mineralògists adept at determining the practical value of the area's geology), and "Synkers of welles and finders of springes" were also required.

The possibility of having to defend the colony was surely also considered, for Hakluyt also advised the investors to take: "Men experte in the arte of fortification," "Capitaines of longe and of greate experience," and "Souldiers well trayned in Flanders to joyne with the younger" (the latter meaning men who had fought in France to support those with little or no battle experience).

Hakluyt even considered the potential to harvest America and dispatch goods back to England. These roles would be important in ensuring the prosperity of the colony. His *Discourse* therefore included a requirement for "Burners of asshes for the trade of sope asshes (Potash)," "Joyners, to cutt oute the boordes into chests to be imbarqued for England," "Tallow chandlers, to prepare the tallowe to be incasked for England," shipwrights "in some number," and oar makers and makers of cable and cordage.[2]

Having identified the skills needed, Raleigh and Grenville set out to recruit their colonists. They and their followers had invested a serious amount of money into the colony. Thus, such a venture had no option but to rely a great deal upon the abilities and loyalty of those sent to do the job some 3,500 miles and several months of perilous journey away. In effect, the investors choices surely, had to be restricted principally to their employees, acquaintances, or perhaps just as likely, those of their private circle of family and friends; essentially, people they could trust. Any trade or skill recommended by Hakluyt but not covered by those connections would then, and probably only then, have required the gamble of selecting those of unknown quality from the general population. In fact, there is strong evidence from John White's own words, which confirm he had persuaded many of his connections to go to Roanoke, and from Pedro Diaz who informs us that Simon Fernando had also conducted something of a personal recruitment drive.[3]

A supporting argument, for want of a better term, is the "demographic" hypothesis, which developed from studying the demographics of the colonist's surnames. Its basis is a study, conducted by Researchers from the UCL Centre for Advanced Spatial Analysis (CASA), which revealed that many English surnames prevail and generally remain, specific to definable geographical areas of England.[4] When applying this study to the colonist's surnames, it becomes apparent that the nucleuses of many of them have a distinct connection to the estates and spheres of influence of the investors.

In detail: There are a number of surnames in the colony with origins in the west midlands. For their connection to an investor, we can refer to the Earl of Shrewsbury, someone known to Raleigh and Grenville not least because his flagship, the *Talbot*, took part in Drake's West Indian adventure, the same adventure that relieved Ralph Lane's military colony from Roanoke in 1585. While, the link between Raleigh and the colonists with surnames originating from the southwest of Scotland probably originates from religious persecution. In the late sixteenth century, Scotland was still a country in its own right. Its queen, Mary, Queen of Scots, was a staunch disciple of Roman Catholicism. There can be no doubt many Protestants suffered eviction from their lands because of their beliefs. Raleigh would have known of their plight. Perhaps he took the opportunity to offer them relocation to his Irish estates during the 1570s as part of the English plan to increase the number of English Protestant families living there. This would certainly explain the prevalence of Scottish surnames appearing in the records of the province at this time. By resettling in Munster, they would have encountered the English settlers transplanted by Grenville, who had already relocated over 100 people there by this time. However, as the English settlements in Ireland began to turn sour, it is reasonable to suggest that Raleigh and Grenville persuaded some of their Irish settlers to relocate once again, this time to the new world, and Roanoke Island.

Further evidence can be found in the west of England where we find the estates of some of the most pivotal players and investors in the colony. Apart from Grenville, the area was home to the Harris family of Plymouth, the Arundells of Cornwall, the St. Legers of Annery (near Bideford), the Carews (who also owned Carisbrooke Castle on the Isle of Wight, a stopping over point for the colonists' voyage of 1587) and, of course, Raleigh whose own family home was in East Devon.

We may observe that many of the investors with estates in the west of England knew each other, often as relatives, and thus made frequent social calls, often lasted several weeks. Such leisurely visits would have allowed more than enough time to discuss the Roanoke colony. These visits must have provided fertile ground for finding potential colonists.

If we make a more specific examination of the hypothesis, we find tantalizing fragments that may confirm the case for the west of England as being home to many of the colonists. Take, for example, the estate of Sir Richard Grenville at Bideford. While as a former Mayor of the town, the author may be somewhat biased, what follows does offer a number of coincidences, almost too many in fact not to have some basis in fact surely?

One of the earliest potential colonist records we find in Bideford relates to the Smith family. A common name indeed, but in 1696 a shipbuilding family of Smiths dispatched some of their employees to develop a ship repair yard on the Chester River in the colony of Maryland, specifically to repair the ships collecting tobacco from plantations, including their own, in Virginia. Could the Thomas Smith of the lost colony been one of their ancestors from barely a hundred years earlier? Might he have even been one of Hakluyt's recommended shipwrights for the colony? One might draw the same conclusion about other shipbuilders associated with the town, specifically the Chapman and Ellis families. Is it just conceivable Thomas Ellis, his son Robert, and John Chapman all worked on converting Grenville's Spanish prize the *Santa Maria de San Vincente*, and then later joined a Thomas Smith to sign up for the Roanoke colony, perhaps even at Grenville's request?

The Berry surname of the lost colony also has links with several villages in the north Devon area, not least with the ancient manor at Eastleigh, barely two miles from Bideford, which served as home for Sir John Berry, Commissioner of the Royal Navy, and many of his family between at least 1501 and circa 1800. A recent discovery in fact confirms that Sir Richard Grenville presided over an Inquisition Post-Mortem for a member of a Berry family who lived just eight miles south of Bideford.

Are all these connections just coincidences, or is there more substance to the demographic hypothesis than we dare hope?

There is of course one obvious source for potential colonists, albeit one that numbers only a very few: those who had travelled previously to Roanoke. While we have no rosters from the 1584 or 1586 voyages, the voyage of 1585 provides several names that appear on Hakluyt's 1587 list of colonists. A cursory glance for example reveals the name Edward Powell. Shortly before he sailed with Grenville and Lane in 1585, he married his wife Winifred (on January 10, 1585). From his time on Roanoke Island with the military colony, he may have considered the island offered a fair prospect for a new life. Thus, he and his wife duly signed up for the civilian colony two years later.

It is important at this point to address the question of involvement by the population of London in the search for colonists. One might consider the crowded diseased streets of London as the obvious place to find colonists, but there are good reasons to cast a note of caution on this hypothesis. London was certainly a commercial center for the landed gentry in Elizabethan times, but it was home to very few of them. One can confirm this with a quick review of the entries in the records of the Middle Temple for example, which clearly demonstrate that most of its members lived in country estates and simply travelled to London to conduct business. This is certainly proven by Grenville's own lifestyle, which confirms his main homes were in the west of England and, when in London he merely lodged at his in-laws' London home by Southwark Bridge. Therefore, with relatively few of the investors having a major influence over the population of London, even allowing for the servants that they may have employed to maintain their London homes, the investors would have had to raise considerable local awareness of the plan to settle America.

Such a large population would hardly know of any such venture, or sign up for it on a whim, without some form of mass marketing. Do we have any posters advertising the voyage? Are there any records from the dozens of communities in London asking for volunteers? Is there anything in the London Guilds recording the request for volunteers in specific trades as recommended by Hakluyt? With such widespread potential for sources of evidence, it would be surprising if nothing survived to support the claim for an exclusive London origin for the colonists, yet, no supporting evidence appears to exist.

Let us consider another possibility for the lack of evidence to raise volunteers for the colony in London. Is it possible that some of them worked indirectly for the investors, for example, as bookkeepers of a commercial accountancy practice? If such generic institutions contributed to the venture, it seems hardly likely they would allow their valuable and trusted employees to go to Roanoke without some form of recompense. Yet, like so much of the London hypothesis, there are no known records of any such correspondence or commercial agreements for services to the colony, or its investors, by these organizations … if indeed they were ever made.

There is also the simple realization that several of the trades Hakluyt recommended for the colony would not exactly find the filthy streets of London a profitable place for their trade—"Hunters," "Warreners," and "Sugar cane, vine and olive planters" for example.

Without intentionally seeking to discredit claims by some that the City of London holds the key to the colonist roster, it is relatively easy to discover colonist surnames among its Elizabethan population of some 200,000 people or more. While some would seem unique enough to qualify as valid, no evidence exists to confirm that any of them did indeed take part in the colony.

While this lack of proof is an equal hindrance for any other location vying for the claim, if finding colonists were a simple case of plucking colony surnames from a Parish Register, one could apply that principle anywhere. A survey of the Bideford Parish records between 1561 and 1630 for example, reveals no less than eight surnames of colonists and this in a town with a population of around 1,000 at the time. Expand that to cover the surrounding parishes, and from a population of approximately 5,000 we get eighteen surnames. On a statistical basis alone, that gives Bideford and the North Devon area an overwhelming case for launching its own claim.

It is important to understand that London's claims as the home of at least some of the colonists are not being denied, but instead that they are being tempered by evidence that suggests the city does not hold the singular—or perhaps even the strongest—claim to be their point of origin.

Finding those you can trust to carry out your bidding is one thing; convincing them to go is another, even given that Raleigh offered a generous incentive to those that signed up. A snippet contained in the Domestic State Papers of Elizabeth, sent from the Lieutenants of Cornwall and Devon, highlights the problem of finding people to settle in a foreign land, in this case Munster in southern Ireland. The entry reads, "We have generally made known through this country, her majesty's offers, and do find none of sufficient ability do offer to undertake the same." Importantly, it goes on to propose a solution: "We suggest it would further the people's willingness if some principal Gentlemen of each county, of whose discretion and fidelity the people are persuaded, be sent with them as their captain or governor, the people then would follow."[5]

This candid plea may have been the impetus for Raleigh and Grenville to form a hierarchical council for the "Cittie of Ralegh." Of the twelve they selected for this duty Hakluyt records that eight of them (Roger Bailie, Christopher Cooper, Ananias Dare, Dyonis Harvie, Roger Prat, John Sampson, Thomas Stevens, and George Howe) arrived and remained on Roanoke Island.

Of the remaining four, Raleigh's "Assignment" of 1589, a document effectively forming a transfer of power to his investors gives some vague clues as to their fate. Two of them, Humfrey Dimmocke and John Nichols, appear therein as "late of London" but it is unclear whether Raleigh was describing them as members of the Roanoke colony, or that they had died en route to Roanoke Island. The other two assistants, William Fulwood and James Plat, described as being "of the other part," appear not to have travelled to Virginia. It may be that they were simply responsible for setting up a London administrative base for the colony.

It is on this point of confusion that we should address the commonplace misinterpretation that Hakluyt's roster is a definitive list of the "lost" colony. Such assumption is evidently incorrect. In Hakluyt's own words, the list is simply "those who remained on Roanoke 1587." Observe that both John White and Simon Ferdinando appear on the list, yet were later recorded by Hakluyt as having returned to England the same year. Sadly, there are no surviving original notes or manuscripts by which to validate Hakluyt's list, a situation that exists because the Elizabethans, including Hakluyt, tended to discard the original documents they were working from when transcribing their content for formal publication. Thus, we cannot be certain precisely how many colonists truly settled on Roanoke Island in 1587. However, for the sake of completeness, herewith the balance of the colony roster according to Hakluyt; the names have been broken down into their known or probable relationships.

The families: Arnold Archard, Joyce Archard and their son Thomas Archar; Ananias Dare (already listed above), Elinor Dare (née White), and their daughter Virginia Dare; Dyonis Harvie (already listed above), Margery Harvie, and their unnamed child "Harvye"; Ambrose Viccars, Elizabeth Viccars, and their son Ambrose Viccars.

The following couples were probably husband and wife, or at least perhaps betrothed: John Chapman and Alis Chapman; Thomas Colman and Joan Colman (Mrs. Colman's Christian name is not given but there is a marriage record of the right period which suggests she could have been called Joan Coleman née Rudd); John Jones and Jane Jones; Edward Powell and Wenefrid Powell; Henry Payne and Rose Payne; Thomas Topan and Audry Tappan (these two could be subject of a possible transcribing error because research cannot find a marriage record for the Topan or Tappan surnames although the latter surname does exist in Parish records. It is simply possible that they are not husband and wife); Thomas Warner and Joan Warren (another possible spelling mistake; a record exists for the marriage of a Joan Barnes to Thomas Warner in London).

The following were probably father and son: Thomas Ellis and Robert Ellis; George Howe (already listed above) and George Howe (Junior); Roger Prat (already listed above) and John Prat; John Sampson (already listed above) and John Sampson (Junior).

The single women were: Elizabeth Glane, Margaret Lawrence, Jane Mannering, Emme Merrimoth, Jane Pierce, and Agnes Wood

The following may have been orphans: Thomas Humfrey, Tomas Smart and William Wythers.

The single men were Morris Allen, Richard Arthur, Marke Bennet, William Berde, Henry Berrye, Richard Berrye, Michael Bishop, John Borden, John Bridger, John Bright, John Brooke, Henry Browne, William Browne, John Burden, Thomas Butler, Anthony Cage, John Cheven, William Clement, John Cotsmur, Richard Darige, Henry Dorrell, William

Dutton, Edmond English, John Earnest, John Farre, Charles Florrie, John Gibbes, Thomas Gramme, Thomas Harris, Thomas Harris (A second man of the same name), John Hemmington, Thomas Hewet, James Hynde, Henry Johnson, Nicholas Johnson, Griffen Jones, Richard Kemme, James Lasie, Peter Little, Robert Little, William Lucas, George Martyn, Michael Myllet, Henry Mylton, Humfrey Newton, William Nicholes, Hugh Pattenson, Thomas Phevens, Henry Rufoote, Thomas Scot, Richard Shaberdge, Thomas Smith, William Sole, John Spendlove, John Starte, John Stilman, Martyn Sutton, Clement Tayler, Richard Taverner, Hugh Tayler, Richard Tomkins, John Tydway, William Waters, Cutbert White, Richard Wildye, Robert Wilkinson, William Willes, Lewes Wotton, John Wright, Brian Wyles, and John Wyles.[6]

The high number of single men may have resulted, in part, from some of them, perhaps up to twenty-five or so, being the crew for the pinnace that remained with the colony. This possibility is not as far-fetched as it might seem, for Hakluyt's *Discourse* contains clear instruction that the colony should have "pinesses with experte Seamen."

The social structure of the colony is perhaps worth a passing mention. Members of a Guild in Elizabethan society would be what we might term today in England as "lower-middle" class. This is contrary to at least one modern source.[7] They probably earned a living wage and resided in modest but comfortable surroundings. It is likely that the twelve assistants to the colony were of this social standing. However, this standing would not have been enough for them to command a significant respect among the remainder of the colonists. It is for this reason that we may suspect Raleigh chose to elevate their standing with the Grant of Arms he bestowed upon them. That elevation, however artificial, would have been enough to ensure the command structure of the colony, however grudgingly the remaining colonists may have felt about it.

Whether the number of "lost" colonists is 117, 119, or 121 depends on clarification of the fate of the four "assistants" unaccounted for. Nevertheless, Raleigh now had his colonists, albeit considerably fewer than he hoped. What he needed now was a leader, a Governor.

There is no evidence as to how he selected John White for the role of Governor of Virginia in 1587, but his profession as a painter would have given him relatively high status in Elizabethan England. Thus, it seems probable that when Grenville and Raleigh reviewed the colony roster, John White was the most senior member of the Colony; he was certainly one of the very few who had previous experience of living on Roanoke Island.

John White's background has been the subject of widespread debate.

His elevation to the status of "Gent of London," according to his Grant of Arms from Sir William Dethick, Garter Principal of the Royal College of Arms,[8] has certainly led to a widespread belief that he was born there. Whether this ever proves to be true or not, White's family origins are Cornish. A study of White's Coat-of-Arms by J.P. Brook-Little, Norrey and Ulster, King of Arms at the Royal College of Arms, London, in 1987, and later by Dr. Kim Sloan of the British Museum in private correspondence with Clive Cheesman, Richmond Herald of the same institute in 2006, confirmed White's Cornish ancestry. His earliest ancestors are in fact Robert White and Alice Wymark of Truro.[9] As an aside, whether distant cousins Grenville and White knew each other during their formative years is unknown.

It is also through the work of the Royal College of Arms that we learn John White had several cousins also named John. It is little wonder therefore that, 400 years on, we are still uncertain of making a positive determination of exactly where he was born, or lived, prior to his appearance in the Parish records of London.

One outcome from the research on John White's origins is that we can dismiss a number of popular candidates. Of note among these, and the most promising was a John White of Plymouth. The will of his uncle, also a John White and described in the Prerogative Court of Canterbury Wills as a "Haberdasher of London,"[10] contains the names of a great many relatives and family connections, included among which are the Golston family of St. Albans (referred to as in-laws in the will). It is reference to this family in particular that allows us to calculate that John White of Plymouth (described as a nephew in the will), must simply have been too young to be our John White, Governor of Virginia.

Other popular candidates also dismissed include John White, Lord of the Manor of Southwicke, and members of the John White family of South Warnborough who were twice Lord Mayors of London. One further John White, noted in his will as being a member of the Inner Temple (London), and one who had overwhelming connections with several of the Colony's investors and principals, can also be dismissed on account of his marriage in 1576, at a time when the John White we seek had already been married for ten years.

There is one last candidate John White we need to mention, one described as a brother to a Bridget White of Pangbourne, Berkshire. This Bridget is widely regarded as being the same Bridget White some historians believe was responsible for obtaining John White's paintings following his death.

The story stems from an entry in the Probate 6, Administration Act Books for May 22, 1606.[11] Various sources declare that it confers the role of "Administrix" upon Bridget for the estate of her brother John White "late of parts beyond the seas." If this were a correct transcription of the record, then on the assumption that we consider America as overseas, it may well implicate this Bridget White in the journey of White's paintings to the British Museum. However, the record, written in Latin, correctly translates as: "On 22nd a commission was issued to Bridget Whate alias Lewes for the administration of the goods of John Whate [White], her brother, sworn by Christopher Lewes, her husband." There is no reference to her brother as being lately of parts beyond the seas.

Further research of Bridget's brother reveals that he was in fact married to an Ann Montague in 1574 at Pangbourne in Berkshire. Our John White was still married to Thomasine at this time. Therefore, this Bridget Whate (White) of Pangbourne cannot have been his sister. This record and its associated story are therefore irrelevant to the biography of John White's life.

If we assume that John White relocated to London from his ancestral home in Cornwall, if indeed he did, then his motive is likely to have been the offer of an apprenticeship, a consideration that readily serves to justify the records we have for him in that city.

Yet, it is not until 1566, certainly at least 18 years after his probable birth, that we may have evidence of his first appearance in public records. On June 30 of that year, a John White married Thomasine Cooper at St. Martin's Ludgate in London. The transcription of the entry in the parish records reads: "The same day was marryed John Whyte and Thomasine Cowper (Cooper) maid."

The entry in the Prerogative Court of Canterbury's Acts of Administration (Probate 6) under May 22, 1606. The inscription makes no mention of John White being "late of overseas" as described by others. The entry actually reads: "On 22nd a commission was issued to Bridget Whate alias Lewes for the administration of the goods of John Whate [White], her brother, sworn by Christopher Lewes, her husband" (translated from the Latin, author's photograph).

As if to confirm this likely marriage, the following year, the same parish register records the christening of John and Thomasine White's only son, Thomas, on April 27, 1567. The transcription of this entry reads: "April 27th, day, was christened Thomas the son of John White."

A little more than a year later, we find that the same register also records the christening of John White's enigmatic daughter, Elinor, on May 9, 1568. The transcription of this entry reads, "The ninth day was christened Elinor the daughter of John White / paynter."

This last entry thus also reveals a pivotal moment in John White's life, for at some point between the christening of Thomas and Elinor, he gained recognition as a painter. If this recognition came from the Worshipful Company of Painters and Stainers (London) the record of that moment does not appear to exist. However, it should be noted that according to J.P. Brooke-Little in 1987, St. Martin's Ludgate was the principal church for the Guild.

John White's young family suffered a tragedy late in 1568 with the death of their son, Thomas, on November 26. The entry in the Parish register reads simply: "The 26th day was buried Thomas White the son of John White paynter." Again, one should note the acknowledgement of John White's profession.

Despite a further extensive search of the parish records of London, the handful of entries in the parish register of St. Martin's Ludgate appear to represent the only evidence for children positively identified with the marriage of John and Thomasine. As to why there appear to have been no further offspring, given the propensity for Elizabethan couples to have

The Christening of Elinor Dare. The inscription in the St. Martin's Ludgate Parish register reads: "The ninth day was christened Elinor the daughter of John White / paynter" (author's photograph).

several children, and that John White knew only two years into his marriage that he had no male heir, remains a mystery.

Between 1576 and 1578, the eventful voyages of Sir Martin Frobisher took place. Frobisher sailed with the objective of finding the Northwest Passage, a route through the myriad of islands and ice flows north of Canada, which many believed offered a shorter route to the Orient. On his second voyage, Inuit Eskimos ambushed Frobisher, an incident graphically recorded by an artist onboard his ship. Despite credible support for the style of the painting, whether this artist was John White remains uncertain. The ships logs of the voyages as transcribed by Richard Hakluyt in 1589 make no mention of his presence on the voyage. What does appear certain is that John White painted the three Inuit that Frobisher brought back to Bristol, England, in 1577.

A year later, there surfaces an intriguing fragment of evidence as to John White's whereabouts, in the records of the Court of Revels. When the court of Queen Elizabeth held one of its greatest spectacles, the "Amasons maske" of 1578, the account for the event reveals a payment of 33 shillings and 4 pence: "To John White ... for the parcell gilding of two armors compleat for Mr Tresham and Mr Knowles being two of the Knightes in the Amasons maske."[12]

"Mr. Tresham" was most likely Thomas Tresham, whose eldest son Francis was later involved with the Gunpowder Plot of 1605, an attempt to blow up the Houses of Parliament, the English seat of government. While "Mr. Knowles" was probably Sir Francis Knollys (his surname was frequently recorded spelled in either form), Treasurer of the Royal Household of Elizabeth. We should note that the order to paint armor for Gentlemen of the Royal Court was a prestigious one to fulfill and therefore only awarded to the most accomplished of painters. John White's work from Roanoke Island may be evidence enough to suggest he is the painter referred to here.

By 1583, John White must have met Ananias Dare. Ananias was a member of the Tylers and Bricklayers Company (of London), a fact confirmed by the will of William Bateman, "Bricklayer and Tiler of London."[13] Quite at what point they discussed Sir Walter Raleigh's venture to America we may never know, but Ananias was later to become an assistant of Raleigh's "Cittie of Ralegh" on Roanoke Island.

On June 24, 1583, Ananias became a son-in-law to John White by marrying his daughter Elinor at St. Clement Danes, in The Strand. The parish register reads simply, "June, Ananias Dare and Elinor Whyte–24."

The use of this church does suggest that the White family had relocated from Ludgate to the more affluent City of Westminster. When that took place, and exactly where they lived, is unknown. Many have cited the Rate Books of the Ward of St. Clement Danes as a method of determining this, yet these only contain the name of the principal householder, without any further reference to the remaining residents of the property or the principal occupation of the owner. Thus, contrary to popular suggestion, it is quite impossible to determine which of the four John Whites in the Rate books for St. Clement Danes refers specifically to our Painter and Governor.

As 1587 dawned, with Grenville on duty for Queen Elizabeth, preparing the defenses in the west of England for the anticipated attack by the Spanish, and his pilot Pedro Diaz "incapacitated" at Bideford,[14] it fell to Raleigh to pass command, and navigation for the colonist's voyage, to John White, and Simon Fernando.

NINE

The "Lost" Colony, 1587

With Charter in hand, his colony of around 120 men, woman, and children,[1] their tools, weapons, supplies, and perhaps some trepidation, John White sailed for Roanoke Island in April 1587. This is his account:

Aprill
Our Fleete being in the number three saile, viz, the Admirall, a shippe of one hundred and twentie tunnes: a flieboat, and a Pinnesse, departed the sixe and twentieth of Aprill from Portesmouth, and the same day came to an anker at the Cowes, in the Isle of Wight,[2] where wee staied eight daies.

May
The 5 of Maye, at nine of the clocke at night, we came to Plymmouth, where we remained the space of two daies.
The 8 we waied anker at Plymmouth, and departed thence to Virginia.
The 16 Simon Ferdinando Master of our Admirall, lewdly forsooke our flie boate, leaving her distressed in the Baye of Portingall.[3]

June
The 19 we fell with Dominica, and the same evening we sailed betweene it and Guadalupe: the 21 the flie boate also fell with Dominica.
The 22 we came to an anker at an Isle, called Santa Cruz,[4] where all the planters were set on land, staying there till the 25 of the same moneth. At our first landing on this Island, some of our women, and men, by eating a small fruite, like greene apples, were fearefully troubled with a sudden burning in their mouthes, and swelling of their tongues so bigge, that some of them could not speake. Also a child by sucking on one of those womens breast,[5] had at that instant his mouth set on such a burning, that it was strange to see how the infant was tormented for the time: but after 24 houres, it ware away of it self.[6]
Also the first night of our being on this Island, we tooke five great Torteses,[7] some of them such bignes, that sixteene of our strongest men were tired with carrying of one of them but from the Sea side, to our cabbins. In this Island we found no watring place, but a standing ponde, the water whereof was so evill, that many of our companie fell sick with drinking thereof: and as many as did but wash their faces with that water, in the morning before the Sun had drawen away the corruption, their faces did so burne, and swell, that their eies were shut up, and could not see in five or six daies, or longer.[8]
The second day of our abode there, we sent foorth some of our men to search the Island for fresh water, three one way, and two another way. The Governour also, with six others, went up to the toppe of an high hill, to view the Island, but could perceave

no signe of any men, or beastes, nor any goodnes, but Parots and trees of Guiacum.[9] Returning back to our cabbins another way, he found in the discent of a hill, certaine potsheards of savage making, made of the earth of that Island: whereupon it was judged, that this Island was inhabited with Savages, though Fernando had tolde us for certaine to the contrarie. The same day at night, the rest of our companie very late returned to the Governour. The one companie affirmed, that they had seene in a valley, eleven Savages, and divers houses halfe a mile distant from the steepe, or toppe of the hill where they staied. The other companie had found running out of a high rocke, a very faire spring of water, whereof they brought three bottles to the companie: for before that time, we dranke the stinking water of the pond.

The same second day at night, Captaine Stafford, with the Pinnesse, departed from our fleet, riding at Santa Cruz, to an Island called Beake, lying neare S. Johns,[10] being directed by Ferdinando, who assured him he should there finde great plentie of sheepe. The next day at night, our planters left Santa Cruz, and came all aboord, and the next morning after, being the 25 of June, we waied anker, and departed from Santa Cruz.

The seven and twentieth we came to anker at Cottea, where we found the Pinnesse riding, at our coming.

The 28 we weighed anker at Cottea, and presently came to anchor at S. Johns in Musketas Bay,[11] where we spent three daies unprofitably, in taking in freshe water, spending in the meanetime more beere, than the quantitie of the water came unto.

Julie

The first we waied anker at Muskitoes Baye, where were left behind two Irish men of our companie, Darbie Glaven, and Denice Carrell,[12] bearing along the coast of S Johns, till evening, at which time we fell with Rosse Baye.

At this place Fernando had promised wee should take in salt, and had caused us before, to make and provide as many sackes for that purpose, as we could. The Governour also, for that he understoode there was a Towne in the bottome of the Baye, not farre from the salt hils, appointed thirtie shotte, ten pikes, and ten targets, to man the Pinnesse, and to goe aland for salt. Fernando perceaving them in a readines, sent to the Governour, using great perswasions with him, not to take in salt there, saying that he knewe not well, whether that the same were the place or not: also, that if the Pinnesse went into the Bay, she could not without great danger come backe, till the next day at night, and that if in the meane time any storme should rise, the Admirall were in danger to be cast away. Whilest he was thus perswading, he caused the lead to be cast, and having craftily brought the shippe in three fathome, and a halfe water, he suddenly began to sweare, and tear God in peeces, dissembling great danger, crying to him at the helme, beare up hard, beare up hard: so we went off, and were disappointed of our salt, by his meanes.

The next day, sailing along the West ende of S. Johns, the Governour determined to goe aland in S. Germans Baye, to gather yong plants of Oringes, Pines, Mameas, and Plantonos,[13] to set at Virginia, which we knewe might easily be had, for that they growe neere the shoare, and the places where they grewe, well knowen to the Governour, and some of the planters[14]: but our Simon denied it, saying: he would come to an anker at Hispaniola, and there lande the Governour, and some other of the Assistants, with the pinnesse, to see if he could speake with his friend Alanson, of whome he hoped to be furnished both of cattell, and all such thinges as wee woulde have taken in at S. Johns: but hee meant nothing lesse, as it plainely did appeare to us afterwards.

The next day after, being the third of Julie, wee sawe Hispaniola, and bare with the coast all that day, looking still when the pinnesse should be prepared to goe for the place where Fernando his friend Alanson was: but that day passed, and we sawe no preparation for landing in Hispaniola.

The 4 of Julie, sailing along the coast of Hispaniola, untill the next day at noone, and no preparation yet seene for the staying there, we having knowledge that we were past the place where Alanson dwelt, and were come with Isabella: hereupon Fernando was asked by the Governour, whether he meant to speake with Alanson, for the taking in of cattell, and other things, according to his promise or not: but he answered that he was now past the place, and that Sir Walter Raleigh tolde him, the French Ambassador certified him, that the King of Spaine had sent for Alanson into Spaine: wherefore he thought him dead, and that it was to no purpose to touch there in any place, at this voyage.

The next day, we left sight of Hispaniola, and haled off for Virginia, about 4 of the clocke in the afternoone.

The sixt of Julie, we came to the Island Caycos, wherein Fernando saide were two salt pondes, assuring us if they were drie, wee might find salt to shift with, until the next supplie, but it prooved as true as the finding of sheepe at Beake. In this Island, whilest Ferdinando solaced himself ashoore, with one of the company, in part of the Island, others spent the latter part of that day in other parts of the Island, some to seeke the salt ponds, some fowling, some hunting Swannes, whereof we caught many. The next day, earely in the morning, we waied anker, leaving Caycos, with good hope, the first lande that wee sawe next, should be Virginia.

About the 16 of July, we fell with the maine of Virginia, which Simon Fernando tooke to be the Island of Croatoan, where we came to anker, and rode there two or three daies: but finding himselfe deceaved, he waied, and beere along the coast, where in the night, had not Captaine Stafforde bene more carefull in looking out, then our Simon Fernando, wee had beene all cast away upon the breache, called the Cape of Feare, for wee were come within two cables length[15] upon it: such was the carelesnes, and ignorance of our Master.

The two and twentieth of Julie, we arrived at Hatoraske, where our shippe and pinnesse ankered: the Governour went aboord the pinnesse, accompanied with fortie of his best men, intending to passe up to Roanoke foorthwith, hoping there to finde those fifteene Englishmen, which Sir Richard Grenville had left there the yeere before, with whome he meant to have conference, concerning the state of the Countrey, and Savages,[16] meaning after he had so done, to returne againe to the fleete, and passe along the coast, to the Baye of Chesepiok, where we intended to make our seate and forte, according to the charge given us among other directions in writing, under the hande of Sir Walter Raleigh[17]: but as soone as we were put with our pinnesse from the shippe, a Gentlemen by the meanes of Fernando, who was appointed to returne for England, called to the sailers in the pinnesse, charging them not to bring any of the planters backe againe, but leave them in the Island, except the Governour, and two or three such as he approved, saying that the summer was farre spent, wherefore hee would land all the planters in no other place.

Unto this were all the sailers, both in the pinnesse, and shippe, perswaded by the Master, wherefore it booted not the Governour to contend with them, but passed to Roanoke, and the same night, at Sunne set, went aland on the Island, in the place where our fifteene men were left, but we found none of them, nor any signe, that they had bene there, saving onely we found the bones of one of those fifteene, which the Savages had slaine long before.

The 23 July, the Governour, with divers of his companie, walked to the North Ende of the Island, where Master Ralfe Lane had his forte, with sundry necessarie and decent dwelling houses, made by his men about it the yeere before, where wee hoped to finde some signes, or certaine knowledge of our fifteen men. When we came thither, wee found the forte rased downe, but all the houses standing unhurt, saving the neather roomes of them,[18] and also of the fort, were overgrowen with Melons of divers sorts, and Deer within them, feeding on those Melons: so we returned to our companie, without hope of ever seeing, any of the fifteene men living.

The same day order was given, that every man should be imploied for the repairing of those houses, which we found standing, and also to make other newe Cottages, for such as shoulde need.

The 25 our flie boate, and the rest of our planters, arrived all safe at Hatoraske, to the great joye, and comfort of the whole companie: but the Master of our Admirall, Fernando grieved greatly at their safe comming: for he purposely left them in the Baye of Portingall, and stole away from them in the night, hoping that the Master thereof, whose name was Edward Spicer, for that he never had bene in Virginia, would hardly finde the place, or els being left in so dangerous a place as that was, by means of so many men of warre, as at that time were aboord, they should surely be taken, or slaine: but God disappointed his wicked pretences.

The eighth and twentieth, George Howe, one of our twelve assistants was slaine by divers Savages, which were come over to Roanoke, either of purpose to espie our companie, and what number we were, or else to hunt Deere, whereof were many in the Island. These Savages beeing secretly hidden among high reedes, where oftentimes they finde the Deere asleepe, and so kill them, espied our man wading in the water alone, almost naked, without any weapon, save onely a small forked sticke, catching Crabs therewithall, and also being strayed two miles from his companie, shotte at him in the water, where they gave him sixteene wounds with their arrowes: and after they had slaine him with their woodden swordes, beat his head in peeces, and fled over the water to the maine.

On the thirtieth of Julie, Master Stafford, and twentie of our men, passed by water to the Island of Croatoan, with Manteo, who had his mother, and many of his kinred, dwelling in that Island,[19] of whome we hoped to understande some newes of our fifteene men, but especially to learne the disposition of the people of the Countrey towards us, and to renew our olde friendshippe with them. At our first landing, they seemed as though they would fight with us: but perceaving us begin to marche with our shot towards them, they turned their backes, and fled. Then Manteo their Countreymen, called to them in their owne language, whom as soone as they heard, they returned, and threwe away their bowes, and arrowes, and some of them came unto us, embracing and entertaining us friendly, desiring us not to gather or spill any of their corne, for that they had but little. We answered them, that neither their corne, nor any other thing of theirs, should be diminished by any of us, and that our comming was onely to renew the old love that was betweene us, and them, at the first, and to live with them as brethren, and friendes: which answere seemed to please them well, wherefore they requested us to walke up to their Towne, who there seated us after their manner, and desired us earnestly, that there might be some token or badge given them of us, whereby we might know them to be our friendes, when we met them any where out of the Towne or Island.

They tolde us further, that for want of some such badge, divers of them were hurt the yeere before, beeng founde out of the Island by Master Lane his companie, whereof they shewed us one, which at that very instant laye lame, and had lein of that hurt ever since: but they said, they knew our men mistooke them, and hurt them insteede of Winginoes men, wherefore they held us excused.

August

The next day we had conference further with them, concerning the people of Secota, Aquascogoc, and Pomiok, willing them of Croatoan, to certifie the people of those townes, that if they would accept our friendship, we would willingly receave them againe, and that all unfriendly dealings past on both partes, should be utterly forgiven, and forgotten. To this the chiefe men of Croatoan answered that they would gladly doe the best they could, and within seven daies, bring the Weroances, and chiefe Governours of those townes with them, to our Governour at Roanok, or their answere. We also understoode of the men of Croatoan, that our man Master Howe, was slain by the remnant of Winginoes men, dwelling then at Dasamongueponke, with whome Wanchese kept companie: and also we understood by them of Croatoan, how that the 15 Englishmen left at Roanok the yeere before, by Sir Richard Grenville, were suddenly set upon by 30 of the men of Secota, Aquascogoc and Dasamongueponke, in manner following. They conveied themselves secretly behind the trees, neere the houses, where our men carelessly lived: and having perceaved that of those 15 they could see but 11 only, two of those Savages appeared to the 11 Englishmen, calling to them by friendly signes, that but two of their chiefest men should come unarmed to speake with those two Savages, who seemed also to be unarmed. Where-fore two of the chiefest of our Englishmen, went gladly to them: but whilest one of those Savages traitorously embraced one of our men, the other with his sword of wood, which he had secretly hidden under his mantell, stroke him on the head, and slewe him, and presently, the other eight and twentie Savages shewed themselves: the other Englishmen perceaving this fled to his companie, whom the Savages pursued with their bowes, and arrowes, so fast, that the Englishmen were forced to take to the house, wherein all their victuall, and weapons were: but the Savages foorthwith set the same on fire, by means whereof, our men were forced to take up such weapons as came first to hand, and without order to runne foorth among the Savages, with whome they skirmished above an houre. In this skirmish, another of our men was shotte into the mouth with an arrowe, whereof he died: and also one of the Savages was shot into the side by one or our men, with a wild fire arrowe, whereof he died presently. The place where they fought, was of great advantage to the Savages, by meanes of the thicke trees, behinde which the Savages through their nimblenes, defended themselves, and so offended our men with their arrowes, that our men being some of them hurt, retired fighting to the water side, where their boate lay, with which they fled towards Hatorask. By that time they had rowed but a quarter of a mile, they espied their foure fellows comming from a creeke thereby, where they had bene to fetch Oysters: these foure they receaved into their boate, leaving Roanoke, and landed on a little Island on the right hand of our entrance into the harbour of Hatorask, where they remained a while, but afterward departed whither, as yet we knowe not.[20]

Having now sufficiently dispatched our busines at Croatoan, the same day wee departed friendly, taking our leave, and came aboord the fleete at Hatoraske.

The eight of August the Governour having long expected the comming of the Weroances of Pomioake, Aquascogoc Secota, and Dasamongueponke, seeing that the seven daies were past, within which they promised to come in, or to send their answers by the men of Croatoan, and no tidings of them heard, being certainly also informed by those men of Croatoan, that the remnant of Wingino his men, which were left alive, who dwelt at Dasamongueponke, were they which had slaine George Howe, and were also at the driving of our eleven Englishmen from Roanoke, he thought to deferre the revenging thereof no longer. Wherefore the same night, about midnight he passed over the water, accompanied with Captaine Stafford, and 24 men, whereof Manteo was one, whome wee tooke with us to be our guide to the place where those Savages dwelt, where he behaved himselfe toward us as a most faithful English man.

The next day, being the ninth of August, in the morning so earely, that it was yet darke, wee landed neere the dwelling place of our enemies, and very secretly conveyed our selves through the woods, to that side, where we had their houses betweene us and the water: and having espied their fire, and some sitting about it, we presently sette on them: the miserable soules herewith amased, fledde into a place of thicke reedes, growing fast by, where our men perceaving them, shotte one of them through the bodie with a bullet, and therewith wee entred the reedes, among which wee hoped to acquire their evill doing towards us, but wee were deceaved: for those Savages were our friendes, and were come from Croatoan, to gather the corne, and fruite of that place, because they understoode our enemies were fledde immediately after they had slaine George Howe, and for haste had left all their corne, Tabacco, and pompions[21] standing in such sorte, that all had beene devoured of the birdes and the Deere, if it had not beene gathered in time: but they had like to have paide deerely for it: for it was so darke, that they being naked, and their men and women apparelled all so like others, we knew not but that they were all men: and if that one of them, which was a Weroans wife, had not had her childe at her backe, she had beene slaine insteede of a man, and as happe was, another Savage knewe Master Stafford,[22] and ranne to him, calling him by his name, whereby he was saved. Finding our selves thus disappointed of our purpose, wee gathered all the corn, pease, Pompions, and Tabacco, that we found ripe, leaving the rest unspoiled, and tooke Menatonan his wife, with the yong childe and the other Savages with us over the water to Roanok. Although the mistaking of these Savages somewhat grieved Manteo, yet he imputed their harme to their owne follie, saying to them, that if their Weroans had kept their promise in comming to the Governour, at the day appointed, they had not knowen that mischance.

The 13 of August, our Savage Manteo, by the commandment of Sir Walter Raleigh, was christened in Roanok, and called Lord thereof, and of Dasamongueponke, in reward of his faithfull service.

The 18 Elenora,[23] daughter to the Governour, and wife to Ananias Dare, one of the Assistants, was delivered of a daughter in Roanok, and the same was christened there the Sunday following, and because this childe was the first Christian borne in Virginia, she was named Virginia.[24] By this time our shippes had unlanded the goods and victuals of the planters, and began to take in wood, and fresh water and to newe caulke and trimme them for England: the planters also prepared their letters, and tokens, to send backe into England.

Our two shippes, the *Lyon* and the flie boate, almost ready to depart, the 21 of August, there arose such a tempest at northeast, that our Admirall then riding out of the harbour, was forced to cut his cables, and put to Sea, where he laye beating off and on, six dayes before hee coulde come to us againe, so that wee feared he had beene cast away, and the rather, for that at the tyme that the storme tooke them, the moste, and best of their saylers, were left aland.

At this time some controversies rose betweene the Governour, and Assistants, about choosing two out of the twelve Assistants, which should goe backe as factors for the companie into England: for every one of them refused, save onely one, which all the other thought not sufficient: but at length, by much perswading of the Governour, Christopher Cooper onely agreed to goe for England: but the next day, through the per-swasion of divers of his familiar friendes, he changed his minde, so that now the matter stoode as at the first.

The next day, the 22 of August, the whole companie, both of the Assistants, and planters, came to the Governour, and with one voice, requested him to returne himselfe into England, for the better and sooner obtaining of supplies, and other necessaries for them: but he refused it, and alleged many sufficient causes, why he would not: the one was, that he could not so suddenly returne backe againe, without his great discredite, leaving the action, and so many, whome he partly had procured through his perswasions, to leave their native Countrey,[25] and undertake that voyage, and that some enemies to him, and the action at his returne into England, would not spare to slander falsely both him, and his action, by saying he went to Virginia, but politically, and to no other ende, but to leade so many into a countrey, in which he never meant to stay himselfe, and there to leave them behind him. Also he alleaged, that seing they intended to remove 50 miles further up into the maine presently,[26] he being then absent, his stuffe, and goods, might be both spoiled, and most of it pilfered away in the carriage so that at his returne, he should be either forced to provide himselfe of all such things againe, or els at his comming againe to Virginia, finde himselfe utterly unfurnished, whereof already he had found some proofe, beeing but once from them but three daies.[27] Wherefore he concluded that he would not goe himselfe.

The next day, not onely the Assistants, but divers others, as well women, as men, beganne to renewe their requests to the Governour againe, to take uppon him to returne into England for the supplie, and despatch of all such thinges, as there were to be done, promising to make him their bonde under all their handes, and seales, for the safe preserving of all his goods for him at his returne to Virginia, so that if any part thereof were spoiled, or lost, they would see it restored to him, or his Assigns, whensoever the same should be missed, and demanded: which bonde with a testimonie under their handes, and seales, they foorthwith made, and delivered into his hands. The copie of the testimonie, I thought be good to set downe.

"May it please you, her Majesties Subjects of England, wee your friendes and Countreymen, the planters of Virginia, doe by these presents let you, and every of you to understande, that for the present and speedie supplie of certaine our knowen, and apparent lackes, and needes, most requisite and necessarie for the good and happie planting of us, or any other in this lande of Virginia, wee all of one minde, and consent, have most earnestly intreated, and uncessantly requested John White, Governour of the planters in Virginia, to passe into England, for the better and more assured helpe, and setting forward of the foresayde supplies: and knowing assuredly that he both can best, and will labour, and take paines in that behalfe for us all, and hee not once, but often refusing it, for our sakes, and for the honour, and maintenance of the action, hath at last, though much against his will, through our importunacie, yeelded to leave his government, and all his goods among us, and himselfe in all our behalfes to passe into Englande, of whose knowledge, and fidelitie in handling this matter, as all others, we doe assure our selves by these presents, and will you to give all credite thereunto, the five and twentieth of August."

The Governor being at the last, through their extreame intreating, constrayned to returne into England, having then but halfe a daies respit to prepare him selfe for the same, departed from Roanoke, the seventh and twentieth of August in the morning: and the same daye about midnight, came aboord the flie boate, who already had waied anker, and rode without the barre, the Admirall riding by them, who but the same morning was newly come thither againe. The same day, both the shippes waied anker, and sette saile for England.[28] At this waying their ankers, twelve of the men which were in the flie boate, were throwen from the capstone, which by meanes of a barre that brake, came so fast about upon them, that the other two barres thereof stroke and hurt most of them so sore, that some of them never recovered it: neverthelesse they assaied presently againe to waigh their anker, but being so weakened with the first fling, they were not able to weigh it, but were throwen downe, and hurt the seconde time. Wherefore having in all but fifteene men aboord and most of them by this infortunate beginning so bruised, and hurt, they were forced to cut their Cable, and leeve their anker. Nevertheless, they kept companie with the Admirall, untill the seventeenth of September, at which time wee fell with Coruo, and sawe Flores.[29]

September

The eighteenth, perceaving of all our fifteene men in the flie boate, there remained but five, which by meanes of the former mischance, were able to stande to their labour: wherefore understanding that the Admirall meant not to make any haste for England, but linger about the Island of Tercera for purchase, the flyboat departed for Englande with letters, where we hoped by the helpe of God to arrive shortly: but by that time wee had continued our course homeward, about twenty dayes, having sometimes scarce, and variable windes, our fresh water also by leaking almost consumed, there arose such a storme at Northeast, which for 6 days ceased not to blowe so exceeding: that we were driven further in those 6 than wee could recover in thirteen daies: in which time others of our saylers began to fall very sicke, and two of them dyed, the weather also continued so close, that our Master sometimes in foure daies together could see neither Sunne nor starre, and all the beverage we could make, with stinking water, dregges of beere, and lees of wine which remained, was but 3 gallons, and therefore now we expected nothing but by famyne to perish at Sea.

October

The 16 of October we made land, but we knew not what land it was, bearing in with the same land at that day: about Sunne set we put into a harbour, were we found a hulke of Dublin, and a pynnesse of Hampton[30] ryding, but we knew not as yet what place this was, neither had we any boate to goe ashoare, until the pinnesse sent off their boate to us with 6 or 8 men of whom we understood we were in Smewicke in the west parts of Ireland: they also releeved us presently with fresh water, wyne, and other fresh meate.

The 18, the Governour, and the master ryd to Dingen Cushe,[31] 5 myles distant, to take order of the new victualling of our flye boate for England, and for reliefe of our sicke and hurt men, but within 4 dayes after the boatswane, the steward, and the boatswanes mate dyed aboord the flye boate, and the 28 the Masters mate and two of our chiefe Saylers were brought sicke to Dingen.

November

The first the Governour shipped him selfe in a ship called the *Monkie*, which at that time was readie to put to Sea from Dingen for England, leaving the flyeboat and all his company in Ireland, the same day we set sayle, and on the third day we fel with the northside of the lands end,[32] and were shut up by the Severne,[33] but the next day we doubled the same, for Monts Bay.

The 5 the Governor landed in England at Martasew,[34] neere Saint Michaels mount in Cornewall.

The 8 we arrive at Hampton, where we understood that our consort the Admirall was come to Portsmouth, and had bene there three weeks before: and also that Fernando the Master with all his company were not onely come home without any purchase, but also in such weaknesse by sicknes, and death of their cheefest men, that they were scarce able to bring their ship into the harbour, but were forced to let fall anker without, which they could not way again, but might all have perished there, if a small barke by great hap had not come to them to helpe them.

The names of the chiefe men that dyed are these, Roger Large, John Mathew, Thomas Smith, and some other their saylers, whose names I know not at the writing hereof. An. Do. 1587.[35]

A list of colonist names follows this last entry, and at the foot of that list, the following note appears: "Savages. That were in Englande and returned home into Virginia with them. Manteo & Towaye."[36]

TEN

The Attempts to Resupply the Colony, 1588

Of John White's return from Roanoke in 1587, Hakluyt records:

After the Governors return out of Virginia the 20 of November 1587 he delivered his letters and other advertisements concerning his last voyage and state of the planters to Sir Walter Raleigh: whereupon he foorthwith appointed a Pinnesse to be sent thither with all such necessaries as he understood they stood in neede of: and also wrote his letters unto them, wherein among other matters he comforted them with promise, that with all convenient speede he would prepare a good supply of shipping and men with sufficiente of all things needefull, which he intended, God willing, should be with them to Sommer following. Which Pinnesse and fleete were accordingly prepared in the West Countrey at Bidforde under the charge of Sir Richard Grenville.

This fleete now being in reddinesse only staying but for a faire wind to put to Sea, at the same time there was spred throughout all England such report of the wonderfull preparation and invincible fleetes made by the king of Spaine joyned with the power of the Pope for the invading of England, that most of the ships of warre then in a readines in any haven in England were stayed for service at home: And Sir Richard Grenville was personally commanded not to depart out of Cornwall. The voyage for Virginia by these meanes for this yere thus disappointed, the Governor notwithstanding labored for the reliefe of the planters so earnestly, that he obtained two small pinnesses the one of them being of 30 tonnes called the *Brave*, the other of 25 called the *Roe*, wherein 15 planters and all their provision,[1] with certaine reliefe for those that wintered in the Countrey[2] was to be transported.

Grenville did indeed attempt to resupply the Roanoke colony from Bideford early in 1588, but with his ships full of victuals and waiting only for a favorable wind; the Privy Council placed a blanket ban on all ships leaving England. With the Spanish Armada now on a war footing and sailing for England, they directed him to take anything capable of putting up a good fight, to Plymouth, in readiness to support the English defense against the Spanish Armada. In effect, he had little choice but to second his intended Roanoke fleet and refit them for a fight with the Spanish. Thankfully, we know from an obscure publication[3] that Grenville had pre-

"The manner of their attire" by John White (© The Trustees of the British Museum).

pared at least five ships for the fight, ships which could only have been originally destined to sail to Roanoke.

The largest, the Galleon *Dudley*, weighed around 300 tons. Beers-Quinn states that it had sailed to Bideford from London in preparation for the fight. However, this latter point seems unlikely for the simple reason that the voyage would have taken the ship directly past the rendezvous point at Plymouth in order to reach Bideford. Whether it was at Bideford for repairs, or was there by order of its owner, the Earl of Leicester as part of an interest in the Roanoke colony, for Leicester was an enthusiastic supporter of exploration and colonization, is unclear. One other possibility is that it is the former Spanish prize, the *Santa Maria de San Vincente* captured by Grenville in 1585 and was named *Dudley* after it had been sold to a new owner, the one and the same, Robert Dudley, Earl of Leicester. James Erisey, its captain, had previously visited the Roanoke colony as one of Drake's captains that conducted the relief of Lane's military colony in 1586. The ship had a contingent of around a hundred men.

Grenville's flagship from the Roanoke voyages, the *Tyger*, was also part of the fleet. This would have been her third sailing for Roanoke. Captained by James Bostock, she carried a compliment of around a hundred men.

Described as a galleasse, the *Virgin God Save Her* was probably of similar build to Grenville's *Tyger*, and weighed around 200 tons. Beers-Quinn offers the opinion that she was the former *Santa Maria de San Vincente*, a ship that contemporary reports suggest weighed around 300 tons. The basis of his argument is that her naming was a parody of the Spanish ship, which, while a valid observation seems unlikely, given the described weight of the *Santa Maria de San Vincente*. Grenville gave the duty of captaining her to his second son, John. She carried eighty men to fight the Spanish.

The fourth ship in the fleet, the *Golden Hind*, described as a pinnace of some 50 tons and captained by Thomas Fleming, played a brave role in the fight against the Spanish Armada by serving as the English fleet's lookout. She was successful, and can claim to be the first English ship to bring news of the Spanish Armada to England. She carried fifty men. There remains a curious but unauthenticated tale regarding this ship involving Sir Francis Drake. Drake apparently objected to her name being that of his now fabled *Golden Hind*. As a result, Grenville's pinnace was renamed *Barke Fleming* after her captain; this is how she appears on early tapestries depicting the battle.

The smallest ship of his fleet, the *Bark St. Leger* weighed around 50 tons and was the charge of his brother-in-law, John St. Leger, who also owned the ship.

It is worth noting that it was because of Grenville's planned voyage to Roanoke that Bideford was able to furnish the third largest contribution in England towards the fight against the Armada. By comparison, Bideford's near and much larger neighbor, Barnstaple, pleaded poverty to the Privy Council when asked to raise support. Receiving short shrift, the Privy Council commanded them to provide one ship. This was the *John of Barnstaple*, of some 40 tons. Its captain remains unknown. It appears the Privy Council allowed Barnstaple to share the cost of providing a ship with another nearby town, Great Torrington, which lies around ten miles to the south.

Grenville duly delivered his ships to Plymouth. With the Spanish Armada still a long way from England, Grenville returned to Bideford, partly to take command of his forces monitoring the Bristol Channel for potential Spanish attacks, but, significantly, to also make alternative arrangements for John White, and an additional seven men and four women colonists, to slip away back to Roanoke. He was certainly there no more than five days prior to John White setting sail.[4] The ships Grenville had left by which to supply John White and the additional colonists, were the *Brave* and the *Roe*.

Hakluyt continues John White's account:

Thus the 22 of Aprill 1588 we put over the barre at Biddiford in the edge of the North side of Cornewal,[5] and the same night we came to an anker under the Isle of Lundy,[6] where some of the our company went on land: After we had roade there about the space of three howers we wayed anker againe and all that night we bare along the coast of Cornewall.

The next day being S. George's Day and the 23 of Aprill stil bearing along the coast we gave chase to 4 ships, and borded them and forced them all to come to anker by us in a smal bay at the lands end, out of these ships we took nothing but 3 men and the same night we waied and put to Sea.

The 24 day we gave chase to 2 ships, the one of them being a Scot and the other a Breton.[7] These we borded also and tooke from them whatsoever we could find worth the taking, and so let them goe.

The 26 of April we escied a ship on sterne of us, for whom we strooke our toppe sayle, and stayed for it. By that time it came with us we saw in his flagge a redd crosse: whereupon we helde him for an Englishman, and gave over our preparation to fight with him. But when he was come near to us we perceived his flagge not to be a right St George: whereupon we were somewhat amazed having so farre mistaken, for it was a very tall ship, and excellently well appointed and now readie to clap us aboord.[8] And it was not now neede to bid every man to bestirre himselfe, for each one prepared with al speed to fight. In the meane time we hayled them whence they were: They answered of Flushing, bound for Barbarie.[9] And they perceiving us to be Englishmen of warre bare from us and gave us a piece,[10] and we gave them two pieces and so departed.

The 27 day in the morning we were come with the height of Cape Finister,[11] the winde being still at Northeast.

The 28 day the wind shifted: about foure of the clocke in the afternoone the same day we escied a sayle to the weather of us,[12] whom we kept so neere unto us as we could all that night.

The 29 in the morning we gave chase to the same ship being then to the wind of us[13] almost as farre as we could ken.[14]

As soone as our Pinnes, came up to them, the Pinnes fought with the ship, and it was an hulke of 200 tonnes and more, but after a few great shot bestowed on both sides, the Pinnesse perceiving her consort not able to come to ayd her left the hulke and came roome with the *Brave* againe.[15] At their comming they desired the Captaine and Master of the *Brave* to lend them some men and other things whereof they had neede. Which things put aboord them they returned again to the chase of the hulke earnestly, and with full purpose to boord her. But the hulke bare all night in with the coast of Spaine, and by morning were so neere land, that we fearing either change of wind or to be calmed gave over the fight and put off to Sea againe.

May

The first day of May being Wedenday the wind came large at Northeast.

The 3 being friday we gave chase to another tal ship, but it was night before we spake with her: and the night grew darke sodenly in such sort, that we lost sight both of the great ship and of our consort also, having thus in the darke lost our Pinnesse, and knowing our Barke so bad of sayle that we could neither take nor leve, but were rather to be taken or left of every ship we met, we made our course for the Isle of Madera, hoping there to find our pinnesse abiding for us.

The same day following being the 5 of May we spake with a man of warre of Rochel[16] of 60 tonnes, very wel manned and bravely appointed being bound, as he said for Peru: having hailed each other, we parted frindly in outward shew, giving each other a voley of shot and a great piece: but nevertheles we suspected by which followed: for this Rocheller having taken perfect view of our ship, men and ordinance, towards evening fell on sterne of us: and as soone as it was darke left us, and returned to his consort which was a tal ship of 100 tonne lying then on hull to weather of us out of ken, having 84 men in her, whereof 50 were smal shot, and 12 muskets, and in the ship 10 pieces of ordinance. This ship being this night certified by her consort that viewed us, of what force we were and how bad of sayle, this greater ship tooke in 20 of the chiefest men that were in the smallest ship, and presently gave us chase.

The next morning being Monday and the 6 of May, we escied them in the weather of us, so that it was in vaine to seeke by flight, but rather by fight to help our selves. The same day about 2 of the clocke in the afternoone they were come with us. We hayled them, but they would not answere. Then we waved them to leewardes of us, and they waved us with a sword amayne,[17] fitting their sailes to clappe us aboord, which we perceiving gave them one whole side: with one of our great shot their Master gunners shoolder was stroken away, and our Master gunner with a smal bullet was shot into the head. Being by this time grappled and aboord each of other the fight continued without ceasing one houre and a halfe. In which fight were hurt and slain on both sides 23 of the chiefest men, having most of them some 6 or 8 woundes, and some 10 or 12 woundes.

Being thus hurt and spoiled they robbed us of our victuals, powder, weapons and provision, saving a smal quantity of biskuit to serve us scarce for England. Our Master and his Mate were deadly wounded, so that they were not able to come forth of their beds. I my selfe was wounded twice in the head, once with a sword, and another time with a pike, and hurt also in the side of the buttoke with a shot. Three of our passengers were hurt also, whereof one had 10 or 12 woundes our Master hurt in the face with a pike and thrust quite through the head. Being thus put to our close fights, and also much pestred with cabbens[18] and unserviceable folkes we could not stirre to handle our weapons nor charge a piece: againe having spent all the powder in our flaskes and charges which we had present for our defence, they cut downe our netting and entred so many of their men as could stand upon our poope and forecastle, from whence they playd extreemely upon us with their shot. As thus we stood resolved to die in fight, the Captaine of the Frenchmen cried to us to yeld and no force should be offred. But after we had yelded, they knowing so many of their best men to be hurt and in danger of present death, began to grow into a new furie, in which they would have put us to the sword had not their Captaine charged them, and persuaded them to the contrary. Being at length pacified they fell on all handes to rifling and carrying aboord all the next day until 4 of the clock: at which time by over greedy lading both their owne boate and ours, they sunk the one and split the other by the ships side: by meanes whereof they left us two cables and ankers, all our ordinance and most of our sayles, which otherwise had ben taken away also. Furthermore they doubting the wind would arise, and night at hand, and a tal ship all that day by meanes of the calme in sight, they came aboord us with their ship, and tookr in their men that were in us, who left us not at their departing any thing worth the carrying away.

The French ship deprived John White of one other important asset, the ship's pilot Pedro Diaz. Diaz recounts his bid for freedom in his deposition:

> They proceeded on their voyage and had reached a point some 30 leagues from the island of Madeira when, having sighted a sail, the faster vessel pursued it and so became separated from the other.
>
> The vessel where Pedro Diaz was, continuing on its course, met a French ship which overhauled it, came alongside and sent aboard 30 men with whom the English fought until most of both parties were killed or wounded. The English vessel surrendered to the Frenchman who looted it, removing what he wanted. He left the vessel to some of the English who on their knees begged him to leave Pedro Diaz with them because without him they could not proceed, and would perish. For his part, Pedro Diaz so exerted himself to persuade the Frenchmen not to leave him with the English that he prevailed and the Frenchman took him with him, promising to set him ashore in the Canaries.
>
> Pedro Diaz escaped from the Frenchman at Isla de Mayo.[19] He reached Havana in the month of March, 1589, where he is at present, intending to go to Spain with the fleet.[20]

John White, having narrowly escaped with his life recounts the journey home:

> Being thus ransacked and used as is aforesaid in all sorts, we determined (as our best shift in so hard a case) to returne for England, and caused all our able and unhurt men, to fal to newe rigging and mending our sailes, tacklings, and such things as were spilled in our fight. By this occasion, God justly punishing our former theeverie of our evil disposed mariners, we were of force constrained to break of our intended voyage for the reliefe of our Colony left the yeere before in Virginia, and the same night to set our course for England, being than about 50 leagues to the Northeast of Madera.

The 7 of May being Wednesday in the forenoone the wind came large at East Northeast and we haled off as farre west and by north as we could[21] until the 10 of May, fearing to meete with any more men of warre, for that we had no maner of weapons left us.

The 11 the wind larged more, and thence forth we continued our due course for England.

The 17 of May we thrust our selves west of Ushant, and sounded, but found no ground at 110 fathoms. The same day at night we sounded againe, and found ground at 80 fathoms.

The 20 being Sunday we fell with the coast of Ireland.

The 21 in the forenoone we saw the Northside of Cornewal at the lands end.

The 22 of May we came to an anker betweene Lunday and Harting point[22] neere unto Chavell key,[23] where we road untill the next tyde, and thence we put over the barre, and the same day landed at Biddeford.

Our other Pinnesse whose company we had lost before the last cruell fight, returned also home into Cornwall within fewe weekes after our arrival, without performing our entended voyage for the reliefe of the planters in Virginia, which thereby were not a little distressed.[24]

The year ended for Grenville on September 14, 1588, when Queen Elizabeth, fearful of another attack by the Spanish now circumnavigating their way around the British Isles, commanded Grenville to undertake the defense of the western approaches. Details of the command ask him to guard the Severn (the Bristol Channel) and fortify Waterford and Cork. Sadly, for Grenville's chance of fame, English storms and the treacherous reefs of the west coast of Scotland and Ireland destroyed the Spanish fleet. However, for his pains in supplying ships and men for the battle against the Spanish Armada, Grenville's financial receipt from Lord Howard and Sir John Hawkins was £1,960 for the hire of seven hundred men for four months; and for providing ships totaling 800 tons, £320.

ELEVEN

The Voyage of
John White, 1590

In 1589, mindful that his Charter to settle America was about to expire, Raleigh assigned it to a number of London merchants and investors. This not only effectively ended his direct involvement in the Roanoke colony, but also that of his cousin Sir Richard Grenville, who went on to occupy his time with his estates in Ireland.

Between October 1588 and 1590, Grenville busied himself with yet another command from his Queen. She wanted "Gentlemen of substance" to undertake the settlement of Southern Ireland with Protestants. This was England's second attempt to subdue the province. Grenville duly obliged, and by May 1589 had settled ninety-nine people, including his son John, his half-brother John Arundell, Christopher Harris of Radford (near Plymouth), Thomas Stukeley, John Facey, and John Bellew. Grenville also made further acquisitions of land including St. Finbar's Monastery, lands at Kilmoney and Kinalmeaky, and Fermoy Abbey, the latter leased to the Grenvilles for forty years.

Sadly, Grenville never saw the legal conclusion of these acquisitions, for when they were finally sealed he was already on his way to the Azores on his last fateful task for his Queen and his country.

John White remained to plead alone for a rescue mission for his colony 3,500 miles away on Roanoke Island. He finally secured that opportunity. This is his account, recorded by Hakluyt:

> The 20 of March the three ships the *Hopewell*, the *John Evangelist*, and the *Little John*, put to Sea from Plymmouth with two small Shallops.[1]
> The 25 at midnight both our Shallops were sunke being towed at the ships sternes by the Boatswains negligence.
> On the 30 we saw ahead us that part of the coast of Barbary, lying East of Cape Cantyn, and the Bay of Asaphi.
> The next day we came to the Ile of Mogador,[2] where rode, at our passing by, a Pinnesse of London called the *Moonelight*.

Aprill

On the first of April we ankered in Santa Cruz rode, where we found two great shippes of London lading with Sugar, of whom we had 2 shipboats to supply the losse of our Shallops.

On the 2 we set sayle from the rode of Santa Cruz, for the Canaries.

On Saturday 4 we saw Alegranza, the East Ile of the Canaries.

On Sunday 5 of Aprill we gave chase to a double flyboat, the which, we also the same day fought with, and tooke her, with losse of three of their men slaine, and one hurt.

On Monday the 6 we saw Grand Canarie, and the next day we landed and tooke in fresh water on the Southside thereof.

On the 9 we departed from Grand Canary, and framed our course for Dominica.

The last of Aprill we saw Dominica, and the same night we came to an anker on the Southside thereof.

May

The first of May in the morning many of the Savages came aboord our ships in their canowes, and did traffique with us: we also the same day landed and entered their Towne from whence we returned the same day aboord without any resistance of the Savages; or any offence done to them.

The 2 of May our Admirall and our Pinnesse departed from Dominica leaving the John our Viceadmirall playing off and on about Dominica, hoping to take some Spaniard outwardes bound to the Indies; the same night we had sight of three smal Ilands called Los Santos, leaving Guadalope and them on our starboord.

The 3 we had sight of St Christophers Iland, bearing Northeast and by East of us.

On the 4 we sayled by the Virgines,[3] which are many broken Ilands, lying at the East ende of S. Johns Iland; and the same day towards evening we landed upon one of them called Blanca, where we killed an incredible number of foules: here we stayed but three houres, and from thence stood into the shore Northwest, and having brought this Iland Southeast off us, we put towards night thorow an opening or swatch, called The Passage, lying betwene the Virgines, and the East end of S. John: here the Pinnesse left us and sayled South side of S. John.

The 5 and 6 the Admirall sailed along the Northside of S. John, so neere the shore that the Spaniards discerned us to be men of warre; and therefore made fires along the coast as we sailed by, for so their custom is, when they see any men of warre on their coasts.

The 7 we landed on the Northwest end of S. John, where we watered in a good river called Yaguana, and the same night following we tooke a Frigate of ten Tunne coming from Gwathanelo laden with hides and ginger. In this place Pedro a Mollato,[4] who knewe all our state, ranne from us to the Spaniards.

On the 9 we departed from Yaguana.

The 13 we landed on an Iland called Mona, whereon were 10 or 12 houses inhabited of the Spaniards; these we burned and tooke from them a Pinnesse, which they had drawen aground and sunke, and carried all her sayles, mastes, and rudders into the woods, because we should not take him away; we also chased the Spaniards over all the Iland; but they hid them in caves, hollow rockes, and bushes, so that we could not find them.

On the 14 we departed from Mona, and the next day after wee came to an Iland called Saona, about 5 leagues distant from Mona, lying on the Southside of Hispaniola neere the East end: betwene these two Ilands we lay off and on 4 or 5 dayes, hoping to take some of the Domingo fleete doubling this Iland, as a neerer way to Spaine than by Cape Tyburon,[5] or by Cape S. Anthony.[6]

On Thursday being the 19 our Viceadmirall, from whom we departed at Dominica, came to us at Saona, with whom we left a Spanish Frigate, and appointed him to lie off and on other five daies betweene Saona and Mona to the ende aforesaid; then we departed from them at Saona for Cape Tyburon, Here I was enformed that our men of the Viceadmirall, at their departure from Dominica brought away two young Savages, which were the chiefe Casiques sonnes of that Countrey and part of Dominica, but they shortly after ran away from them at Santa Cruz Iland where the Viceadmirall landed to take in ballast.

On the 21 the Admirall came to the Cape Tyburon, where we found the John Evangelist our Pinnesse staying for us: here we tooke in two Spaniards almost starved on the shore, who made a fire to our ships as we passed by. Those places for an 100 miles in length are nothing els but a desolate and meere wildernesse, without any habitation of people, and full of wilde Bulles and Bores, and great Serpents.

The 22 our Pinnesse came also to an anker in Aligato Bay at cape Tyburon. Here we understood of M. Lane, Captaine of the Pinnesse; how he was set upon with one of the kings Gallies belonging to Santo Domingo, which was manned with 400 men, who after he had fought with him 3 or 4 houres, gave over the fight and forsooke him, without any great hurt done on eyther part.

The 26 The *John* our Viceadmirall came to us to cape Tyburon, and the Frigat which we left with him at Saona. This was the appointed place which we should attend for the meeting with the Santo Domingo fleete.

On Whitsunday eve at Cape Tyburon one of our boyes ran away from us, and at ten days end returned to our ships almost starved for want of food. In sundry places about this part of Cape Tyburon we found the bones and carkases of divers men, who had perished (as wee thought) by famine in those woods, being either stragled from their company, or landed there by some men of warre.

June

On the 14 of June we took a smal Spanish frigat which fell amongst us so suddenly, as he doubled the point at the Bay of Cape Tyburon, where we road, so that he could not escape us. This frigat came from Santo Domingo, and had but 3 men in her, the one was an expert Pilot, the other a Mountainer, and the third a Vintener, who escaped all out of prison at Santo Domingo, purposing to fle to Yaguana which is a towne in the West parts of Hispaniola where many fugitive Spaniards are gathered together.

The 17 being Wednesday Captaine Lane was sent to Yaguana with his Pinnesse and a Frigat to take a shippe, which was there taking in fraight, as we understood by the old Pylot, whom we had taken three dayes before.

The 24 the Frigat returned from Captaine Lane at Yaguana, and brought us word to Cape Tyburon, that Captaine Lane had taken the shippe, with many passengers and Negroes in the same: which proved not so rich a prize as we hoped for, for that a Frenchman of warre had taken and spoyled her before we came. Neverthelesse her loading was thought worth 1000 or 1300 pounds, being hides, ginger, Cannafistula,[7] Copper pannes, and Casava.

July

The second of July Edward Spicer whom we left in England came to us at Cape Tyburon, accompanied with a small Pinnesse, whereof one M. Harps was Captaine. And the same day we had sight of a fleete of 14 sail all of Santo Domingo, to whom we presently gave chase, but they upon the first sight of us fled, and separating themselves scattered here and there: Wherefore we were forced to divide our selves and so made after them untill 12 of the clocke at night.

But then by reason of the darknesse we lost sight of ech other, yet in the end the Admirall and the *Moonelight* happened to be together the same night at the fetching up of the Viceadmirall of the Spanish fleete, against whom the next morning we fought and tooke him, with losse of one of our men and two hurt, and of theirs 4 slaine and 6 hurt. But what was become of our Viceadmirall, our Pinnesse, and Prize, and two Frigates, in all this time, we were ignorant.

The 3 of July we spent about rifling, romaging and fitting the Prize to be sailed with us.

The 6 of July we saw Jamayca the which we left on our larboard, keeping Cuba in sight on our starboord.

Upon the 8 of July we saw the Iland of Pinos, which lieth on the Southside of Cuba nigh unto the West end or Cape called Cape S. Anthony. And the same day we gave chase to a Frigat, but at night we lost sight of her, partly by the slow sayling of our Admirall, and lacke of the *Moonelight* our Pinnesse, whom Captaine Cooke had sent to the Cape the day before.

On the 11 we came to Cape S. Anthony, where we found our consort the *Moonelight* and her Pinnesse abiding for our comming, of whom we understood that the day before there passed by them 22 saile, some of them of the burden of 300 and some 400 tunnes loaden with the Kings treasure from the maine, bound for Havana; from this 11 of July until 22 we were much becalmed: and the wind being very scarse, and the weather exceeding hot, we were much pestered with the Spaniards we had taken: wherefore we were driven to land all the Spaniards saving three, but the place where we landed them was of their owne choice on the Southside of Cuba near unto the Organes and Rio de Puercos.

The 23 we had sight of the Cape of Florida, and the broken Ilands thereof called the Martires.[8]

The 25 being St James day in the morning we fell with the Matancas, a head-land 8 leagues towards the East of Havana, where we purposed to take fresh water in, and make our abode two of three days.

On Sunday the 26 of July plying too and fro between the Matancas and Havana, we were espied of three small Pinnesses of S. John de Ullua bound for Havana, which were exceeding richly loaden. These 3 Pinnesses came very boldly up unto us, and so continued untill they came within musket shot of us. And we supposed them to be Captaine Harps pinnesse, and two small Frigats taken by Captaine Harpe: wherefore we shewed our flag. But they presently upon the sight of it turned about and made all the saile they could from us toward the shore, and kept themselves in so shallow water, that we were not able to follow them, and therefore gave them over with expense of shot and powder to no purpose. But if we had not so rashly set out our flagge, wee might have taken them all three, for they would not have knowen us before they had bene in our hands. This chase brought us so far to leeward as Havana: wherefore not finding any of our consorts at the Matancas, we put over again to the cape of Florida, and from thence thorow the channel of Bahama.

On the 28 the Cape of Florida bare West of us.

The 30 we lost sight of the coast of Florida, and stood to Sea for to gaine the helpe of the current which runneth much swifter afarre off than in sight of the coast. For from the Cape to Virginia all along the shore are none but eddie currents, fetting to the South and Southwest.

The 31 our three ships were clearly disbocked,[9] the great prize, the Admirall, and the *Moonelight*, but our prize being thus disbocked departed from us without taking leave of our Admirall or consort, and sayled directly for England.

August

On the first of August the winde scanted, and from thence forward we had very fowle weather with much raine, thundering, and great spouts, which fell round about us nigh unto our ships.

The 3 we stoode againe in for the shore, and at midday we tooke the height of the same. The height of that place we found to be 34 degrees of latitude. Towards night we were within three leagues of the Low sandie Ilands West of Wokokon. But the weather continued so exceeding foule, that we could not come to an anker nye the coast: wherefore we stood off againe to Sea untill Monday the 9 of August.

On Monday the storme ceased and we had very great likelihood of faire weather: therefore we stood in againe for the shore: and came to an anker at 11 fathom in 35 degrees of Latitude, within a mile of the shore, where we went on land on the narrow sandy Iland, being one of the Ilandes West of Wokokon[10]: in this Iland we tooke in some fresh water and caught great store of fish in the shallow water. Betweene the maine (as we supposed) and that Iland it was but a mile over and three or four foote deep in most places.

On the 12 in the morning we departed from thence and towards night we came to an anker at the Northeast end of the Iland of Croatoan, by reason of a breach which we perceived to lie out two or three leagues into the Sea: here we road all that night.

The 13 in the morning before we wayed our ankers, our boates were sent to found over this breach; our ships riding on the side thereof at 5 fathomes; and a ships length from us we found but 4 and a quarter, and then deeping and shallowing for the space of two miles, so that sometimes we found 5 fathome, and by and by 7, and within two casts with the lead 9, and then 8, next cast 5, and then 6, and then 4, and then 9 againe, and deeper; but 3 fathom was the least, 2 leagues off from the shore. This breach is in 35 degree and a half, and lyeth at the very Northeast point of Croatoan, whereas goeth a fret out of the maine Sea into the inner waters, which part the Ilandes and the maine land.[11]

The 15 of August towards Evening we came to an anker at Hatorask, in 36 degrees and one-third, in five fathom of water, three leagues from the shore. At our first coming to anker on this shore we saw a great smoke rise in the Ile Roanoke neere the place where I left our Colony in the yeere 1587, which smoake put us in good hope that some of the Colony were there expecting my returne out of England.

The 16 and next morning our 2 boats went ashore, and Captain Cooke, and Captain Spicer, and their company with me, with intent to passe at Roanoke where our countreymen were left. At our putting from the ship we commanded our Master gunner to make readie 2 Minions and a Falkon well loden, and to shoot them off with reasonable space between every shot, to the ende that their reportes might be heard to the place where wee hoped to finde some of our people. This was accordingly performed, and our two boats put off unto the shore, in the Admirals boat we sounded all the way and found from our shippe until we came within a mile of the shore nine, eight, and seven fathome: but before we were halfe way betweene our ships and the shore we saw another great smoke to the Southwest of Kindrikers Mountes[12]: we therefore thought good to goe to that second smoke first: but it was much further from the harbour where we landed, than we supposed it to be, so that we were very sore tired before wee came to the smoke. But that which grieved us more was that when we came to the smoke, we found no man nor signe that any had bene there lately, nor yet any fresh water in all this way to drinke. Being thus wearied with this journey we returned to the harbour where we left our boates, who in our absence had brought their caske ashore for fresh water, so we deferred our going to Roanoke until the next morning, and caused some of those saylers to digge in those sandie hilles for fresh water whereof we found very sufficient. That night wee returned aboord with our boates and one whole company in safety.

The next morning being the 17 of August, our boates and company were prepared againe to goe up to Roanoke, but Captaine Spicer had then sent his boat ashore for fresh water, be meanes whereof it was ten of the clocke afore noone before we put from our ships which were then come to an anker within two miles of shore.

The Admirals boat was half way towards the shore, when Captaine Spicer put off from his ship. The Admirals boat first passed the breach, but not without some danger of sinking, for we had a sea brake into our boat which filled us halfe full of water, but by the will of God and carefull steyerage of Captaine Cooke we came safe ashore, saving onely that our furniture, victuals, match and powder were much wet and spoiled. For at this time the winde blew at Northeast and direct into the harbour so great a gale, that the Sea brake extremely on the barre, and the tide went very forcibly at the entrance. By that time our Admirals boate was halled ashore, and most of our things taken out to dry, Captaine Spicer came to the entrance of the breach with his mast standing up, and was halfe passed over, but by the rash and undifferent steyerage of Ralph Skinner his Masters mate, a very dangerous Sea brake into their boate and overfet them quite, the men kept the boat some in it, and some hanging on it, but the next sea set the boat on ground, where it beat so, that some of them were forced to let goe their hold, hoping to wade ashore, but the Sea still beat them downe, so that they could neither stand nor swimme, and the boat twice or thrice was turned the keele upward, whereon Captaine Spicer and Skinner, hung untill they sunke, and were seen no more. But four that could swimme a little kept themselves in deeper water and were saved by Captain Cookes meanes, who so soone as he saw their oversetting, stripped himselfe, and foure other that could swimme very well, and with all haste possible rowed unto them, and saved foure. They were 11 in all, and 7 of the chiefest were drowned, whose names were Edward Spicer, Ralph Skinner, Edward Kelley, Thomas Bevis, Hance the Surgion,[13] Edward Kelborne, Robert Coleman. This mischance did so much discomfort the saylers, that they were all of a one mind not to goe any further to seeke the planters. But in the end by the commandement and perswasion of me and Captain Cooke, they prepared the boates: and seeing the Captain and me so resolute, they seemed much more willing. Our boates and all things fitted againe, we put off from Hatorask, being the number of 19 persons in both boates: but before we could get to the place, where our planters were left, it was so exceeding darke, that we overshot the place a quarter of a mile: there we espied towards the North end of the Iland the light of a great fire thorow the woods, to the which we presently rowed: when wee came right over against it, we let fall our Grapnel neere the shore, and sounded with a trumpet a Call and afterwards many familiar English tunes of Songs, and called to them friendly; but we had no answere, we therefore landed at day breake, and coming to the fire, we found the grasse and sundry rotten trees burning about the place.[14]

From hence we went thorow the woods to that part of the Iland directly over against Dasamongwepenk, and from thence we returned by the water side, round about the Northpoint of the Iland, untill we came to the place where I left our Colony in the year 1586.[15]

In all this way we saw in the sand the print of the Savages feet of 2 or 3 sorts trooden by night, and as we entred up the sandy bank upon a tree, in the very browe thereof were curiously carved these faire Romane letters C R O: which letters presently we knew to signifie the place, where I should find the planters seated, according to a secret token agreed upon betweene them and me at my last departure from them, which was, that in any wayes they should not faile to write or carve on the trees or posts of the dores the name of the place where they should be seated; for at my coming away they were prepared to remove from Roanoke 50 miles into the main.[16]

Therefore at my departure from them in An.1587 I willed them, that if they should happen to be distressed in any of those places, that then they should carve over the letters or name, a Crosse + in this forme, but we found no such signe of distresse. And having well considered of this, we passed towards the place where they were left in sundry houses, but we found the houses taken downe, and the place very strongly enclosed with a high palisado of great trees, with cortynes[17] and flankers very Fort-like, and one of the chiefe trees or postes at the right side of the entrance had the barke taken off, and 5 foote from the ground in fayre Capitall letters was graven CROATOAN without any crosse or signe of distresse; this done, we entred into the palisado, where we found many barres of Iron, two pigges of Lead, four ironfowlers, Iron sacket-shotte, and such like heavie things, throwen here and there, almost overgrown with grasse and weedes. From thence wee went along by the water side, towards the poynt of the Creeke to see if we could find any of their boates or Pinnesse,[18] but we could perceive no signe of them, nor any of the last Falkons and small Ordnance which were left with them, at my departure from them. At our returne from the Creeke, some of our Saylers meeting us, told us that they had found where divers chests had bene hidden, and long sithence digged up againe and broken up, and much of the goods in them spoyled and scattered about, but nothing left, of such things as the Savages knew any use of, undefaced.

Presently Captaine Cooke and I went to the place, which was in the ende of an olde trench, made two yeeres past[19] by Captaine Amadas: where wee found five chests, that had bene carefully hidden of the Planters, and of the same chests three were my owne, and about the place many of my things spoyled and broken, and my bookes torn from the covers, the frames of some of my pictures and Mappes rotten and spoyled with rayne, and my armour almost eaten through with rust; this could bee no other but the deede of the Savages our enemies at Dasamongwepeuk, who had watched the departure of our men to Croatoan; and as soone as they were departed, digged up every place where they suspected any thing to be buried: but although it much grieved me to see such spoyle of my goods, yet on the other side I greatly joyed that I had safely found a certaine token of their fate being at Croatoan, which is the place where Manteo was born, and the Savages of the Iland our friends.[20]

When we had seene in this place so much as we could, we returned to our Boates, and departed from the shoare towards our Shippes, with as much speede as we could: For the weather beganne to overcast, and very likely that a foule and stormie night would ensue. Therefore the same Evening with much danger and labour, we got our selves aboard, by which time the winde and seas were so greatly risen, that wee doubted our Cables and Ankers would scarcely holde untill Morning; wherefore the Captaine caused the Boate to be manned with five lusty men, who could swimme all well, and sent them to the little Iland on the right hand of the Harbour,[21] to bring aboard five of our men, who had filled our caske with fresh water: the Boate the same night returned aboard with our men, but all our Caske ready filled they left behinde, umpossible to bee had aboard without danger of casting away both men and Boates; for this night prooved very stormie and foule.

The next Morning it was agreed by the Captaine and myself, with the Master and others, to way anchor, and goe for the place at Croatoan, where our planters were: for that then the winde was good for that place, and also to leave that Caske with fresh water on shoare in the Iland untill our returne. So then they brought the cable to the Capston, but when the Anker was almost on deck, the Cable broke, by meanes whereof we lost another Anker, wherewith we drove so fast in to the shoare, that wee were forced to let fall a third Anker; which came so fast home the Shippe was almost aground by Kendricks Mounts: so that we were forced to let slippe the Cable ende for ende. And if it had not chanced that wee had fallen into a chanell of deeper water, closer by the shoare then wee accompted of,[22] wee could never have gone cleare of the poynt that lyeth to the Southwardes of Kendricks Mounts.

Being this cleare of some dangers, and gotten into deeper waters, but not without some losse; for we had but one Cable and Anker left us of foure, and the weather grew to be fouler and fouler; our victuals scarce, and our caske and fresh water lost: it was therefore determined that we should goe for Saint John or some other Iland to the Southward for fresh water. And it was further purposed, that if wee could any wayes supply our wants of victuals and other necessaries, either at Hispaniola, Saint John, or Trynidad, that then wee should continue in the Indies all the Winter following, with hope to make 2 rich voyages of one, and at our returne to visit our countreymen at Virginia.

The captaine and the whole company in the Admirall (with my earnest petitions) thereunto agreed, so that it rested onely to knowe what the Master of the *Moonelight* our consort would doe herein. But when we demanded them if they would accompany us in that new determination, they alleged that their weake and leake Shippe was not able to continue it; wherefore the same night we parted, leaving the *Moonelight* to goe directly for England, and the Admirall set his course for Trynidad, which course we kept two dayes.

On the 28 the winde changed, and it was sette on foule weather every way: but this stormè brought the winde West and Northwest, and blewe so forcibly, that wee were able to beare no sayle, but our fore-course halfe mast high, wherewith wee ranne upon the winde perforce, the due course for England, for that wee were dryven to change our first determination for Trynidad, and stoode for the Ilands of Azores, where wee purposed to take in fresh water, and also there hoped to meete with some English men of warre about those Ilands, at whose hands wee might obtaine some supply of our wants.

September

And thus continuing our course for the Azores, sometimes with calmes, and sometimes with very scarce windes, on the fifteenth of September the winde came South Southeast, and blew so exceedingly, that wee were forced to lie atry[23] all that day.

At this time by account we judged our selves to be about twentie leagues to the West of Cuerno and Flores, but about night the storme ceased, and fayre weather ensued.

On Thursday the seventeenth wee saw Cuerno and Flores, but we could not come to an anker that night, by reason the winde shifted. The next Morning being the eighteenth, standing in againe with Cuerno, we escied a sayle ahead us, to whom we gave chase: but when wee came neere him, we knew him to be a Spaniard; and hoped to make sure purchase of him; but we understood at our speaking with him, that he was a prize, and of the Domingo fleete already taken by the *John* our consort, in the Indies. We learned also of this prize, that our Viceadmiral and Pinnesse had fought with the rest of the Domingo fleete, and had forced them with their Admirall to flee unto Jamaica under the Forte for succour, and some of them ran themselves aground, whereof one of them they brought away, and tooke out of some others so much as the time would permit. And further wee understood of them; that in their returne from Jamaica about the Organes neere Cape Saint Anthony, our Viceadmiral met with two Shippes of the mayne land, come from Mexico, bound for Havana, with whom he fought; in which fight our Viceadmirals Lieutenant was slaine, and the Captaines right arme strooken off, with foure other of his men slaine, and fifteene hurt. But in the end he entred, and tooke one of the Spanish shippes, which was so sore shot by us under water, that before they could take out her treasure, she sunke; so that we lost thirteene Pipes of silver which sunke with her, besides much other rich merchandize. And in the mean time the other Spanish shippe being pearced with nine shotte under water, got away; whom our Viceadmiral intended to pursue: but some of their men in the toppe made certaine rockes, which they saw above water neere the shoare, to be Gallies of Havana and Cartegena, comming from Havana to rescue the two Ships; Wherefore they gave over their chase, and went for England. After this intelligence was given us by this our prize, he departed from us, and went for England.

On Saturday the 19 of September we came to an anker near a small village on the North side of Flores, where we found ryding 5 English men of warre, of whom wee understood that our Viceadmiral and Prize were gone thence for England. One of these five was the *Moonelight* our consort, who upon the first sight of our comming into Flores, set sayles and went for England, not taking any leave of us.

On Sunday the 20 the *Mary Rose*,[24] Admirall of the Queenes fleete, wherein was Generall Sir John Hawkins, stood in with Flores, and divers other of the Queenes ships, namely the *Hope*, the *Nonpareilia*, the *Raynebow*, the *Swiftsure*, the *Foresight*, with many other good merchants ships of warre, as the *Edward Bonaventure*, the *Merchant Royal*, the *Amitie*, the *Eagle*, the *Dainty* of Sir John Hawkins, and many other good ships and Pinnesses, all attending to meete with the King of Spaines fleete, comming from Terra firma of the West Indies.

The 22 of September we went aboard the *Raynebow*, and towards night we spake with the *Swiftsure*, and gave him 3 pieces. The captaines desired our company; wherefore we willingly attended on them: who at this time with 10 other ships stood for Faial. But the Generall with the rest of the Fleete were separated from us, making two fleetes, for the surer meeting with the Spanish fleete.

On Wednesday the 23 we saw Gratiosa,[25] where the Admiral and the rest of the Queenes fleet were come together. The Admirall put forth a flag of counsel, in which was determined that the whole fleete should go for the mayne, and spread themselves on the coast of Spaine and Portugal, so farre as conveniently they might, for the surer meeting of the Spanish fleete in those parts.

The 26 we came to Faial, where the Admiral with some other of the fleete ankered, othersome plyed up and downe betweene that and the Pico until midnight, at which time the Antony shot off a piece and wayed, shewing his light: after whom the whole fleete stood to the East, the winde at Northeast by East.

On Sunday the 27 towards Evening we tooke our leave of the Admirall and the whole fleete, who stood to the East. But our shippe accompanied with a Flyboate stoode in againe with S. George, where we purposed to take in more fresh water, and some other fresh victuals.

On Wednesday the 30 of September, seeing the winde hang so Northerly, that wee could not attaine the Iland of S. George, we gave over our purpose to water there, and the next day framed our due course for England.

October

The 2 of October in the Morning we saw S. Michaels Iland on our Starre board quarter.

The 23 at 10 of the clocke afore noone, we saw Ushant in Brittany.

On Saturday the 24 we came in safetie, God be thanked, to an anker at Plymouth.

John White submitted this transcript about three years after the voyage. With it came the following letter:

To the Worshipful and my very friend Master Richard Hakluyt, much happinesse in the Lord

Sir, as well for the satisfying of your earnest request, as the performance of my promise made unto you at my last being with you in England, I have sent you (although in a homely stile, especially for the contentation of a delicate eare) the true discourse of my last voyage into the West Indies, and partes of America called Virginia, taken in hand about the end of February, in the yeare of our redemption 1590. And what events happened unto us in this our journey, you shall plainely perceive by the sequele of my discourse.[26] There were at the time aforesaid three ships absolutely determined to go for the West Indies, at the speciall charges of M. John Wattes of London Marchant.[27] But when they were fully furnished, and in readinesse to make their departure, a generall stay was commanded of all ships thorowout England. Which so soonw as I heard, I presently (as I thought it most requisite) acquainted Sir Walter Ralegh therewith, desiring him that as I had sundry time afore bene chargeable and troublesome unto him, for the supplies and reliefes of the planters in Virginia: to likewise, that by his endevour it would please him at that instant to procure licence for those three ships to proceede on with their determined voyage, that thereby the people in Virginia (if it were Gods pleasure) might speedily be comforted and relieved without further charges unto him.

Whereupon he by his good meanes obtained licence of the Queenes majestie, and orders to be taken, that the owner of the 3 ships should be bound unto Sir Walter Ralegh or his assignes, in 3000 pounds, that those 3 ships in consideration of their releasement should take in, and transport a convenient number of passengers, with their furnitures and necessaries to be landed in Virginia. Neverthelesse that order was not observed, neither was the bond taken according to the intention aforesaid. But rather in contempt of the aforesaid order, I was by the owner and Commanders of the ships denied to have any passengers, or any thing els transported in any of the said ships, saving only myself and my chest; no not so much as a boy to attend upon me, although I made great sute, and earnest entreatie as well to the chiefe Commanders, as to the owner of the said ships. Which crosse and unkind dealing, although it very much discontented me, not withstanding the scarcity of time was such that I could have no opportunity to go unto Sir Walter Ralegh with complaint: for the ships being then all in readinesse to goe to the Sea, would have bene departed before I could have made my returne. Thus both Governors, Masters, and sailers, regarding very smally the good of their countreymen in Virginia; determined nothing lesse than to touch at those places, but wholly disposed themselves to seeke after purchase and spoiles, spending so much time therein, that Summer was spent before we arrived at Virginia.[28] And when we were come thither, the season was so unfit, and weather so foule, that we were constrained of force to forsake that coast, having not seene any of our planters, with losse on one of our ship-boates, and 7 of our chiefest men: and also with losse of 3 of our ankers and cables, and most of our caskes with fresh water left on shore, not possible to be had aboord.

Which evils and unfortunate events (as wel to their owne losse as to the hinderance of the planters in Virginia) had not chanced, if the order set downe by Sir Walter Ralegh had been observed, or if my dayly and continual petitions for the performance of the same might have taken any place. Thus may you plainely perceive the successe of my fifth and last voiage to Virginia, which was no lesse unfortunately ended then frowardly[29] begun, and as lucklesse to many, as sinister to my selfe. But I would to God it had bene as prosperous to all, as noysome to the planters; and as joyful to me, as discomfortable to them. Yet seeing it is not my first crossed voyage, I remaine contented. And wanting my wishes, I leave off from prosecuting that whereunto I would to God my wealth were answerable to my will. Thus committing the reliefe of my discomfortable company the planters in Virginia, to the merciful help of the Almighty, whom I most humbly beseech to helpe and comfort them, according to his most holy will and their good desire, I take my leave: from my house at Newtowne in Kylmore the 4 of February, 1593.

Your most wel wishing friend
JOHN WHITE[30]

White was never to see his daughter, or the colonists, again.

Twelve

A Review of the Roanoke Voyages, 1584–1590

The Roanoke voyages were a period of quite extraordinary endeavor, and it is thanks to the endeavors of Richard Hakluyt that we have such a complete record of those events. However, there remain a great many questions and varied interpretations of his record. Before dealing with subsequent events, it may be prudent therefore to review and analyze at least some of the conflicting opinions and interpretations of Hakluyt's record of the voyages associated with the first attempt by the English to settle a colony on American soil.

In chronological order, let us first review the voyage of Amadas and Barlowe that took place in 1584.

To begin with, the location of the first anchorage Amadas and Barlowe chose is confused. Although they gave a latitude that greatly assists modern interpretation, the landing site has still been variously determined as Ocracoke ("Wokocon" in Hakluyt's works); at least two locations on Hatteras Island (Croatoan); and, as the author now deduces, somewhere close to Bodie Island, a location near to the current Oregon Inlet, some sixty miles north of Hatteras Island.

We can determine the location of their first landing from the words of Captain Barlowe, who, when later identifying Roanoke Island and referring to their ships in context, states that Roanoke was "distant from the harbor by which we entered seven leagues." This, in nautical parlance is approximately twenty-one miles. The Ocracoke (Wokocon) inlet is in excess of eighty miles distant while Chacandepeco at Hatteras Island is around sixty miles distant. Only an inlet that existed near present day Bodie Island would have been close enough to meet the observed "seven leagues" distance to Roanoke.

In 2011, during the archaeological excavations on Hatteras Island that year, the author conducted an unpublished study of the shell middens on the island. This study concluded that Hatteras Island (Croatoan) could sustain a year round population, contrary to suggestions that it was only a seasonal habitation for the Native Americans.[1] This point is relevant because, if Amadas and Barlowe had landed near the former Chacandepeco inlet on Hatteras Island, why indeed would it take two days for an inquisitive and unafraid Native American to make an appearance, and why then would he arrive to view them by canoe, rather than simply walk down to the shoreline? We also know that the Croatoan people burned the stubble from their crops. Widespread burning of stubble was a common practice until very recently in England; Barlowe and Amadas would have recognized any such burned fields for what they represented. Of this practice, they make no mention.

Today, the inlet used by Amadas and Barlowe no longer exists. The entire Outer Banks region is highly unstable, with inlets opening and closing periodically throughout history. In fact, according to Dirk Frankenburg's *The Nature of the Outer Banks* and David Stick's *The Outer Banks of North Carolina 1584–1958*, the only opening anyone from the lost colony period would recognize today is the opening to the south of the village on Ocracoke Island. Little wonder then that the location of the inlet through which Amadas and Barlowe first entered the inland sea of North Carolina has proven so difficult to establish.

Continuing with the 1584 voyage, we should acknowledge the moment when Amadas and Barlowe made contact with the Indians and learned of at least two previous encounters with white men. There are, to date, no known accounts of English, French, or Spanish ships foundering in these waters. Yet, given the proximity of the area to Florida, it seems logical to believe these "white men" were probably Spanish, a thought that must have crossed the minds of Amadas and Barlowe. Given the heightened situation between England and Spain at the time, it seems odd they did not attempt to establish more about these mariners or locate any remnant of their ships in an attempt to identify their origin. Evidently, they took the Indians' story entirely on trust, a risky decision considering the planned arrival of English settlements and the potential for their early discovery at a time when they would have been at their most vulnerable.

Amadas and Barlowe returned home to England with rather inflated stories of a bountiful land, enough at least for Raleigh to finance the next step in his colonization attempt. Due to the attentions of Queen Elizabeth, however, Raleigh had to defer charge of these attempts to his cousin, Sir Richard Grenville. Thus, 1585 dawned with Grenville's extraordinary voyage and the detailed accounts of Lane's ill-fated stay on Roanoke. These accounts not only give us a great deal of commentary on Grenville and his character, but also significant information on the forts, explorations and discoveries of Ralph Lane. For now, let's analyze the information regarding those forts.

We know, from John White's paintings, the design of the fort Ralph Lane built at Tallaboa Bay, and the elaborate one he built at Cabo Rojo. However, these forts are not the only ones the industrious Lane built. Apart from Fort Raleigh on Roanoke, we know from his own letters that Lane built something of substance at Port Ferdinando on Bodie Island, and, most intriguingly, may have built one somewhere near Chesapeake Bay. Historians have not recognized the potential for the existence of this latter fort, even though the shape and style of the fort at Jamestown is typical of the preferred English military style of fort at that time. This, of course, begs the question: Is it possible that another fort lies undiscovered on the James River? We may never know, but it is certain that Lane's reports of 1585 influenced the location of the 1607 settlement. As an aside, these fortress designs also provide us with a compelling image of what to expect at the site of Lane's Fort Raleigh on Roanoke Island. Yet a visit to this site today reveals nothing of the kind. This is essentially because what is visible to the public today is not Lane's fort, a fact that can readily be determined mainly by studying John White's account from his voyage in 1587—an account perhaps overlooked by those searching for the fort today.

Exactly where Lane's fort was located is uncertain at this time. John White merely provides us with a generalization that it stood on the northern part of Roanoke Island. However, Pedro Diaz's deposition goes further. He claimed that Lane had built the fort near the water's edge, a claim we must temper, because Grenville had forbidden Diaz from leaving his ship. Therefore, he could only have gained this information third hand. Given that Diaz was a prisoner, it is also highly unlikely that anyone from Grenville's crew would have given him its precise location, in case he escaped to relay that information to the Spanish, which of course is precisely what he did in 1588. It is just possible that Diaz interpreted a fort on Bodie Island, Port Ferdinando, as the English fort.

One curious observation to close the discussion on Lane's forts comes from re-reading the transcription, which makes it clear Lane's officers lived separately from the men, with the Native Indians in the nearby village in fact, a point we shall discuss later.

Elsewhere in the account of Grenville's 1585 voyage, we have fascinating stories of their encounters with the Spanish. The first encounter occurred during their stay on the island of St. John, and the meeting held under a flag of truce between the English and Spanish soldiers. Grenville claimed he sent his men out to meet the Spanish to tell them that they were merely replenishing supplies and making repairs, signaling that they did not seek any trouble with the Spanish. Yet, from the Spanish archives, we get a slightly different picture. Their version states that the English had declared they were in possession of Spanish hostages who they were intending to ransom in New Spain (Florida), unless they were free to make their repairs.[2] As to which version is correct, we will never know. However, it is possible the Spanish Governor would not have wished to answer awkward questions at the Spanish court as to why he did not attack Grenville, thus by alluding to a hostage situation he had a reasonable excuse for not doing so.

There followed the landing at Roxo Bay (Cabo Rojo, Puerto Rico) where Ralph Lane showed his bravado by instructing twenty of his men to surround a salt hill on the beach and dig in for an expected skirmish with the Spanish. Salt was a valuable commodity and essential for the existence of both the Spanish and the English colonies. What followed with the arrival of the Spanish forces can only be described as an extraordinary standoff as the Spaniards watched Lane's men quite literally steal the valuable salt in front of their eyes while the men of both sides waited, probably only a few yards apart, for the order to attack, facing certain bloodshed.

We arrive now at the great feast of Hispaniola. It took place at a time when relations between England and Spain were rapidly deteriorating. In boldly coming ashore, was it Grenville's plan to intimidate the Spanish into thinking the English he commanded were so powerful as to be able to act with an almost belligerent impunity? Alternatively, did the Spanish simply take Grenville's offer of a feast as an opportunity to break the monotony of their existence? It is perhaps more likely the event took place simply because the Spanish governor considered himself a man of Grenville's equal. Hence, the reason why, in complement to Grenville's feast, he offered what must have been a magnificent sporting sight as both sides' finest rode together during the hunt that followed. Again though, the English and Spanish accounts differ slightly in what Grenville wanted from the visit. The English account states Grenville intended to barter for horses, cattle and victuals; the Spanish account states that he demanded these. Either way, he obviously got what he came for. Perhaps the most revealing note from this encounter is the Spanish observations of the Native Americans (Manteo and Wanchese), described as wearing fine clothes, being familiar with the English language and, apparently, having a love of music. This is the only known description we have of them.

The journey to Roanoke was not without other dangers. The record of Grenville's voyage includes an account wherein the fleet had anchored at an island in order to take seals for food. In making the attempt Grenville and several others "were in very great danger to have been cast away," although the precise reason why is not revealed.

The voyage continued to suffer further mishap when the *Tyger*, Grenville's flagship and no doubt his pride and joy, for it appears several times in his life history, ran aground at the entrance to the inlet between Ocracoke and Hatteras (Croatoan) Island and was damaged sufficient for Hakluyt's eyewitness to declare that it had sunk. It had not sunk but had evidently suffered damage severe enough to warrant drastic and urgent repairs.

The *Tyger* was likely to have been one of the ships carrying the horses Grenville acquired from Hispaniola. It was certainly one of the few ships large enough to hold this cargo. Assuming the horses did not simply escape we can be certain they were removed from the ship while the repairs took place. An intrigue from the consequence of this action is that Grenville could be responsible for one of Ocracoke Island's great mysteries. The island today has a dwindling population of genetically confirmed Spanish Mustangs, and no one knows where they came from or when they arrived.

There are two principal hypotheses regarding their origin. First, that when Lucas Vazquez de Ayllon's Spanish colony, established near the Santee River in South Carolina failed, they left their horses behind. Second, that Grenville was unable to recapture his bartered horses following the repair of his ship, the *Tyger*. Of the two, Grenville seems to be the obvious choice. Any horses left behind by de Ayllon's colony would have had to travel many miles northward along the coast and negotiate at least three open sea inlets in order to arrive on Ocracoke; whereas the grounding of Grenville's ship merely required those on board to do little more than canter ashore or break free from their tethering. It may be no more than pure fancy to suggest, but it is a rather intriguing concept to consider, that the term "Banker" horse, the description by which these horses are known today, is a corruption of "Barter" horse; after all, Grenville bartered for his horses at Hispaniola.

One popular misconception we must dispel in the Grenville and Lane accounts of 1585 is the incident involving the theft of a silver cup. It is a popular misconception that in reprisal for the theft, the native Indians were slayed. The truth is they had not been slain but had in fact fled from the village. Given the vagaries of Elizabethan typeset, wherein the letter "s" of this handwriting form is regularly mistaken for an "f," it is not surprising that such an interpretation, however incorrect, has been made. We must also realize skirmishes were a way of life among the Indians, and thus, their scattering into the reeds and nearby woods amounted to a well-rehearsed evacuation from the attack. It is also unlikely that Lane, a man who displayed compassion on occasion, would have seen genocide as an appropriate punishment for the silver cup, which in reality had probably just been lost. Of course, it is not entirely clear that Lane was the culprit in this instance. Amadas could have carried out the attack by the English, but that moot point remains unclear in Hakluyt's texts.

When Grenville finally left Lane's colony on Roanoke later that same eventful year and proceeded home, luck was with him for he came upon a Spanish treasure ship lying at Bermuda. The capture of the ship, witnessed by one of its passengers, Enrique Lopez, is arguably one of the most extraordinary accounts of piratical activities known.

It was also aboard this Spanish ship that Grenville captured a Portuguese pilot, Pedro Diaz. The consequences of which, could hardly have been more fortuitous for the historian. Grenville held Diaz captive for four years, during which time he visited Roanoke at least once before finally escaping from Grenville's clutches while piloting John White's ill-fated voyage of 1588. When Diaz made his deposition to the Spanish authorities in Havana recalling his extraordinary adventure, he spoke not only about Grenville's voyage home in 1585, but also of the voyage in 1586 and about his time as a prisoner of Grenville.

Of his time in Grenville's hands, perhaps the most intriguing note in his account is being made to help, along with around forty Spanish prisoners, build Grenville's new house on the quay at Bideford. It is extraordinary to consider that Spanish slaves were working on projects in the rural tranquility of small-town Elizabethan England, not to mention the question of where they lie buried today.

Let us return though for a moment to Ralph Lane and his military colony back at Roanoke. We know from his account that he travelled some considerable distances in exploration of the surrounding region, quoting 130 miles on at least two occasions. Even allowing for some inaccuracies, there is evidence in his accounts that give us clues to the areas he reached; these make for significant reading. For example, from his own description of the voyage north, he records the existence of a barren channel also running north. What Lane is in fact describing is modern day Currituck Sound. Given a short overland crossing at its furthest reaches, Lane could have reached Chesapeake Bay and the James River by this route if his measurement was even only vaguely accurate.

The other great journey Lane made was to find the source of what he thought was some type of gold found at the fabled location of Chaunis Temoatan, a location he seems to have been very close to finding, judging by the Indian reception he got. Nevertheless, what Lane got close to was, in reality, probably not gold, but a rich vein of copper ore, possibly bornite (peacock ore) and/or chalcopyrite (the latter a source of iron pyrites, or "fool's gold"). Since both of these ores have impurities in them, it is likely from Lane's description of how the Natives extracted the metal, that what constituted for Indian copper contained a significant percentage of iron, and therefore would not have been as refined as the English were accustomed to producing. It is perhaps worth noting that the source of the Roanoke River, which Lane was probably traversing, is in the center of the Virginian pyrite ridge. This area is therefore, the most likely site for the Indian "Chaunis Temoatan."

Perhaps the greatest question many historians ask of the military colony is why Lane chose to abandon Roanoke when offered a lift home by Drake. In his account, he pleads a great deal about the sorry state of his men, yet Drake had evidently already brought in some supplies to alleviate their plight by the time Lane made the decision to abandon the settlement. While the condition of his men must have played on the mind of Lane, he does give away another reason in his account: his clear intent to have abandoned Roanoke in "but three months" time regardless. If he truly believed Grenville, a man he evidently despised, was not coming, why therefore prolong the inevitable?

We close the examination of the 1585 military colony with another fortuitous eyewitness account, that of William Bigges, who was on board Drake's relieving fleet. It contains confirmation of Lane's account on the relief of the military colony, but with one notable difference. Bigges records Lane left with 103 men, four fewer than the list Hakluyt prepared of those Grenville had left with Lane the previous year. Lane states that he accounted for all of his men, yet clearly, there is a discrepancy. Many historians suggest the four may simply have been left behind, for we know Lane scattered his men to at least three other locations in the hope of finding food, and that three had been tasked with taking Okisko back to his village. The truth about what happened to them comes from the deposition of Pedro Diaz, which declares they had died and, in part, from the account of Grenville in 1586, wherein he discovers at least one of their bodies, albeit, hanging from a tree.

Now we come to the 1586 voyages. The ship that arrived barely a week after Lane left remains a mystery. With none of the more learned scholars of past years having discovered its origins, there seems little chance of ever finding out who she was, the name of the man who captained her, or the location of the port from where she set sail. However, it does seem feasible she could have been part of Grenville's fleet that arrived at Roanoke a few days after her. This is not an unrealistic hypothesis, for we know from the diary of Philip Wyot, Town Clerk of Barnstaple, Grenville's flagship was stranded on the Bideford Bar while attempting to leave port; the mystery ship in essence may simply have been part of the fleet and light enough to pass safely over the bar and hence go on ahead.

Hakluyt only generically covers Grenville's belated voyage from Bideford. It is from the invaluable deposition of Pedro Diaz that we learn more. There is also no detailed account of Grenville's time on Roanoke, although it is clear he spent time searching for Lane's colony. He eventually obtained the astonishing truth from the Croatoan Indians. Realizing his cousin Raleigh's claim was in jeopardy, Grenville decided to leave a small garrison of fifteen men (eighteen in Diaz's account) in charge of Queen Elizabeth's new possession of Virginia, an area already perceived to have been many times the size of England, whilst he returned to Bideford for yet more men and more supplies. When Grenville arrived back in England, we should have little doubt that the words exchanged between him, Lane, and Drake, perhaps all in the presence of Raleigh, must have been positively hostile. It is for this fool's errand he had sailed over four hundred leagues; not only in the attempt to resupply the Roanoke colony but also because of sickness on board his ships. The lack of relief when he arrived in the Azores forced Grenville to waste even more time crossing and recrossing the Atlantic in search of a place of respite for his men, and for a prize to make the voyage profitable. When Grenville finally found that prize, it was little more than a passenger ship upon which he evidently acted in the manner of a man who had been simmering with rage for many weeks. It was from this ship Grenville obtained additional labor to build his new house on Bideford quay.

If Grenville's voyage had been a wasteful one, it was a fortuitous one for history and the town of Bideford, for we can now explain the curious entry in the Parish Register of "Rawley (Raleigh), a Winganditoian." Rawley was, according to Diaz's account, one of three native Indians captured during a skirmish Grenville had while looking for Lane's colony. Two of them escaped leaving just one who Grenville brought back to England and baptized a little over eighteen months later. However, "Rawley's" new life was short-lived. Barely a year after his christening, he died and now lies in an unidentified grave in the parish churchyard of Bideford. His

Baptismal record of "Raleigh" (appears later as "Rawly" and "Rawley"), a "Winganditoian," the Native American captured and brought back to England by Sir Richard Grenville in 1586 (from the Parish Register of St Mary's, Bideford, author's photograph).

death ironically making him the first Native American buried on English soil. He probably died from the same illness that tragically claimed Grenville's twelve-year-old daughter Rebecca a few weeks later, and his black African indentured servant "Lawrence."

Grenville's attempts to hold Virginia also proved to be in vain, for by the time the civilian colony arrived, his fifteen men had disappeared without trace. What we learn of their fate comes only from the Indians who told John White in 1587 that at least two had been killed and the remainder relocated to the fort at Hatorask (Port Ferdinando on Bodie Island), from where they simply vanished.

The year 1587 dawned with Grenville in London organizing a colony of planters for Roanoke with his cousin Raleigh. Diaz states he was looking for 210 people. He got barely half that number.

The departure of the colonists ships from Portsmouth raises yet more questions, for we know from the Hakluyt transcription the ships sailed for barely an hour across the Solent to Cowes on the Isle of Wight, where they were to spend no less than eight days at anchor. It makes no sense to consider that this stay was purely for want of a favorable wind, for the busy port of Portsmouth would have had an adequate network of captains coming and going and possessing well-informed reports of sea conditions. Such a resource should have enabled White and Ferdinando to set a more favorable departure date and negate the risk of wasting valuable on-board supplies while languishing in the Solent, if indeed this was the reason for this delay.

There is, however, an alternative possibility as to why the ships stayed over at Cowes for so long. The Carews, a westcountry family, owned Carisbrooke Castle on the island, and were resident at the time of White's departure. Renowned for their involvement in several transatlantic ventures, and being related to Raleigh and Grenville, it is not a giant leap of logic to consider White may have been instructed to stop off for a social call and to ask the Carews if they could add to the number of colonists already in transit. We may never know the truth, but it is difficult to believe White, and perhaps some of his administrators, spent eight days riding at anchor within swimming distance of the shore and never made that journey. We should also observe that some days later the fleet arrived at Plymouth, where they stayed for a further two days. There should be no doubt it was to top up supplies, but it could equally have been, and most likely was, to take on yet more colonists.

Later in the voyage and after wasting a great deal of time in the West Indies, Captain Simon Ferdinando (sometimes written Fernando or Fernandez) finally headed for Chesapeake Bay, the place first suggested by Amadas and Barlowe three years earlier, and the destination which Raleigh had charged Ferdinando to deliver the colony to. However, Ferdinando, feigning a lack of time to get to the Chesapeake, simply left the entire colony at Roanoke. His motive for doing so has been widely debated. Ideas today range from conspiracy theories to a belief he may have known the Spanish knew of the English plans to settle in Chesapeake Bay. Whatever his reasons, the colonists on Roanoke expected Grenville's fifteen men stationed there the previous year to greet them, but as we know, there was no sign of them.

John White's account of the colony of 1587, the so-called "lost" colony, is precise enough so there is little one can add, yet there are a few observations worth noting.

The first one is that the transcriptions of the names of the 1587 colonists in Hakluyt's 1589 volumes include Captain Simon Ferdinando, yet at the conclusion of the same account, Hakluyt declares Ferdinando had in fact arrived back at Portsmouth. It is upon re-reading Hakluyt's narrative that one realizes Captain Edward Stafford has to be the one who remained at Roanoke, and he almost certainly remained to Captain the pinnace the colonists possessed. What happened to the pinnace remains a great mystery, but we can be certain its discovery would provide a major clue as to what became of at least some of the colonists.

Second, why did the colonists persist so intently in their wish to make John White return to England, and why did he finally decide to do so alone? The answer to this question is that we simply have no idea. The most widely held belief is that his status was of such significance that on arrival in England, he would probably have had no trouble convincing the colony's investors to provide it with even more supplies. Yet one could also speculate that, because this was probably White's third voyage, he may have felt the act of sailing over three thousand miles across the hazardous Atlantic Ocean was one he was accustomed to while others feared the very real risk of dying on the voyage. At a more basic level, given the perils of such sea crossings and the high mortality rate associated with them, the colonists may simply have considered him lucky and, therefore, the most likely among them to return safely. Certainly, of those who remained, few if any probably had the stomach for undertaking such an arduous voyage again. One final possibility is that a number of the colonists were actually criminals and simply saw the offer of settling America as an opportunity for freedom. If true, then by disposing of John White they could simply vanish into the interior of America. Although White evidently did not trust all of them, the investment made in the colony by a number of prominent and wealthy backers makes it nonsense to suggest they would have allowed Raleigh to risk their investment in criminals; therefore we can dismiss this claim. Whatever the reason for White's decision to return to England, he could not possibly have predicted that the Spanish Armada would interrupt his return to Roanoke.

One final observation from the narrative of 1587 is the realization Ralph Lane's fort was no more. John White specifically states: "we found the fort raised down, but all the houses standing unhurt, saving the nether rooms of them." He goes on to inform us, "The same day order was given, that every man should be employed for the repairing of those houses, which we found standing, and also to make other new Cottages, for such as should need." There is no mention of the rebuilding of Lane's fort.

After the premature relief of the military colony, the disappearance of Grenville's fifteen men in 1586, and the stranding of the colony in the wrong place in 1587, the year 1588 brought the untimely arrival of the Spanish Armada. They arrived just as Grenville was waiting only for a fair wind to set sail from Bideford with relief supplies for Roanoke!

Before exploring the events of 1588, it is worth pausing for a moment to realize what an extraordinary year 1588 must have been for the town of Bideford.

Picture the quayside.... Grenville's brand new manor house presiding over it; the quay, filled with at least three galleons and other assorted sea-going ships, each being prepared for the relief of Roanoke, all no doubt under the watchful eye of Grenville. Meanwhile, John White, who probably lodged with the Grenvilles, may have spent his time pacing up and down the quay worrying over the plight of his daughter and grandchild; while Rawley, the now baptized Native American, may have been busy preparing to make his own hoped-for return to Roanoke. Elsewhere, in a quayside public house, Philip Amadas and Grenville's captive pilot Pedro Diaz, perhaps hoping for his own freedom, were probably debriefing the other captains and masters about the intended voyage. To add to the general hustle and bustle, there should be no doubt the streets of Bideford would have been home to the comings and goings of many of the westcountry landed gentry. The St. Legers, the Queen's commanders of Munster in Ireland, the Arundells, one of the most powerful families of Cornwall, and conceivably even Sir Walter Raleigh may well have paid a visit. One wonders just how many of those intrinsic to the story of the lost colony were entertained by the Grenvilles at their new manor house, and, or, were being accommodated by them.

As Grenville and his fleet for Roanoke waited for that fateful break in the weather, news arrived from the Privy Council sequestering the fleet with instructions to sail for Plymouth under Grenville's command, and make ready to fight the Spanish Armada. The precious supplies and colonists for Roanoke were abandoned on the quayside and replaced by men of war and ammunition.

Grenville did not forsake his commitment to the Roanoke colony though, for he returned to Bideford from Plymouth in order to meet with John White and organize the slipping away of the *Brave* and the *Roe*, ships that also carried additional colonists for Roanoke. The voyage, as we know, was tragically doomed, although and with some irony, if Pedro Diaz had not escaped via its misfortune, we may not have known nearly as much about Raleigh's colonization attempt, or about how significant Grenville's involvement really was.

By 1589, aware his Charter to develop a colony in Virginia had nearly expired; Raleigh had his assignment drawn up. Its use of the flowery Elizabethan legal language of the day makes it confusing as to who was given what, yet what it does give us is the names of two more individuals who may yet number among the colonists not mentioned in Hakluyt's 1587 account: John Nichols and Humfrey Dimmocke.

Raleigh's "Assignment," effectively creating what today might be termed a "Holding" company, moved the financial powerbase firmly into the hands of London merchants and those in their service. It is probably for this reason that Sir Richard Grenville also takes no further part in the attempts to settle Roanoke.

The year 1590 arrived, and with Raleigh and Grenville no longer officially involved, John White made one last desperate attempt to find the colony. As we can see from White's letter of 1593, the arrangements for the voyage were ill conceived. The captains and backers were clearly getting involved only for personal and piratical interests, the search for the colony merely a flag of convenience under which to conduct their desired activities. Nevertheless, there are several fragments of interest in White's account of the voyage, mostly from the point when he finally arrives at Roanoke.

First, the mention of "Haunce the Surgion" who first travelled on the 1585 voyage and the trench dug by Amadas in 1587, confirm that there was a substantial nucleus of individuals willing enough to take on the dangers of crossing the Atlantic on more than one occasion for this quest. Philip Amadas, although not on the 1590 voyage, may have sailed to Roanoke at least three times, for example. To undertake such a voyage when there were probably far safer options available to reputable seafarers suggests they were either well paid, or perhaps had been promised a valuable stake in the venture.

Second, White made an extensive search of the northern end of Roanoke Island for his colonists. His notes from that exploration provide the most accurate information modern researchers have as to where the colonists may have set up home, and where they may have moored their boats. His description of the colonists palisade also provides a useful indication as to the most significant feature that may remain today for archaeologists to uncover.

Lastly, we obtain the greatest epitaph of the Roanoke voyages, the sign left by the colonists: "CROATOAN." White's instructions to the colonists were to leave a message as to where they had gone, and to add a simple cross beneath it if they had to flee under duress. No cross was evident; they clearly left of their own accord.

On seeing the sign, White was convinced his colonists had moved to be with the relative safety of the friendly Croatoan Indians down at Hatteras Island. However, the stormy intervention by Mother Nature, the loss of men already sustained while trying to land the first time, and with more being injured when the capstan gave way, the journey was too much for the crews to endure. White's captains set sail for Trinidad to overwinter and make repairs, or so White thought. The cruel reality was this was just a ruse to persuade White they would return; they never did.

John White last saw his daughter and grandchild in 1587 as he sailed away from Roanoke. His hopes raised and dashed twice in 1588, and now in 1590, he once more found himself looking back at Roanoke as he sailed away yet again.

History records that John White was the last European person to see the colonists alive—or was he?

Thirteen

From Roanoke
to Jamestown

The year 1591 dawned with the genuine threat of a second attempt by the Spanish to invade England. Spain was still pillaging its way through Mexico and South America and bringing much of what it took back to Spain to fuel the country's expansion plans, plans that posed a very real threat to the English intentions to settle America. The Privy Council of England realized that if it was to prevent the creation of the second Armada, it had to cut the Spanish supply lines from the New World. Thus, plans were drawn up to send a fleet of warships to intercept the Spanish treasure fleet in the Azores, a key refueling point for the fleet on its way back from Florida and the West Indies. Grenville was appointed as Vice-Admiral of the English fleet, and given the command of the *Revenge*, a ship regarded as one of the finest in the fleet and one owned by the Queen, recognition indeed of Grenville's skills as a sea captain and military commander. Unfortunately, Spain, aware of the English plan, had sent its own warships to the Azores to counter the threat posed by the English fleet. The subsequent engagement, the Battles of Flores, was to prove pivotal to both nations.

Prior to the onset of battle, it seems the Spanish fleet knew the English were at anchor on the northward side of the island. With that knowledge, they split into two flotillas and circumnavigated the island hoping to catch the English in a pincer movement. On sight of the Spanish, the English Admiral, Lord Howard, fled, taking his fleet with him, except Grenville and the *Revenge*. Accounts from the later repatriated Englishmen inform us that Lord Howard commanded Grenville to anchor in the bay on the north side of the island and send men ashore to find fresh water. Grenville also landed an unknown number of English mariners ashore so that they might recover from a sickness that had swept through the fleet. When Howard fled, Grenville, ever loyal to his men, had either miscalculated the time he had left to escape from the Spanish, or had simply refused to leave English men ashore for the Spanish to torture and enslave as prisoners of war.

Accounts of what then took place have always thought to follow the rather flowery report produced for England by Sir Walter Raleigh. We should now conclude that it is only partially accurate. Alternative evidence from a number of sources, not least from the first-hand Spanish account of Don Alonso de Bazan's flagship, but also from the testimony of the fifty-ton *Foresight*, and from Grenville's own men repatriated by the Spanish and subsequently interviewed at the request of Queen Elizabeth, provide a more complete and quite extraordinary picture.

With Lord Howard already a long chase away, records suggest the Spanish saw the capture of both Grenville and the *Revenge* as the best possible prize from their action against the English. Grenville and the *Revenge* each had already accumulated a great deal of previous history with the Spanish. The Spanish account on Grenville declares "Almirante Ricardo de Campo Verde gran corsario y de mucha estimacion entrellos" (Admiral Richard Grenville, a great corsair and of great estimation among them). Of the *Revenge*, the same account states "This Admiral Galleon was one of the best there were in England; they called her the *Revenge*. She was the flagship that carried Drake to Corunna."

The battle began when the *San Felipe* grappled the *Revenge* and boarded her with around a dozen men. In the following hand-to-hand combat, seven died in the attempt to take Grenville's ship. The ships broke free. Vice-Admiral Aramburu then made an attempt with his flagship to board the *Revenge* but was also repelled. His ship, according to Aramburu's own admission, suffered severe damage in the engagement. It was then the turn of the crew of the *Ascencion*, under Don Antonio Manrique, to make their attempt to board the *Revenge*, but they too failed. The Spanish account goes on to state that by now the *Revenge* had become unrigged and dismasted but was still fighting. She continued to fight and in the continuing battle sent Vice Admiral Luis Cuitinho's ship, the *La Serena*, and Manrique's *Ascencion* to the bottom of the sea. These same accounts also record that several other ships in the Spanish fleet suffered damage in the engagement.

At some time around midnight, a musket shot hit Grenville in the head. Some accounts claim that one of Grenville's own men fired the shot. This is incorrect. Throughout the extensive records we have of Grenville and his various commands, he appears to have remained loyal to his men, giving them no cause to conduct such action.

What actually occurred is revealed through the interviews conducted by Sir Francis Godolphin of two men who arrived home at Lyme Regis, Dorset, sometime after the Spanish set them free. In their account, the men stated that Grenville had remained on the upper decks of the Revenge until he was shot "into the bodie" shortly before midnight, and while his wound was being dressed where he fell, he received a further shot, this time to the head (probably from the same Spanish sharpshooter). Confirmation of their story came a few days later when four more mariners from the Revenge arrived home in England and gave the same account.

In fact, the first inkling we have of any thoughts by Grenville's men to rebel against him does not appear to have occurred until the following morning. It was at this point the *Revenge* was almost out of gunpowder and had no pikes left to repel boarders. As an aside, there is a somewhat gruesome account that describes the decks of the *Revenge* as being littered with the bodies of forty men. The ship was also slowly sinking from a catalogue of cannon and artillery shot it had received during the battle.

Grenville's final command, as reported by the subsequently repatriated mariners, was to order his men to use the remaining gunpowder to sink the ship so the Spanish would not take her as a prize. It is at this point some of the crew finally mutinied. There can be little doubt that they hoped by handing the ship over, their act would save their own lives. With his crew not prepared to sink the ship, and having nothing left to fight with, Grenville had no choice but to surrender. In doing so, he first sought assurances his men would come to no harm, and be repatriated, a condition the Spanish evidently honored.

The Spanish took Grenville onboard the *San Pedro*, the Spanish flagship, where he was dressed of his "multiple wounds" and given a meal of his choosing. The Spanish account states that while Grenville sat at the table, "Don Alonso would not see him yet all the rest of the captains and Gentlemen did visit him to comfort him and to wonder at his courage and stout heart, for that he showed not any sign of faintness or changing of color."

Grenville died sometime around the first of September and was buried at sea on the way to Terceira, another island in the Azores. The *Revenge* also sank on route, possibly after breaking free. The account of Von Linschoten claims she broke up against the cliffs of the island of Terceira following a storm, but the Spanish records do not confirm this.

Following Grenville's death, the Spanish admiral, Don Alonso, wrote,

"El Almirante de los mayors marineros y cosarios de inglaterra gran hereje y perseguidor de catholicos" (The admiral of the master mariners and corsairs of England [was] a great heretic and persecutor of the Catholics). He added, "Mas la herida era grande y murio otro dia" (But his wounds were grievous and in a day or two, he died).

The Spanish quoted their official losses as a hundred men, two captains and two ships. However, the same Spanish record subtly notes that several more ships suffered severe damage.

English accounts suggest up to fifty-three Spanish ships were involved in the battle but this is technically incorrect as only twenty-nine actually took part. The remainder stayed back, presumably as a reserve.

The events surrounding the Battle of Flores had a consequence that rippled across the Atlantic and throughout the Spanish Empire for many years afterwards. The single-handed battle Grenville had fought not only severely hampered their expansion plans, but also provided sufficient delay to the arrival of their treasure ships from the West Indies that they were caught in the worst storm for a century. Grenville's actions, in effect, also curtailed Spanish plans to prevent the English from settling in America. Spanish maritime power never recovered. For the next three centuries, it was England's turn to become the greatest naval power in the world.

Of all the commentary made by various sources, it is the succinct words of Sir Francis Bacon, in his book *Considerations Touching a War with Spain*, which seem the most fitting. Therein, he describes Grenville's actions as "that memorable fight of an English ship called the Revenge, memorable I say even beyond credit and to the height of some heroic fable."[1]

*   *   *

The closing days of John White's life were certainly less spectacular. He had not long been home from his dispiriting voyage to Roanoke Island when Thomasine, his wife of 24 years, died on February 6, 1591. The Burial register of St. Clement Danes reads simply "February–Thomasin Whyte ye wyfe of John–6."

Sometime between the death of Thomasine and his letter of 1593 to Richard Hakluyt, John White relocated to Ireland. The catalyst for doing so might have been an unrecorded offer from Sir Walter Raleigh to assist in the surveying and drawing of his vast estates in the Blackwater valley in County Cork. Certainly, his skills there would have been useful to Raleigh. The house he lived in, "at Newtowne, Kylmore," as quoted in his letter to Hakluyt, has been subject to several attempts at identification.

Many have assumed that "Newtowne" is the settlement of that name near the present day town of Charleville in County Cork, probably because it stands in the Barony of Kylmore, the same "Kilmore" as also referred to in White's letter. However, the correct identification of "Newtowne" is the modern day village of Ballynoe, some miles further south. W.A. Wallace, who studied the English in Ireland, points out that Ballynoe is Irish for Newtown, and that it would have reverted to the Gaelic spelling shortly after Sir Walter Raleigh's estates passed to Irish hands through their sale to Robert Boyle, 1st Earl of Cork.[2] Wallace also states that Ballynoe was part of Raleigh's estates, and within easy distance of Thomas Harriot's residence at Molana Abbey, someone White collaborated with on the Roanoke Voyages and therefore probably later in the detailing of Raleigh's Irish estates. The author's own research has further cemented the connection by discovering that from as early as 1464; the village of Ballynoe was part of the Diocese of Cloyne, which functioned under the collegiate church of St. Mary of Youghal where Sir Walter Raleigh was Mayor in 1588 and 1589. A mere twelve miles away, and still within the Diocese, was the town of Lismore where a John Prendergast resided as the Dean of Lismore, relevant because a John Prendergast appears in transactions between a John White and Robert Boyle 1st Earl of Cork in 1606, more of which, later. As to which house in Ballynoe was John White's residence, we can only guess. It would seem logical that the Parsonage, undoubtedly a house of status, would have been the most likely candidate. The house is sadly no longer there.

From John White's life in Ireland, apart from a debated contribution to the Mogeely Estate Map of Henry Pyne, there are no known works that attributable to him.[3] A document held in the Lismore Castle Papers could resolve whether John White was still alive in Ireland at the end of the sixteenth century though, for it contains, among other items, "notes of the horse and footmen to be provided by Sir Walter Raleigh (20th Jun 1598)."[4] However, archivists at the National Library of Ireland have advised the author that the document is extremely fragile and wholly illegible due to water ingress. It is unlikely, therefore, that this document will ever be able to provide supporting evidence to the last days of John White. However, the author discovered another document in the catalog for the Lismore Papers, and one which gives the strongest indication yet that John White may well have still been alive in Ireland as late as 1606. It is a series of transactions between a John White and Robert Boyle, 1st Earl of Cork.

There are two inscriptions on the reverse (outside) of the document. The upper notation reads: "John Whites acquittances uppon which he receives to my use £15 & uppon taking in of this acquittance I received of the Dean of Lysmore £5.10s & gave the Dean an acquittance for £20.10s so Mr White is to pay me the £15 sterling." The second (lower) notation reads "John Whites bill for £10 delivered by him to sir Richard Boiles use the last of January 1606."

While on the obverse (inside) of the document there are two further inscriptions: The upper notation reads: "I have received of John Prendergast Dean of Lysmore the sum of ten pounds curraunt money of England to the use of Sir Richard Boyle knight, witness my hand herewith subscribed third day of January 1606." The lower notation reads, "I have received also of the said John Prendargast to the use of Sir Richard Boile aforesaid the sum of fyve pounds per curraunt money of England witness my hand here unto subscribed this second of March 1606." A John White signs both of these notes.[5]

Whether this document is credible evidence of John White's presence in Ireland as late as 1606 is indeed debatable, but one should note that whoever this John White is, he must have had the status of Gentleman, for only someone of that status would have had the necessary prominence to be able to correspond with an Earl in person. It is also reasonable to assume that if he were alive when Sir Richard Boyle purchased Sir Walter Raleigh's lands in County Cork and Wexford in 1602, his knowledge of the estate would have been invaluable to the Earl, thus making him a natural candidate to employ in his own plans for the estate. If this document does relate to John White, painter and Governor of Virginia, then the signatures on it are the only ones by John White of which we are presently aware.

John White's last days must have been lonely ones; he had lost his wife, his only son, and his daughter, now presumed dead, somewhere in the distant and foreign land of Virginia. Certainly his Coat-of-Arms, given to him and "his heires ofspring and (for) posterity" according to William Dethick, has never been carried forward by any known descendant. It appears, therefore, that when he died he probably died alone and without a direct heir.

Whatever the accepted date of John White's death, he probably lived out his days at Ballynoe and almost certainly lies in a quiet corner of the former English Parish church situated a few yards southeast of the village. Sadly, this unmarked church was already in ruins by 1615, the graveyard long neglected.[6] Thus, any pretense towards identifying his grave today would seem highly unlikely.

Questions remain about John White's life. Further research towards

Possibly the signature of John White, from a document detailing a transaction between a John White and Robert Boyle, 1st Earl of Cork (courtesy of the National Library of Ireland).

establishing his place of birth (pending the release of more UK Parish records) and where in London he lived (he must have moved house at least twice) needs to be conducted. Confirmation of his house at Ballynoe, his burial date, and the location of his grave are also key elements of his story. There is also the matter of his work as a painter, a discipline he held by 1568. There appears to have been very little work attributed to him until the Roanoke voyages, yet he must have had some form of income from his profession. We should therefore expect to discover further works attributable to his hand from the period between 1568 and 1584.

John White's legacy is his paintings. Dr. Kim Sloan's research has identified that many began to circulate among his connections long before his death, and yet there remains some confusion as to exactly which of the paintings purchased by the 1st Earl of Charlemont in 1788, and those that came into the possession of Hans Sloane sometime later, are actually attributable to John White's hand. A discussion on this question is beyond the scope of this book but for a more detailed examination of the history and study of the paintings, one should refer to Sloan's excellent book and also to that written by Paul Hulton. Nevertheless, by whatever route those paintings of the Native Indians of the outer banks of North Carolina came to be rescued, they survive today to provide a glorious epitaph and legacy to an enigmatic man of such extraordinary circumstance, if, alas, a man of such tragedy.

*   *   *

With the key players now no longer part of the colonization attempt, and the colonists and Indians perhaps determining the fate of Raleigh's Charter between them, one might be encouraged that others had not given up searching for them back in England. However, the first attempt to do so was not of English origin and actually took place two years before John White's final voyage in 1590. Ironically, it may have resulted from the deposition made to the Spanish by Darby Glande, one of the colonists stranded on Puerto Rico during the 1587 landing there on the way to Roanoke Island. Most probably because of his deposition, the Spanish promptly sent Vincente Gonzales to look for the English colony. Crucially, Darby Glande would have known only that the intended destination of the Colony was Chesapeake Bay, and not that they had been deserted by Simon Ferdinando on Roanoke Island. Thus, Gonzales headed directly to Chesapeake Bay, a location already known to the Spanish, and spent some considerable time there exploring the creeks and river estuaries looking for signs of the English settlement. It was only on his return voyage that he discovered the English settlement on Roanoke Island, of which he noted: "...there was a ship-yard, indicated by the presence of sloops, while on the land there were some remains of English barrels. Besides, there were other signs of debris, indicating that people had been there."[7]

However, according to the same account by de Ore, the Spanish believed the Roanoke colony incorporated 300 men and an equal number of women. Therefore, Gonzales probably considered himself ill equipped to confront the English, to which end, the Spanish governor sent a messenger to Spain intent on obtaining sufficient troops to mount an attack. For reasons unknown, the plan was never acted upon. Had they carried out this intention, the course of English settlement in America may never have succeeded.

As a footnote to the Darby Glande story, according to at least one source,[8] it is suggested that he was an indentured servant of some of the 1587 colonists. A source for this interpretation could be the account he gave Governor Canzo of Florida, in 1600.[9] In his account, he claimed Grenville captured him near Nantes in 1584. As far as we know, Grenville was nowhere near Nantes in 1584. It would seem therefore that Glande was trying to convince the Spanish that he was a victim of the English by concocting a story to suggest he had been a prisoner of theirs, probably in an effort to save his own life. Evidently, they believed him.

Over the following years, the English sent a number of voyages to America, but it is not until 1602 that one appears to have had the express purpose of finding the Roanoke colony. However, for all its significance, it appears only as a footnote in John Brereton's account of Bartholomew Gosnold's exploration of New England in 1602. The note, found in Samuel Purchas's *Purchas his pilgrimes* reads:

> A briefe Note of the sending of another barke this present yeere 1602, by Sir Walter Ralegh, for the searching out of his Colonie in Virginia.
>
> Samuel Mace of Weymouth, a very sufficient Mariner, an honest sober man, who had beene in Virginia twice before, was employed thither by Sir Walter Ralegh, to finde those people which were left there in the yeere 1587. To whose succour he hath sent five severall times at his owne charges. The parties by him set forth, performing nothing; some of them following their owne profit elsewhere; others returning with frivolous allegations. At this last time, to avoid all excuse, he bought a barke, and hired all the company for wages by the moneth: who departing from Weymouth in March last 1602, fell fortie leagues to the Southwestward of Hatarask, in 34 degrees or hereabout; and having there spent a moneth; when they came along the coast to seek the people, they did it not, pretending that the extremitie of weather and losse of some principall ground-tackle, forced and feared them from searching the port of Hatarask, to which they were sent...[10]

The final voyage we presently know about which refers specifically to Raleigh's Colony, and also found in "Purchas his Pilgrimes," sailed from Southampton on April 17, 1603, under the captaincy of Bartholomew Gilbert. The voyage recorded by crewmember Thomas Canner "of Bernards Inn" states that they landed at several locations in the West Indies and, after weighing anchor, proceeded northwards "towards our long desired Countrey Virginia." When they arrived in the Outer Banks, Canner describes the area as "very fine low land, appearing far off to be full of tall trees, and a fine sandie shoare" but that, "...we saw no harbour." Perhaps the most defining comment Canner makes though, is "if the winde should stand, then we should fetch the Bay of Chesapian (Chesapeake), which Master Gilbert so much thirsted after, to seeke out the people for Sir Walter Raleigh left neere those parts in the yeere 1587."

What this tells us is that for all the efforts of Samuel Mace, Bartholomew Gilbert and perhaps of others, the searches conducted for Raleigh's colony were looking in the wrong place. Is it just possible Simon Ferdinando did not tell Raleigh the entire truth about where he had left the Colonists? Certainly by the time of these later voyages, few, if any, knew precisely where Roanoke Island was.

By the time Jamestown had become the focus of English intentions in America, politics—the risk of realizing the Roanoke colony, if found, could have a prior claim to the riches of the new world—almost certainly played on the minds of those capable of mounting a serious attempt to find them. In fact, there is the strongest evidence some of the Jamestown colonists actually knew the whereabouts of some of Raleigh's settlers quite early on. One clue, somewhat blatantly revealed in the instructions given to Sir Thomas Gates, Governor of the colony in 1609, by the Council of the Virginia Company in London, states:

> (at) Peccarecamicke where you shall find foure of the English alive, left by Sr Walter Rawely wch (which) escaped from the slaughter of Powhatan of Roanocke, upon the first arrival of our Colonie, and live under the protection of a wiroane called Gepanocon enemy to Powhaton, by whose consent you shall neuer recover them, one of these were worth much labour, and if you find them not, yet search into this Countrey it is more probably then towards the north.[11]

Before jumping to the conclusion these English captives were from the lost colony of 1587, we should analyze the statement "slaughter of Powhatan of Roanocke." Contrary to popular opinion, this cannot be a reference to a slaughter of the 1587 colony. Brandon Fullam, in his three-part paper, "The Slaughter at Roanoke,"[12] provides a very sound case for this determination. His research concluded that the Native Indian propensity to try to curry favor and reputation by elaborating upon stories of bravado, suggest that the story may be a development of the rout of Grenville's fifteen men he left behind on Roanoke Island in 1586. Thus, there is every possibility that these four men were the survivors of that rout and not lost colonists.

As the English developed their settlement at Jamestown, Powhatan, a local Indian Chief, presented John Smith with a matchlock and several other English artifacts, claiming they were proof his tribe had wiped out the first English settlers in the area. Sometime around this point, Christopher Newport fueled the claim by reporting the appearance of English style fields, and some areas of burning. It is possible that what Newport saw were the remains of Powhatan's attack on Raleigh's colonists, but surely far more likely that he was mistaking the same Indian practice of burning crop stubble that Amadas, Barlowe, and others had observed in the Outer Banks of North Carolina.

However, what then of William Strachey's comment in his book *The Historie of Travaile into Virginia Britannia*, which only adds to the mystery:

> ...where at Peccarecamek ... and Ochanahoen, by the relation of Machumps, the people have howses built with stone walles, and one story (storey) above another, so taught them by those Englishe whoe escaped the slaughter at Roanoak ... and where at Ritanoe, the Weroance Eyanoco preserved seven of the English alive—fower men, two boyes, and one younge mayde (who escaped and fled up the river of Chanoke), to beat his copper...[13]

Is it possible that Strachey is informing us that there were other English colonists from Roanoke Island also in the custody of local Indian tribes, a point borne out by his reference to an additional "two boyes" and a "younge mayde," or is he simply taking literary license with Sir Thomas Gates's instructions? Either way, if only one of these references is accurate, we are assured that at least some of Grenville's men of 1586, and, or, quite possibly a few members of the 1587 colony were still alive around 1610, some twenty-three years after the landing of the lost colony on Roanoke Island.

FOURTEEN

The Search for Descendants

Almost another ninety years were to pass before there were any further direct references to the people of Raleigh's colony. It fell to John Lawson, a land surveyor sent from England in 1701 to survey North Carolina, to make the startling observation when, of the Hatteras Island Indians, he comments:

> These (Indians) tell us, that several of their ancestors were white people, and could talk in a book, as we do; the truth of which is confirm'd by gray eyes being found frequently amongst these Indians, and no others. They value themselves extremely for their affinity to the English, and are ready to do them all friendly offices.[1]

Crucially, by this time, there is also no suggestion that any of the colonists' descendants survived as recognizable Europeans, a point not lost on Lawson who draws the conclusion that:

> It is probable, that this Settlement miscarry'd for want of timely supplies from England; or thro' the treachery of the natives, for we may reasonably suppose that the English were forced to cohabit with them, for relief and conversation; and that in process of time, they conform'd themselves to the manners of their Indian relations.

Even given the significance of his observations, Lawson did not publish details of his discoveries until eight years later. Sadly, it seems the events of the 1580s had long been forgotten by then, and with Lawson dying barely a year after publication, his account simply went unnoticed for what it represented to the lost colony story.

The connection between the lost colony and the Hatteras Island Indians continued a little less than a decade later, with the Reverend John Urmstone of Bath, North Carolina, who wrote to his superiors complaining that his parishioners from Hatteras and Ocracoke Islands were:

> ...half indian and half English, (and) are an offense to my own ... and I gravely doubt the Kingdom of Heaven was designed to accomodate such. They stunk and their con-

dition was not improved by the amounts of sacramental wine they lapped up nor by sprinkling with baptismal waters.[2]

By 1715, the entire native Indian population of the eastern seaboard of America had become embroiled in the Tuscarora Indian War. The resulting genocides left fragments of tribes littering the entire area. How badly the war affected the Hatteras Island Indians we simply do not know. It seems likely that some of them may have become absorbed into neighboring tribes, and/or into the European immigrations that were by now spreading rapidly throughout North Carolina. Equally, it is also possible that the relative difficulty in reaching the island, secured them from becoming directly involved in the conflicts. If the latter consideration proves correct then it is an intriguing possibility their descendants could have been among those privy to a land grant given to William Elks on March 7, 1759, on that island.

Today, the island is still home to many who continue to claim lost colony ancestry. As to whether their claim, or for that matter, claims by any individuals, tribal group, or community to being descendants of the lost colony is valid, will depend on science, and specifically, DNA testing.

In mentioning DNA tests, we should perhaps pause to look at the efforts of The Lost Colony Research Group. One of the prime directions of their research is to investigate the potential for colonist DNA to exist among the American population. Over a number of years, the group has not only built up the largest and most credible database of information on the colonists and their origins, but has also amassed the largest DNA database of prospective descendant candidates, all of whom still await a match with a positively identifiable lost colonist.

The use of DNA testing, though, is an emotive one. There are many wild claims DNA could end up in the hands of insurance companies, which in turn could use this data to assess what illnesses, and therefore insurance risk, you would represent. Such claims, if true, would lead to such a catastrophic backlash against the insurance industry that the risk is surely too great for them to take. However unlikely, it is still enough to discourage participation of many candidates, a critical component in compiling potential matches to lost colonists.

There is also the question of risk, not a medical risk, but a political one. Some members of one group claiming to be lost colony descendants, the Melungeons, submitted themselves to DNA testing to establish their claim. The results effectively destroyed their claim when the tests revealed that their origins could only be the progeny of a relationship involving West African slaves.[3]

Meanwhile, another group, the Lumbee, despite providing consistent oral histories connecting them to the colonists, have refused to submit to DNA testing. Thus, no matter their oral claim, without the scientific support, it is impossible to reconcile their claim.

Regardless, the ability of DNA to provide irrefutable and conclusive evidence in unravelling many of history's great questions has become widely accepted both academically and publicly. Indeed, two very recent examples of success using the technique include confirmation of the identity of the father of Egyptian pharaoh Tutankhamen, and, at a less significant level, the discovery of two people living over three thousand miles apart whose common ancestor had sailed from Bideford to start a new life in Canada almost three hundred years ago. DNA testing is, therefore, a technique that really must achieve a higher acceptance amongst the populous, and certainly among the Native American tribes, if the quest to find descendants of the lost colonists is to progress.

The costs involved with this technique though, does require us to focus on its most effective use, and that means searching for a colonist using the uniquely male possessed "Y" chromosome. This chromosome, being also much less complex than the female "X" chromosome, is easier to study and significantly, remains relatively unchanged over generations of males of the same family line. If not too obvious a statement, with significantly more male lost colonists than female ones, the odds of finding a male heir to the colonists are therefore also substantially higher.

In order to increase the potential for identifying descendants of colonists, Genealogists are actively mining through old English records in order to find anything that may provide evidence of modern day descendants. However, one has to accept that the difficulty faced with identifying prospective families is just where would you start searching for colony surnames like Smith (as in colonist Thomas Smith) and Jones (as in colonist John Jones)?

A recent search through the Prerogative Court of Canterbury records, for example, revealed around 300 late-sixteenth-century wills with colonist surnames, yet of the ninety or so studied by the time this book went to print, none have yielded anything remotely confirming a connection to the colony. It is possible the colonists simply did not have estates of sufficient value to warrant the Court's involvement. This lack of evidence challenges a popular perception that many of the colonists were from the middle classes of London. The Court covered the London area and sat on all cases where the value of the goods involved was greater than five pounds, and where property was held in two (or more) dioceses within

Great Britain. When these colonists were declared lost therefore, we should find a number of Wills for their estates appearing in the records in quick succession. There are none.

In the search for colonists, many genealogists have attempted to identify records using a variety of methods. For example, the naming of a first-born son in honor of a parent or grandparent in Elizabethan times was as much a tradition then as it is today. Thus, we might hypothesize that Robert Ellis, lost colonist son of Thomas, took his grandfather's name, while it is quite clear that George Howe, and others, bestowed their own Christian name on their sons. Armed with this rudimentary information, genealogists have searched the English Parish records and wills for an earlier parent, usually in the hope of finding that a lost colonist had a brother or sister. It is through finding that proven direct male line via a sibling that we can secure an authenticated DNA sample of a lost colonist.

Would-be genealogists should note though, despite it being a legal requirement to maintain Parish Registers in England since 1538, they were rarely completed and the law equally rarely enforced. Additionally, many of those that were dutifully completed have since been lost, damaged beyond legibility, or destroyed during times of war; those stored at the City of Exeter's Devon County Archives being one such casualty of World War II. That act alone decimated the records of wills for most towns in Devon. Bideford, for example, has only six surviving wills from the critical lost colony period. Thus, we learn that a great many gaps exist in English birth records, particularly for the period in question. Most, we have to accept, will never be recovered.

The interrogation of wills and the disappointing lack of evidence from every other source whatsoever, added to the genealogical evidence in America being largely based on oral histories, which, while some remain credible, have yet to provide any substantiated claim, highlight the potential scale of the task.

Nevertheless, many continue the quest, and in this quest, the most pivotal name and the greatest prize for genealogists and DNA specialists remains that of Ananias Dare.

His unusual Christian name should make for easy discovery among the fragments of early English parish records, but there are surprising only a handful of possible references, the most likely of those so far discovered, is a half illegible entry in the parish register of North Curry, a small village in Somerset, some sixty miles east of Grenville's Bideford.

Wherever Ananias was born, what we do know of him is limited to the period between his marriage to Eleanor White, John White's daughter, at St. Clement Danes in London on June 24, 1583, and ends, in the Roanoke voyage of 1587.

Therefore, to discover a descendant of Ananias, the strongest line of enquiry would be through his children. Quinn believed Virginia was the first child of Ananias and Elinor; this is incorrect. Elinor had already given birth to two other children, John and Thomasine.[4] Why the Dares did not take both John and Thomasine with them to Roanoke is probably because they thought them too young for such an arduous journey. They probably also believed either they could return for them later, or that they could undertake the journey, probably in the care of John White's wife, Thomasine, once the colony had established itself. Certainly, Eleanor must have known she was pregnant when she set sail too, thus the burden of a new child to add to her two others may have made the decision to leave them behind that much easier.

Sadly, daughter Thomasine died on March 13, 1588, the parish entry simply reading "Thomasin Dare ye daughter of Ananias." Her death, recorded in St. Clement Danes parish register, strongly indicates that John White's wife, Thomasine had cared for John and Thomasine in Elinor's absence.

With John White's wife subsequently dying in 1591, White must have considered he was too old to raise the Dare's remaining son, John, alone. It is likely therefore, that he would have been encouraged to find foster parents or perhaps an apprenticeship for him. White himself, after all, must have undergone a similar induction in his life as a painter. John, however, appears to have been subject of a custody battle between a John Nokes and a Robert Satchfield (or Sackville). The case began a year after White first appears in Ireland and did not resolve itself until 1597. The evidence for the resolution lies in the Canterbury Administrations, which contain the rather cryptic entry: "[Dare, Ananias, St. Bride, Lond. To Jn. Nokes, k., dur. min. of Jn. D., s., (by Decree), (prev. Gnt. Apr 1594, p.95)]" This translates as: "Dare, Ananias, St Bride, London. To John Nokes kin, during minority of John Dare, son (by decree); previously granted April 1594 Page 95."[5]

The entry essentially confirms John Dare became an adopted son, by law, of John Nokes in 1597. This means we have our first confirmed, and potentially traceable descendant of a colonist, and one who is none other than the one most seek, excepting that, as a legally adopted son, his name would undoubtedly have been changed to John Nokes and not remained as John Dare. One must wonder, therefore, just how many genealogists have been looking for a descendant in England of John Dare when it is a John Nokes they should really be seeking.

Many questions still surround Ananias Dare, but it is difficult to ignore one tenuous record that corroborates the hypothesis that the colony investors may have known many of the colonists—a Martin Dare is named as an executor in Sir Richard Grenville's last will and testament drawn up shortly before he set sail for Roanoke in 1585. Whether he was a relative of Ananias is at present impossible to prove, but it is nevertheless yet another tantalizing fragment that with further research might just lead us to a colonist descendant today.

However, an alternative route by which to answer the question did the lost colonists survive to become undeniably the first successful English settlers of America; would involve the discovery of a skeleton by which to compare DNA records.

A lost colonist skeleton has proven elusive, but given that it is likely any surviving colonists probably integrated with the Native customs and lifestyle within a generation or two, it is wholly unrealistic to expect to find a recognizable "English" grave complete with the obligatory "Here lies ..." grave marker. The more likely burial will be in the Native American form for the tribe, which the colonist became a part. In the case of the prime candidate "Croatoan" or "Hatteras Island" Indian tribe, we know from John White's paintings, and the descriptions brought back to England, that whilst detailed in its preparation at a Charnel house, ultimately skeletal remains were disposed of into a simple pit or tossed into their field system, evidence of which has already been uncovered.

Because of this likely assimilation, the desire to sample skeletal DNA has become embroiled in a bureaucratic jungle, involving, not least, the Commissions representing the interests of various Native American groups, particularly among those who continue to claim to be descendants of the lost colonists. The laws surrounding Indian burials permit these groups to veto such a test, and they frequently do, citing it would disturb ancient spirits. While it is appropriate to respect such beliefs, scientists will need to conduct these tests if the tribe is to establish its claims of ancestry. Obtaining permission to conduct skeletal DNA sampling, therefore, will require the greatest of diplomacy.

The discovery of a Native American skeleton lying in the English "crouch" style, on Hatteras Island in 2010, has brought the issue of DNA testing into sharp focus. The discovery, in an area regarded by the archaeologists as being a colonist's settlement, was of a woman, estimated to have been around forty year of age. Significantly, she was uncovered in a context suggesting that either she, or her children, may have lived to see the colonists. The recovery of an adjacent fragment of what appeared to be part of a scabbard adds to the intriguing possibility she may have even been a wife to one of the colonist's single men. If this claim seems fanciful, then consider what we already know of the Hatteras Indian burial practices and how this one differs from those.

If the wholesale disturbance of potentially Native American skeletons is such an emotive one though, might we not negotiate for a simple tooth? Tooth enamel forms in the first few years of life. During this time, it stores a chemical record of the environment in which a child grows up; and it remains in the enamel, even after death.

The two chemical elements found in teeth enamel that provide the environmental data are oxygen and strontium. Most of the oxygen in teeth and bone comes from drinking water. In warm climates, drinking water contains a higher ratio of heavy oxygen (O-18) to light oxygen (O-16) than it does in cold climates. By comparing the oxygen isotope ratio in teeth with that of drinking water from different regions, we can build a picture of the climate in which a child grew up. Strontium on the other hand, is present in most rocks, and permeates from them into the water table. The ratio of strontium 87 and strontium 86 isotopes varies according to local geology. Testing the isotope ratio of strontium in a person's teeth can provide information on the geological setting where an individual lived in childhood. By combining these results, we can ascertain the origin of a skeleton. For example, the local geology and drinking water of the Outer Banks of North Carolina will ensure that the results for someone raised there will be significantly different from those of someone raised in England. The oxygen and strontium tests, therefore, would prove whether any skeletal remains are Native American ... or English. At the time of writing, no tooth remains have been recovered through which to negotiate for this test.

While discussing skeletal remains of colonists, we should recall one last and most extraordinary story. It occurred in the 1950s in an area known as Beechlands, just a few miles into the mainland from Roanoke. While excavating a channel through the area, the operator of an excavator, or drag-liner as they are more correctly referred to, uncovered four, some sources suggest five, wooden caskets, each of which had been made by inverting two canoes and pegging them together. The operator, according to some sources, stated that the caskets were marked with a holy cross, and had the initials "INRI" inscribed upon them. When the drag-liner told his supervisor of his find, the supervisor's immediate reaction was to deduce, perhaps wrongly, that they had stumbled upon an unmarked cemetery. The crew reburied the caskets in such indecent haste; that today no one knows the burial location. Whether they were lost colonists or simply other unidentified early explorers or settlers, we simply do not, and may never know. Beechlands however, will continue to remain an area of interest for seekers of the lost colony until (if) proven otherwise.

*   *   *

When John Lawson surveyed North Carolina in 1701, he employed a Native American of the Eno tribe as a guide; his name was Enoe Will. During his exploration, Lawson's party came upon a river. When he asked Enoe Will where it disgorged, Lawson reported that Enoe declared it emptied into a bay "near his country, which he had left when he was a boy." From this statement and the fact it emptied into the Neuse River, a major outlet to the inland sea between the mainland and the Outer Banks, Lawson deduced Enoe Will's family were descendants of the Coranine, or Coree, Indians; Lawson's exact words—"...by which I perceiv'd he was one of the Cores by birth."

Perhaps the most striking point of John Lawson's deduction regarding Enoe Will's origins is the "CORA" tree of Hatteras Island. This ancient live oak tree has the singular word, "CORA," inscribed in Romanized capitals, deep into its bark. Although one story suggests the word could refer to the legend of a girl of the same name who was alleged to have been hung from a branch of the tree, it could equally refer to the Coranine, or Coree Native American Indians, a tribe who lived by Lake Mattamuskeet on the nearby mainland. Sadly the heart of the tree has long since rotted out, making it impossible to conduct a dendrochronological examination to determine the tree's age and thus confirm a possible dating for the inscription.

So, the perhaps not so fanciful question is, did the colonists decide to leave Hatteras Island and therefore inscribed that tree with their intended destination, just as they had when carving the word "CROATOAN" at Roanoke? If so, then it is the first tangible clue as to what happened to them, and one that has been visible to everyone for perhaps the last four hundred years and on the hypothesis that the Corees most likely included some of the former Croatoan Indians; and knowing that the Eno merged with the Catawba Indian Nation sometime around the period of the Yamassee War of 1715; the Catawba nation, however tenuously, most likely hold the clues to the fate of at least some of the lost colonists.[6]

FIFTEEN

Irrefutable Evidence

Archaeologists and historians (so it seems from one with personal experience) often struggle to agree upon the point where historical evidence and archaeological evidence are in accord. Nowhere is this more apparent today than in the search for irrefutable evidence of the lost colony's foothold on American soil, as we shall see.

Historians inform us that when searching for evidence of Raleigh's colonization attempts, we should expect to find the remains of a number of forts, a small collection of simple housing, a ship large enough to have undertaken an ocean voyage, and of course, a smattering of personal effects, and maybe skeletal remains. If historians can go further and identify prospective locations for the archaeologist to investigate, they, in all their forms, should then be able to determine answers to our questions. In the case of the Roanoke colonists, we seek to learn where and how they lived, how they died, what became of them after they left Roanoke Island, and perhaps, just how stable their relationship was with the Native Americans, the latter, no doubt, a critical element in their survival.

In order to try to answer the historians' questions, we should examine each element individually. We start with the search for the forts and settlements.

The earliest evidence for the existence of a fort dates to a mid–seventeenth century account given by Travis Yardley, a beaver trader, but a man recorded as "Governor" Yardley by J.C. Harrington in 1962, who travelled to Roanoke in September of 1653. Yardley reported that during his time on Roanoke Island, the local Native Indians showed him the ruins of Sir Walter Raleigh's fort. There is sadly no further description.

In 1701 John Lawson wrote in his journal about the "ruins of a fort" on Roanoke Island and the discovery of "English coins" and "a brass gun, a powder horn, and one small quarter deck gun made of iron staves and

A finds tray from the LCRG archaeological excavations on Hatteras Island, 2011 (author's photograph).

hooped with the same metal."[1] Frustratingly, he gives no description of the fort, or its specific location.

More than a hundred years were to pass before Francois-Xavier Martin wrote, in 1828, that as late as 1778 people on Roanoke Island would refer to the stump of a live oak tree inscribed with the letters "CRO." Martin aided the archaeologist by informing us that the stump lay six yards from the shore of Shallowbag Bay, on land then owned by a Daniel Baum. Over two hundred years later, we are hardly likely to be able to still find this stump, it, no doubt, having rotted away long ago.

By 1850, historian B.J. Lossing observed that the remains of what he believed was Fort Raleigh, amounted only to "slight traces."[2]

It is not until 1860 that we get our first observation of the fort's location, when Edward C. Bruce described it as being "half a mile from the north-eastern shore and a little further from the northern point of the island." He added, "it was just far enough inland to be sheltered from the heavy winds by the bluffs and woods, without sacrificing facility of watch over the adjacent waters."[3] This is a good description of the National Park Service site known today as Fort Raleigh. Bruce, however, while noting the existence of bricks and mortar, still failed to furnish us with a detailed description of the fort, merely describing it as a low quadrangular mound. An observation to make here is whether this description is appropriate to

Lossing's "slight traces," or whether these gentlemen are in fact describing two different features.

During the American Civil War, extensive damage certainly occurred in and around the site of the fort noted by Bruce, including some physical destruction and pilfering of artifacts discovered there. The situation became so desperate that in 1863, the local landowner, on whose property the fort stood, complained to the Army commander, who subsequently imposed a twenty-four hour guard upon the site.

In 1895 Talcott Williams, an amateur archaeologist from the University of Pennsylvania, obtained permission to conduct a number of excavations on the site of the fort Edward Bruce had observed. Williams described the site as being "on the higher ground at the northern end of the island."[4]

Between 1947 and 1963, further excavations in and around the site were conducted by J.C. Harrington. As part of his work, Harrington reconstructed a series of earthworks, marketed today as an interpretation of what Fort Raleigh may have looked like in 1587. Faced with some criticism, Harrington defended his earthwork interpretation by stating it could have been an outwork, or "sconce" for the main fort. Ivor Noel Hume, perhaps in a political maneuver, finally sided with Harrington in 1992 by suggesting Grenville's men may have built the original earthwork in 1586. Perhaps Harrington's most controversial legacy, though, is his labeling of a smattering of industrial archaeology he discovered as a "science center" for Thomas Harriot and the metallurgists who travelled with Ralph Lane in 1585.[5]

After a period of relative inactivity, David Phelps from East Carolina University conducted a further array of excavations in the 1980s. He was followed in 1991/92 by English archaeologist Ivor Noel Hume, and finally by the First Colony Foundation between 2005 and 2011.

This list is not definitive. In all, over forty surveys and excavations, involving the sifting of hundreds of tons of soil and sand, have taken place in search of evidence for the English forts and settlements on Roanoke Island. In fact, by the time Hume conducted his excavations, he lamented that the whole area had been so heavily excavated, much of the artifacts he found were in the backfill from previous investigations.[6]

Hume's complaint registers an important point. Artifacts found in backfill are usually termed as being found "out of context," meaning that, because they were not found in their original location and/or at their original depth in the soil, it cannot be determined as to what point in history they were dropped or buried where they were later found. Of further note in Hume's report, is that he declared J.C. Harrington's "science center" as having been much destroyed by at least three modern intrusions. Nonetheless, Hume did concur with Harrington over William's assessment of 1895, that the fort everyone over the last hundred years had all been working on or around, was too small to be the true Fort Raleigh.

For all the hypothesizing surrounding their excavations, what Harrington, Hume and later the First Colony Foundation all agreed upon was that Lane's fort and the colonist's village had to be located further west, or south, of the current interpretation site.

With such uncertainty over the precise location of Lane's fort and the lost colony village there is a need to revisit Hakluyt's original texts to see if they can direct us to the correct sites...

Ralph Lane built his "Fort Raleigh" in 1585 as a focal point for the military base. It was from this base he explored much of the nearby continent, and from where he sent a number of men to establish outposts. With more than a hundred men at his disposal, including numerous titled Gentlemen, scholars and scientists, this leads us to perceive Fort Raleigh would have been an impressive structure. One therefore, that should be relatively easy to find the remains of; yet, it is in Lane's account of "the conspiracy of Permisapan" we obtain the first clue to perhaps question that perception. In this, he makes the comment, "for them of the fort, as for us at the town."

This clearly indicates there were two encampments. Because Lane refers to "us" as being at the town, it would seem likely the senior officers, Gentlemen and the non-military personnel were living in their own accommodation, either nearby or perhaps in the Native American village we know was on the island at that time. It is, therefore, unlikely Lane embarked upon a substantial structure because there was clearly, at least in the initial stages of the military settlement, no obvious threat from the Native Americans and thus little need to protect his army. Lane probably built what we might simply term as a stockade made from the local trees, something that would serve as a refuge in times of need.

When Lane abandoned Roanoke in 1586, he certainly did not have time to dismantle the fort. Grenville confirmed this on his arrival two weeks later, where it is recorded that "finding the place which they inhabited deserted...." Grenville left fifteen men in charge of the English foothold on Roanoke. However, when John White arrived at Roanoke in 1587 expecting to find the fort and village still intact, and dutifully guarded by Grenville's men, he recounts:

> The 23 July, the Governour, with divers of his companie, walked to the north ende of the Island, where Master Ralfe Lane had his forte, with sundry necessarie and decent dwelling houses, made by his men about it the yeere before, ... When we came thither, wee found the forte rased downe, but all the houses standing unhurt

John White's use of the term "rased downe" makes it very clear that he found Lane's fort burned to the ground. Since it had been intact when he last saw it in 1585, the fort could only have suffered this fate either in the presence of Grenville's men, or more likely, after they had fled. Therefore, Native American Indians probably set fire to the fort as a symbolic gesture of having defeated the English (Grenville's men) in 1586. The 1587 account goes on to state: "The same day order was given, that every man should be employed for the repairing of those houses, which we found standing, and also to make other new cottages, for such as should need."

There is no reference in the account confirming the colonists of 1587 rebuilt Fort Raleigh. Nevertheless, what White's account does tell us is that, the colonists repaired some of houses, houses that we may presume to have been the residences of the Gentlemen and non-military personnel of 1585. There was in essence, an English village on Roanoke Island in 1587, one evidently built close to the original site of Lane's Fort Raleigh.

Our final reference to forts and settlements on Roanoke Island, come from John White's detailed but complex account of his search for the colonists in 1590. In that account, he states:

> ...we passed towards the place where they were left in sundry houses, but we found the houses taken down, and the place very strongly enclosed with a high palisade of great trees, with cortynes and flankers very fort-like, and one of the chief trees or posts at the right side of the entrance had the bark taken off, and 5 foot from the ground in fair capital letters was graven CROATOAN without any cross or sign of distress; this done, we entered into the palisade, where we found many bars of iron, two pigs of lead, four iron-fowlers, iron sacket-shot, and such like heavy things, thrown here and there, almost overgrown with grass and weeds.

From this narrative, it would appear John White, with some surprise, discovered a fort of considerable strength, and one evidently built by the colonists. He also noted the houses had been taken down, and that there were signs the colonists had been making shot for weapons, a clear indication they had need to defend themselves

Following a detailed examination of these accounts, we can conclude that:

a. Ralph Lane's "Fort Raleigh" existed for no longer than a year or so before being burned to the ground;

b. the colonists did not rebuild Fort Raleigh but did build their own palisade sometime after 1587, and,

c. that both the military men and the settlers built or rebuilt a number of houses, all of which had evidently been systematically taken down and removed by the time John White arrived in 1590.

Furthermore, despite what was evidently a very thorough search by John White, he makes no mention of the earthworks Hume suggested Grenville's men had built in 1586. Thus, the only building we can be certain of that specifically relates to the Roanoke Colonies, which was still standing by the time of John White's departure in 1590, was the colonist's "high palisade of great trees." It is an intriguing possibility that what Travis Yardley actually observed in the summer of 1653 was the colonists' fort.

Part of the struggle identifying the locations associated with the forts and colonist settlements today is that the northern end of Roanoke Island has altered quite significantly since the sixteenth century. For example, what we know today as the northern or northwestern tip of Roanoke has receded, and an inlet called Otis Cove, which existed on the northeastern side as late as the nineteenth century, is essentially no longer there, being little more than a sand bank barely visible at low tide.

It is worth reporting at this point the extraordinary announcement in May 2012, of what was widely circulated by the media as the discovery of a mark painted and then hidden beneath a small paper patch on John White's highly detailed "Virginia Pars" map of 1585. Despite the sensationalist approach, it was nevertheless an intriguing discovery. Indeed, many were convinced it was the site of the mysterious reference in Hakluyt's texts, which alluded to the colonists relocating "50 miles into the main."

The fact that the location is marked on White's map makes it certain it must have been a location under serious consideration, however, its proximity to the hostile tribes that had already made incursions onto Roanoke Island must surely have made it unsuitable. Nevertheless, there is no denying the colonists clearly still considered the site as a possible alternative to Roanoke Island. Yet, if we are to consider the colonists did relocate to this location, then why did they leave such clear messages to the contrary for John White? Was it an elaborate hoax on their part to evade him, and, if so, why? They were hardly likely to have been able to do so, for if White had visited Croatoan and not found his colonists there, he would surely have made the "hidden" fort "50 miles into the main" his next port of call, especially as he had drawn it on his own map.

The technical report on the map, conducted on behalf of the First Colony Foundation by the British Museum, actually reveals a catalogue of amendments and changes throughout the map. These include a much larger patch applied to the coastline further to the south of the "hidden fort" patch. The report confirms that both patches applied by John White used the same paper and inks as the underlying original.

Embedded in the patch overlaying the fort-like mark are some very faint lines. It is these lines which are subject to the publicized claims involving the use of invisible ink by John White. The technical report actually states: "One other possible, if rather romantic, explanation is that these lines could reflect the use of an 'invisible' ink (an ink which would only be revealed when treated in some way, usually by applying heat)." It concludes, "the use of an initially visible, but now much faded, substance is probably more likely."[7]

The notion therefore of invisible ink being applied to the map, to say nothing of an obvious patch are unlikely to have prevented Spanish eyes from discovering the cover-up, had the map fallen into their possession, therefore one must view the publicity surrounding this discovery with some disdain. Ultimately, one has to realize that 400 years before the invention of correction fluid, the application of a small piece of paper to mask an error would surely have been John White's only solution to the making of amendments to his map; the alternative would be to throw away perhaps weeks of work and start again.

A far more significant observation to make about John White's map is that first noted by Talcott Williams. In his narrative, Williams declared that an "o" mark on the map denoted the location of the colony's settlement on Roanoke. He deduced that the "o" mark differentiated the English settlement from the Native American villages, because the latter are denoted by a dot that has been filled in. When we examine White's map closely, there is indeed an "o" mark is clearly discernible above the letter "n" of "Roanoke." However, the singularity of this on the map has led to it being largely dismissed as a small stain or unintended mark. Yet, when we look more closely at the "hidden" mark discovered under the patch in 2012, we find immediately adjacent to it is another "o" mark. Williams could not possibly have known about the existence of this mark a hundred years before the British Museum discovered it, and therefore may have been entirely correct in his deduction that White differentiated the colonist's village from the Native American villages on his map.

By overlaying White's map of 1585 with a modern map, although the process can only be approximate, it becomes somewhat ironic to discover the heavily urbanized area of Mother Vineyard sits on top of the location White drew for the colonist's village on Roanoke Island. While, the "o" mark adjacent to the "hidden" fort, appears to lie to the south of the golf course currently subject of ongoing archaeological excavations. Nevertheless, White's corrective actions surely indicate that the "hidden fort" settlement never developed.

*　*　*

We now focus our attention on the pinnace left with the colonists. There have been no discoveries of a ship, of this significance, anywhere in the coastal waters of Roanoke Island. We must therefore assume it lies elsewhere.

We can hypothesize on where it may lie by considering the position of the colonists in 1587. They knew the intended destination for the English settlement was Chesapeake Bay, a location visited by Lane and some of the colonists who had served under him, in 1585. The pinnace had already proved its seaworthiness by crossing the Atlantic; it would have been seen as a relatively risk free venture through which to explore a potential new location for the colony. It is reasonable to consider that the colonists, or at least some of their number, would therefore have attempted to reach that location with the pinnace.

If those colonists did indeed attempt to make this journey, then they could have followed Lane's route, finally abandoning the pinnace in what is today the Great Dismal Swamp National Wildlife Refuge, and continuing the remainder of their journey on foot. The alternative and far riskier option was to venture through one of the inlets to the open sea and follow the coastline northward to the entrance of Chesapeake Bay. Is it just possible the pinnace lies undiscovered in the Great Dismal Swamp, or perhaps even in Chesapeake Bay?

An alternative hypothesis for the location of the pinnace is that it could lie somewhere between Roanoke Island and Hatteras Island, an area that, while filled with shallows, was and is navigable. The shallow draft of the pinnace would have been invaluable for moving a colony, its possessions and an entire collection of buildings to Hatteras (Croatoan) Island. Perhaps, therefore, it lies buried somewhere in the sand and mud that makes up the inland sea of the Outer Banks region.

There is, however, one last, perhaps obvious, theory…. The ship had made it to Roanoke from England, so it was reasonable for the colonists to think she could make the return journey.

If Edward Stafford and his crew elected to attempt the return journey, there are no records of her return, or of her being shipwrecked. If they made such a voyage, then the ship and all those on board perished in the attempt.

Finding Stafford's pinnace could give us the clearest possible indication of where at least some of the colonists headed after deserting Roanoke. Sadly, given the vastness of the area we would need to search, and the likelihood of the pinnace's decay over the centuries, the chance of its discovery remain remote.

*　*　*

Finally, we should examine the possibility of discovering the personal possessions of the colonists. Recent archaeological excavations by the Lost Colony Research Group and others, on Hatteras Island, the island identified by John White's map, and by the colonists' own message as "Croatoan," identified numerous items of English origin. Many of these were uncovered in context with Native American artifacts. These finds included metal fragments of buckles, firing mechanisms from matchlocks, a substantial array of European pottery and ceramics, numerous ships nails, and, more recently, an inscribed piece of slate, part of a rapier, a fascinating re-use of a piece of glass as an arrowhead, and a copper ingot.

Of these finds, a handful of the items are positively identifiable as sixteenth-century. Their presentation with the Native American finds, however, while representing clear evidence of English influence some considerable time before John Lawson's account of "gray-eyed Indians" in 1701, could simply represent traded goods. Having said this, if they were traded goods, then one must ask why there are no records of gray-eyed, English-speaking Indians wandering into an English township to barter for them. Alternatively, did traders visit the Hatteras area, but chose to make no mention to their colleagues of the English traits of the Indians they traded with, for fear of ridicule, or more likely, the risk of one of them poaching their lucrative business?

It is of course possible, these fragments came from ships wrecked on their way to trade with the English settlements that had become established further north by the early seventeenth century. If, this was the case, the quantity of finds from such a relatively small area uncovered to date represent an awful lot of Elizabethan and early shipwrecks, far more than have been recorded.

One facet of the Native American Indian's life which has led to a great many finds is a wild form of tobacco known as "Uppowoc." To smoke the tobacco, they produced their own pipes. Yet, among the many discoveries

A large piece of daub from the LCRG 2011 archaeological excavations on Hatteras Island, showing the use of crushed seashell in the manufacturing process. Embedded in the find is a piece of very early 18th century salt-glazed pottery (photograph by Roberta Estes).

on Roanoke and Hatteras Islands, there are also a range of very early English clay pipes; the unique use of kaolin or Marland clay in their manufacture marking them out as English, as opposed to the local clays used in the construction of the more robust Native American designs. The presumption is that the English also smoked the native "Uppowoc" tobacco, yet the argument stands that these "English pipes," too, could simply be traded or shipwrecked goods.

When discussing personal artifacts, one must examine the myth of the so-called "Kendall" ring. This was a significant find of David Phelps's digs on Hatteras Island in the 1980s and one that has remained generally hidden from public view. Analysis of the engraving on the ring by the author identifies it as a stylized lion. It does not match either of the coats-of-arms of the two known Kendall families of the period.[8] It could be a simple representation of a portion of the English Royal coat-of-arms, which consists of three lions, perhaps signifying that it was a signet ring used to impress wax seals on official documents. While we can be certain that it does not have any connection to the Kendall family, it is certain that its design and construction confirms it as being Elizabethan in origin.

What is perhaps more important than confirming the ownership of the ring is that such an item would have had a substantial value and is therefore highly unlikely to have been traded. It was therefore either inadvertently dropped by a member of Lane's military colony, which we know had an outpost on the Island, or, it belonged to a lost colonist....

Discussion on finds relating to the lost colonists would not be complete without considering the possible clues they themselves may have deliberately left behind for us to discover.

We may no longer have the post or tree with "CRO" or "CROATOAN" inscribed upon it at Roanoke Island, and the "CORA" tree as discussed earlier, no longer possesses the heartwood required for testing, but we do have the so called "Eleanor Dare Stones."

The first one, discovered in 1937 sixty miles west of Roanoke Island, on the Chowan River, caused a sensation. Over the following years, a further forty-seven were uncovered, including some from over five hundred miles away in the state of Georgia.

The fundamental problem with the stones, however, is one of authenticity. For example, the language used on all but the first stone is inconsistent with the style and prose of Elizabethan English. Paul Green, the author of the play *The Lost Colony*, also reportedly declared that the story related by the stones largely followed that of his play. Curious, then, that the colonists knew what variations on their story Paul Green would put into his play 350 years later! The author, too, seriously questions their authenticity, for one of the stones carries on its reverse side the names of several English families, including "Pole-Carew," a hyphenated name that was not used before the eighteenth century.

A closer examination of the stones' history reveals a number of notorious hoaxers linked to their discovery. This fact naturally calls their entire authenticity into question ... and yet it is worth noting that the first stone discovered is quite different in many respects from those later brought forward for public scrutiny. The message written upon it states on one side:

> Ananias Dare & Virginia
> Went Hence Unto Heaven 1591
> Anye Englishman Shew
> John White Govr Via

While the reverse contains an even more compelling message:

> Father soone After you goe foe Englande we cam hither
> Onlie misarie and warretow yeare Above halfe DeaDe ere
>   tow yeere moore from sickenes beine fovre and twentie

salvage with mesage of ship unto us
smal spac of time they affrite of revenge ran al awaye
wee bleeve yt nott you
soone after ye salvages faine spirits angrie
suddaine murther al save seaven
mine childe ananias to slaine wth much misarie
burie al neere foure myles easte this river upon small hil
names writ al ther on rocke
putt this ther alsoe
salvage shew this unto you & hither wee promise you to give
   greate plentie presents

The inscription ends with the letters "EWD."

We can make an interpretation of the inscription on the reverse by suggesting it would read something like this in modern English:

"Soon after you left for England father, (we suffered) only misery and war (for) two years. About half died there. (After) two (more) years twenty-four (more) died from sickness. A savage (native Indian) (came) with a message of a ship to us. In a small space of time, they were afraid of revenge and ran away. We believe (the ship) was not you. Soon after, the savages feigned that the spirits were angry, and suddenly murdered all save seven of us. My child (Virginia), Ananias too, (were) slain with much misery (pain?) (We) buried all (of them) near four miles east of this river, upon a small hill, (and) wrote their all their names on a rock there. (Please) put this (stone) there also. (If the) savages show this to you, we promised you would give (them) many presents."

The stone, like the other forty-seven, has been analyzed numerous times, but it is this first stone, and in particular the accuracy of the Elizabethan language used, that remains the singular stone of interest. The story it relates is certainly feasible. Count out the years and one could suggest that the ship really was a case of mistaken identity of John White's 1590 return. The likelihood of sickness among the colonists is also highly probable. However, the colonists' burial hill remains undiscovered, regardless of the quite specific directions inscribed on the stone and the required size of the plot needed for so many bodies. There are, though, two fundamental problems with the inscription.

First, the complex construction of the inscription makes it difficult to believe that an Elizabethan woman would have attained the required level of English education to write it. In a male dominated society accustomed to passing off their female children to eligible bachelors, Elizabethan fathers tended not to invest in the education of their daughters.

Second, the belief that Elinor Dare would sign herself "EWD" is unfathomable. We know that she had no second Christian name (the Parish record of her christening would record that if she did), and candidly, any suggestion the "W" represented "White," thus suggesting she signed herself Elinor White-Dare is, frankly, laughable. It simply did not occur in Elizabethan England—however, the practice is prevalent in the southern states. Thus, however compellingly different it is from the other forty-seven, which all still exist in a private collection today, strong doubts as to its authenticity must remain.

* * *

In 2014, one archaeological group searching for the lost colony declared that they had substantial (yet) circumstantial evidence of colonist habitation on Hatteras Island. Their finds, like those of the LCRG excavations between 2009 and 2011 which had already indicated lost colony habitation on Hatteras Island, and those of David Phelps thirty years previously, all the excavations on Roanoke Island, and even those recently undertaken at the "hidden fort" site, remain precisely that—circumstantial.

It is beyond reasonable doubt that the story of the Roanoke colonization attempt is true, and yet if Talcott Williams can be considered as having conducted the first serious investigation into the search for the colonists' settlements way back in 1895, then 120 years later there is still not one shred of irrefutable evidence of their forts or their homes. As for the claims made by some that the artifacts they have uncovered relate directly to the colony period, they, too, remain legitimately open to challenge. The oft joked golden chalice of lost colony archaeology would indeed appear to be Virginia Dare's "pinkie" ring.

Sixteen

The Grenville Legacy

Today, the National Park Service facility on Roanoke Island receives over 300,000 visitors a year. They flock to see J.C. Harrington's recreation of "Fort Raleigh" and to learn about the lost colony. Many of them subsequently go on to patronize other attractions in the area that have developed to take advantage of the footfall created by the National Park Service; not least the adjacent Lost Colony Theater, which, remarkably, has been staging its version of the lost colony story since the 1930s. Because of this patronage, the host, and delightfully picturesque town of Manteo, prospers accordingly, although it must be pointed out that Manteo's existence as a town, unlike Bideford, its transatlantic twin town is a relatively new one, being recognized as such since 1899. Regardless of what is available to visitors to the island, they will not witness anything positively connected to Raleigh's colony. Perhaps, though, that is not the point; many will consider it sufficient to know they are treading on the ground once walked upon by the first English settlers in America.

Across the Atlantic Ocean, in the town of Bideford, the sense that one is standing on ground that played host to much of the story simply does not exist. That is a disappointing state of affairs considering the town was the birthplace and home to Sir Richard Grenville, and a town where, without any reasonable doubt, many of the lost colony players, Governor and painter John White included, must have spent at least part of their lives visiting or perhaps living.

The town also still possesses streets that Sir Richard Grenville, John White, and others connected with the lost colony story must have walked upon and might still recognize today, for some of these streets were already at least 350 years old by the time their story unfolded.

There is no need to retell the life of Sir Richard Grenville here of course, but following his death in 1591, it is worth noting that the resulting Inquisition Post-mortem confirmed his Indenture of 1585. It granted his

Some of the Spanish "Armada" cannons at Bideford arrayed around a children's play fort (author's photograph).

wife Mary the right to live in some comfort at the house he built for her on the quayside at Bideford in 1585, until her death, unless she remarried. There were also strict instructions requiring family connections to ensure she was cared for in later life. Mary died aged about eighty on November 23, 1623, having remained a widow for some thirty-two years.

Of Sir Richard's heirs, his eldest son and heir Bernard, alas, appears to have been something of a shadow of his father. We know very little about his tenure except that he yielded considerable powers to Bideford's Town Council in 1607, and that he appears to have invested in a major refurbishment of the original Grenville manor house in Bideford, sometime around 1610–1620.

Bernard's son Bevil followed his father into the Lordship of the town. He was a much-loved hero of the English Civil War but died at the Battle of Lansdowne in 1642. Despite his frequent duties away from home, the letters between him and his wife Grace both before and during the English Civil War reveal a deep and loving relationship, one that, despite those long absences, found time to raise at least fourteen children…

Bevil's son John became the next Lord of the Manor of Bideford following his father's tragic death. John appears to have been somewhat reckless with money. He mortgaged almost everything he had in the campaign to have King Charles II reinstated to the English throne, and while he was then released from all debt by a gratefully re-instated King, he subsequently created more debt by having the family's other manor house at Stowe, near Kilkhampton in Cornwall, pulled down and lavishly rebuilt, around 1670.

For a short time, and despite legal dispute, John also held lands in North Carolina. Those lands later passed into the ownership of George Carteret via his marriage to John's sister, Grace.

John left such debt that his son and heir, Charles, committed suicide in 1701, the same year his father died. When Charles's only son William died from smallpox barely ten years later, in 1711, it marked a rather ignominious ending for the direct male lineage of the Grenvilles of Bideford.

The surviving sisters of Sir John Grenville, Grace and Jane, pulled down the new Stowe Manor in around 1720, barely fifty years after John had completed it. They disposed of much of it through auctions. A staircase belonging to it exists, built into the fabric of a house near Great Torrington in North Devon, while other features exist in South Molton's Town Hall, also in North Devon, and in Prideaux Place in Cornwall. There are also odd fragments, including an over-mantle, long but erroneously thought to have contained an image of Bevil Grenville (it is in fact John Grenville), that resides in a house now converted into apartments on the quayside at Bideford.

The other manor houses the Grenvilles owned; the two in Bideford, suffered widely differing fates. The grandiose one Sir Richard built in 1585 on the town quayside, had faded into obscurity and become something of an enigma by the early nineteenth century. Local historians and archivists, past and present, have erroneously described it as any number of buildings on Bideford's quayside.

Thankfully, we do possess just one image of what it looked like. In 2011, and with the author present, Professor Mark Horton examined a painting dated around 1640, which has hung in the Mayor's parlor of Bideford Town Council since at least 1851. It contains an image of the manor house in the background of the main subject, former mayor John Strange.

From this painting, we know the house was a substantial building of six gables and three stories in height, with what appear to be storage cellars below. Later images of the house have been uncovered and reveal its various fortunes and alterations over the next three centuries. Sadly, the last remaining section of what, if Sir Richard's work at Buckland Abbey is anything to go by, must have been a truly fabulous example of Elizabethan architecture was ignominiously pulled down in 1937, the town at the time evidently entirely ignorant of its significance, for no attempts appear to have been made to save it.

It is just possible that two superbly carved Elizabethan doors, which now serve as rather elegant entrances to cupboards standing sentinel either side of the same over-mantle mentioned above, are the only surviving features from this house.

The original "Old Place," Grenville Manor in Bideford, which probably served the Grenvilles since the thirteenth century, ironically, still stands, albeit much altered. Of its history, following the major alterations embarked upon by Sir Bernard Grenville, the family appears to have used it only occasionally, Sir John Grenville and his wife Jane Wyche being the last of the family to occupy it between 1652 and 1656, shortly after their marriage. It appears that the Grenvilles sold the property to either the Town Council or to the Town Clerk, John Hill, a man whose infamous claim to fame is his persecution of the "Bideford Witches," the last people in England to be hung for practicing witchcraft. Following his demise, the building served as a parsonage, the local post office sorting room, and more recently, as a variously named public house (or bar), some of whose owners appear to have had free range to destroy much untold architectural treasures during their tenure. What remains inside the building, includes fragments of a coat-of-arms intrinsically linking Sir John and Lady Jane Grenville to the property, several Elizabethan fragments of windows, oak beams, a solitary door, and a fragment of an ancient spiral staircase. Further surveys have also revealed the footprint of the original medieval manor house still visible in the foundations, and an extensive range of cellars, parts of which still exist beneath a number of properties in the adjacent Church Walk and a neighboring property in Bridge Street.

An attempt to save this manor house from redevelopment fell well short of the required target, a target that was actually less than the cost of a three bedroomed house in the town. Perhaps the reason for that failure is best interpreted from a comment overheard at a secret meeting of the town's multi-million pound Bridge Trust, to whom the charity attempting to save the building had appealed to for support. One of its members, another former Town Mayor at that, declared that the manor house was in the wrong place to attract tourist revenue. The building actually lies adjacent to the Parish church, the Town Hall, and opposite the ancient bridge that has been the primary entrance into the town for 750 years...

At the time of writing, the building had sold for redevelopment into apartments, its treasures unprotected. Only the tenuous existence of a plaque mounted upon its external wall gives any indication as to the building's former significance.

Ironically, it is Buckland Abbey, a former monastery, re-designed and rebuilt almost entirely by Sir Richard and his grandfather, which has fared best in terms of its preservation—ironic because the Abbey is noted only for its connection to Sir Francis Drake, who purchased it via a Grenville intermediary in 1580, some forty years after the Grenvilles originally obtained it. It is only recently, perhaps due to an increased awareness of to whom it owes its existence, that one can visit the Abbey and find at least some modest homage to the Grenville family. Nevertheless, it serves as a painful reminder of just what has been lost on Bideford's quayside.

With their homes destroyed, neglected, or accredited to others, our search for what remains of the Grenvilles and connections to the lost colony turn to the Bideford Town Council, a vehicle surely for the remembrance of a family to whom the town owes so much. Yet, when the council moved to its new edifice in 1851, ironically next door to the original Grenville manor house in Bridge Street, the town clerk of the day was rumored to have taken the opportunity to clear out the cupboards and dispose of countless documents that had lain there for centuries. If true, for nothing of those documents exists today, it appears he burned everything ... almost certainly including many invaluable documents concerning Grenville's involvement in the colonization of America, and the Roanoke voyages. It is therefore perhaps ironic that the Town Council was later awarded its own coat-of-arms, which show the clarion or "horseman's rest" symbols of the Grenville family coat-of-arms emblazoned across theirs in the form of a chief, signifying the council also owed its existence to the Grenville family.

However, the council does retain a King Charles II mace, no doubt given for Sir John Grenville's role in his restoration to the throne, and a most extraordinary pair of Elizabethan lesser maces. Given their provenance, it is quite realistic to believe that Grenville presented these lesser maces to the town council sometime shortly after its formation in 1574.

Having so far drawn a near blank in search of the Grenville legacy in Bideford, we should perhaps retire to the Parish Church of St. Mary's in the town. St. Mary's was, after all, the last resting place of many of Sir Richard's family and his ancestors. It was very likely the place of worship for many of the colonists too. However, when the Victorians remodeled the church in the 1850s, its rector appears to have cleared out what was the Grenville family crypt, and cremated all the remains he could find. Probably several generations of the family literally went up in smoke. The crypt was finally broken into again in December 2015 when a core sample revealed a substantial deposit of soil had either fallen into the crypt, or, and much more likely, the crypt had been filled in during the Victorian remodeling.

Only two Grenville residents appear to have survived this travesty, Mary, Sir Richard Grenville's wife, who was reputedly buried somewhere, at present unidentified, under what was the Grenville Chapel floor; and the mausoleum of Sir Thomas Grenville, Sir Richard's great-great-grandfather, which lies to the north side of the same chapel. The observant visitor may also spot a commemorative plaque to Sir Richard's wife Mary, albeit inscribed with Sir Walter Raleigh and Alfred Lord Tennyson's rather erroneous version of the events surrounding her husband's death.

With some relief, we can at least view the font used to christen "Rawley," Sir Richard's Native American. However, the whereabouts of "Rawley's" burial place remain lost. The sad story relating to this loss revolves around a persistent rumor that the Victorian masons who rebuilt the church accidentally broke his marker stone. Whether a handful of curiously marked stones found randomly re-used within the cemetery walls surrounding the church burial ground are its remains is uncertain.

There is however, one final, and glorious treasure in the church, a screen made from the pew ends of the original Elizabethan benches that once adorned the church before the Victorian restoration. The screen provides a fascinating glimpse into the world as the Elizabethans perceived it to be, filled with exotic people, including what we may consider to be an interpretation of the Native Americans Grenville met. Naturally, among the pew ends are several with the blazon of the Grenville family carved upon them.

For this entire lament, there may be one other and unique connection to Sir Richard and the lost colony in Bideford, and one that is accessible to the visitor throughout the year...

Masquerading as part of a children's play fort in the town's municipal park, there are around a dozen cannons, erroneously labelled as "Armada Cannons" from 1588. While at least four of them are certainly nowhere near old enough to have any relevance to the period in question, the remaining eight, identifiable as Sakers and Minions, are of sixteenth century origin, and almost certainly have a far more significant provenance than their present accreditation.

These cannons, subject of a report made by a Captain Enthoven shortly after five of them were discovered lying in the mud adjacent to Bideford's quay during remodeling works undertaken in 1894/5, were declared by him to be from a Spanish Armada ship, which sank off Hope Cove in South Devon. The other three existed as mooring posts on Bideford's quay long before anyone could remember. However, in 1929 Inkerman Rogers, a geologist and self-styled archaeologist noted his measurements of the cannons conflicted with those of Enthoven, and went on to suggest they had only a tenuous link to the Spanish Armada.

It is only now, following the author's own investigations, that their origin may be far more significant. To make the claim, we have to first refute the Armada connection. The cannons are certainly not from Hope Cove, as a cannon raised there from the same wreck is quite different in design; being of much sturdier and finer quality. A much more likely and therefore startling possibility is that they came from the treasure ship the *Santa Maria de San Vincente* Sir Richard Grenville captured in 1585.

Spanish cannons, particularly the earlier designs such as those under discussion here, suffered firing damage around the muzzles due to their poor build quality. In the modification plans of the *Santa Maria de San Vincente*, the Spanish cannons would probably have been useless. Rather than have them melted down and re-cast, Grenville probably chose to re-use some of them as mooring posts, a sort of trophy to remind passers-by of the capture of the ship, if you wish, and placed the remaining five as protection to the quayside from the scouring action of the tidal River Torridge, an action still occurring today. We should note that the location of the cannons when discovered was immediately opposite the location of Sir Richard Grenville's new Manor house on the quay. Some of the cannons on display today also possess damaged muzzles, no doubt sustained during firing.

As a footnote to the cannon story, Inkerman Rogers described them as "Priceless." Their value today can be recognized by the occasional beer cans wedged in their muzzles.

When considering the Grenville legacy, the greatest Sir Richard left behind is arguably the Port at Bideford he secured a Charter for in 1574. Local archivists will argue the port existed long before this time, but while this may be true, Watkins, in his 1792 essay on Bideford's port, states that what trade existed was negligible prior to Sir Richard's time. It is Sir Richard who changed the port's fortunes by recognizing its potential value as the nearest embarkation point to Southern Ireland, a territory he, Sir Walter Raleigh and many of their colleagues were in the process of settling at the time of Grenville's Charter. If the Irish settlements had fared better, this would obviously have led to a lucrative and convenient income for the town, and ultimately for the Grenvilles. We cannot be certain Sir Richard's vision for the port stretched as far as the shores of Roanoke Island, but the potential for trade with the new colony could not have been lost on him as he sallied back and forth from there during the 1580s. Although the Roanoke colony failed, and the potential trade from it thus never materialized, Bideford's port ultimately went on to prosper, and prosper far beyond what even Sir Richard could have foreseen. Ironically, that prosperity occurred primarily with the very country he and Raleigh hoped to colonize.

By the mid seventeenth century, there were extensive shipbuilding and repair yards along Bideford's shoreline. At one point, the port boasted over one hundred registered vessels. The port was also highly successful in the importation of tobacco from North Carolina and Virginia, while in return it sent out tons of pottery and general mercantile goods for trading with the new settlers, much of which is being systematically unearthed during archaeological digs from Jamestown to Roanoke and further up the coast in New England today. Of tobacco, Watkins notes that between 1700 and 1755 Bideford was second only to London in its trading of the commodity and in several of those years actually outstripped the English capital city.

The value of Sir Richard's charter and its impact on Bideford is best summed up by viewing the grandiose houses of Bridgeland Street today. Built originally for wealthy seventeenth and eighteenth century merchants, they are testament to the astonishing level of trade Bideford generated during this time. In 1735 for example, imports landed at Bideford amounted to 3,337 hogshead barrels of tobacco valued in duty revenue at £15,101 15s 7d. By 1742 this revenue had jumped to £22,679 13s 9d, almost £2 Million in today's terms. The port's impact on the American colonies was such that economists in the United States of America acknowledge Bideford's pivotal role in the development of their country during this period.

Ironically, for Bideford, the town's almost singular focus on trade with America became its downfall. Following the American (Revolutionary) War of Independence in 1776, Bideford's port, and the town that depended upon it, went into steep decline and never really recovered from the sudden loss of trade.

Indeed, in 1855, Charles Kingsley, then living in Bideford and writing his novel *Westward Ho!*, commented that the port was so desperate to rejuvenate its trade it had taken to shipping lime, the fine white powder

Earliest known image of the manor house Grenville built on the quayside at Bideford, using Spanish prisoners of war captured during his voyages to Roanoke Island. In this detail from a painting of Bideford mayor John Strange (circa 1640, artist unknown) the house's six gables and what appear to be arched storage cellars are faintly visible, behind the silhouette of the partially obscured ship in the center of the image (photograph by Graham Hobbs, Bideford, England).

coating much of the quayside and surrounding houses. This observation duly encouraged Kingsley to refer to Bideford in his novel as a "little white town," a title many of its inhabitants endear themselves to today, but appear not to understand its derogatory context.

It is perhaps even more ironic that the full title of Kingsley's book reads, *Westward Ho! Or The Voyages and Adventures of Sir Amyas Leigh, Knight of Burrough, in the County of Devon, in the reign of Her Most Glorious Majesty, Queen Elizabeth, Rendered into Modern English by Charles Kingsley* ... revealing it is based entirely on Sir Richard Grenville and the lost colony of Roanoke. Sir Amyas Leigh was of course Grenville, and Kingsley's hero, Rose Salterne, was Elinor Dare, mother of the first-born American, Virginia Dare. The novel also openly refers to "Rawley" the Native American buried in St. Mary's Parish Church.[1]

The decline in Bideford's shipping trade eventually resulted in the town losing its status as a Port in 1882; a status only tenuously reinstated in 1928, ironically by a man from the neighboring port of Appledore.

Despite a brief period of significance during World War II when the town became the headquarters of some relatively secret government organizations, and the nearby beaches became practice grounds for the D–Day landings, Bideford slumped to such a level that in 2010 the British Government recorded that Bideford had become one of the most deprived towns in England. It remains so today.

SEVENTEEN

Considered Opinions

It is customary for authors of historical works to include their own thoughts and opinions on the subject of their research. I offer mine here, if only to satisfy that requirement.

Of Sir Richard Grenville, I note that history has branded him as something of a tyrant with a fiery temper and of possessing a great deal of arrogance. Indeed, Ralph Lane wrote to Walsingham on September 8, 1585, declaring Grenville as "tyrannical" and a man of "intolerable pride" and "insatiable ambition."[1]

Van Linschoten recorded what he understood from the Spanish who captured Grenville at the Battle of Flores, to be his dining habit of "crashing the glass between his teeth until the blood ran from his mouth," an act apparently witnessed by "several and diverse persons." Yet, one might interpret this act as simple entertainment value to a man who knew that he was dying or would probably be tortured to death by the Spanish. Few who have repeated Van Linschoten's comment over the intervening years, however, observe that he also acknowledged that Grenville had "performed many valiant actes."[2]

To add to the records blighting Grenville's character we have the report of Sir William Monson; he defined Grenville as being rash and stubborn. His account goes on to praise Lord Howard, who was otherwise widely condemned by many others for effectively fleeing the very target of his command at the Battle of Flores. What motive Monson had for denigrating Grenville while promoting Howard may be understood by his proximity as a neighbor to the Howards. He may also have seen his comments as an opportunity to curry favor for a planned marriage that eventually took place between the Howards and Monsons a few years later.

A confidential letter written by Thomas Phelippes, a decipherer employed by Sir Francis Walsingham during the Babbington conspiracy, further undermines Monson's report. The letter, written to Thomas

Barnes, states: "Can write no good news from hence; the loss of the *Revenge* with Sir R. Grenville is stale ... they condemn the Lord Thomas (Howard) for a coward, and some say he is for the King of Spain." He adds: "Supposes he has heard of the quarrel and offer of combat between the Lord Admiral (Howard) and Sir Walter Raleigh."[3]

In truth, Grenville had a great deal of respect among his fellow Elizabethans. The notable Sir Richard Hawkins described him as a man of "eternal honour and reputation of great valour, and of an experimented (experienced) soulder chusing rather to sacrifice his life, and to pass all danger whatsoever, than to fayle in his obligation."[4] While unproven, there also persists a story that Queen Elizabeth bestowed a gilded four-poster bed upon the Grenvilles, in gratitude for his services to the country. Certainly when Grenville's wife Mary died, the bed she shared with her husband was by far and away the most valuable personal possession she had.

Taken together, these accounts allow us to build a picture of a man who was undoubtedly short tempered and probably quite short on negotiation skills. However, in his defense, the loss of his father and siblings by the time he was three years old would have failed to provide him with an environment conducive to the development of social skills, which, as modern sociologists tell us about those formative years, tend to shape our interactions with others in later life. Yet it is clear Grenville did possess some compassion for others. The transcripts in this book reveal, for example, occasions when he set prisoners free and when, as at the Battle of Flores, he showed concern for the sick, and sought assurances from the Spanish that his men would be returned to England unharmed.

However, Grenville was also a man born of military genes, whose life accustomed him to making tactical and potentially lifesaving decisions, it is for this reason that he probably never suffered fools gladly. Whatever problem he encountered, he responded with a solution that was clear in vision and decisive in action, and as a former mayor, I speak from experience when I say that decisive actions always lead to criticism from those you brush aside.

In considering Grenville's character, we should also review his evident desire to improve the town of Bideford. It was a desire he achieved by creating self-government through his council and by gaining recognition for the port, which allowed revenue duty to be extracted from wealthy ship owners. Such actions would certainly have contributed to his wealth, but they would also have provided employment and therefore relative prosperity for even the most beggarly of the town's inhabitants.

The observations I have made from years of researching the life and times of Sir Richard Grenville draw me to conclude that he was a man who, without any doubt, possessed an incessant drive, acted with honor and dedication, and remained throughout his life wholly committed to serving his Queen and his country. It is perhaps because of the way he conducted his life that the English nation has almost completely overlooked Grenville's contributions to its history. Even in the light of new evidence he remains out of favor, while those who, it could be argued with some justification, stole his rightful credit, have become history's heroes.

\

*   *   *

Of Bideford, the town he left behind, I have perhaps already offered some strong criticisms, but I cannot close on the subject without declaring that despite the almost certain role it plays as the true home to the founding fathers of America, very little has occurred to elevate its status from its present, and wholly embarrassing position. For that, district and county council bureaucrats, self-serving and perhaps myopic commissioners, many property owners, and a largely disenfranchised population, which believed that National Lottery Funds and other charitable sources would provide the handouts needed to improve the town's status, have only themselves to blame.

*   *   *

As to the colony for which Grenville tried so valiantly to secure success, one that he had planned and made two voyages for and organized two further abortive voyages for, I believe some of them did succeed in raising descendants—not many, but enough to secure their claim as the founding fathers of America. Moreover, they achieved this despite a truly disheartening catalog of misfortune.

Consider that:

• If only Ralph Lane had not decided to take the opportunity to return to England with Sir Francis Drake.
• Perhaps, if only Sir Francis Drake had not offered Lane and his men passage home.
• If only the unnamed ship sent in 1586 had arrived a few days earlier, or Grenville's ships of the same year a couple of weeks earlier. Perhaps if Grenville himself had not become stranded on the sandbar at the mouth of the Bideford estuary on his way to Roanoke Island.
• If only Grenville's men had remained defensive of the English foothold in Virginia.

- If only Simon Ferdinando had followed instructions and left the 1587 colony at Chesapeake Bay.
- If only the foolhardy captain of the *Brave* in 1588 had not engaged in futile warfare with every ship he could find, all invariably, so much larger than his command; and from the same voyage, if only Captain Amadas on board the *Roe* had carried on with the mission rather than simply giving up and returning to England. He had made the journey at least twice before, after all.
- One could argue too that if only Mother Nature had been a little kinder to John White in 1590, or to Sir Francis Drake and Ralph Lane in 1585.
- Finally, if only the Spanish Armada had not chosen 1588 as the year to attack England, something that, perhaps beyond all factors, probably changed the course of the history of English colonization in America.

What became of the colony after they arrived on Roanoke Island in 1587 is a subject of popular debate. My personal opinion is that the colony began to fragment when it became evident that relief was not going to appear in 1588. However, they must have stayed on the island long enough to build the evidently substantial palisade that White observed in 1590.

Factors in this fragmentation would have been simple hardship caused by the scarcity of food, and the increasing desperation of having to defend themselves, the latter evident from John White's observations of their attempts to produce more ammunition. Some of the colonists probably died in that defense at the hands of Wanchese's men.

The colony probably suffered further depletion from sickness and misfortune from encounters with the myriad poisonous plants, animals and natural hazards still present in the Outer Banks region today.

At some point in the late summer of 1588, Edward Stafford and the crew of the pinnace probably either tried to reach Chesapeake Bay, or perished in an attempt to re-cross the Atlantic. If they reached Chesapeake Bay then the survivors of that journey could well be those referred to by William Strachey, or acknowledged by the Virginia Company in their instructions to Sir Thomas Gates, albeit that we must consider what potentially remained of Grenville's men could have equal claim on this point. In either of these cases, their position as slaves to the Indians make it unlikely they raised a family of their own, excepting of course that Strachey's "younge mayde" could have been married off among the tribesmen.

I also believe that a further group of colonists may well have decided to relocate "50 myles into the maine," to the "hidden" site on John White's map. However, I am not convinced they survived very long, if at all. The fickle nature of the Native American alliances would have made the arrangement unsafe; we have only to study Lane's accounts to confirm this. In any case, we should not overlook the situation with Wanchese. It was his men surely, that killed George Howe and launched the attacks on the colony at Roanoke. He would surely have pursued the colonists.

Principal of my personal beliefs however, is that many of the remaining colonists, and certainly all the families and betrothed couples, headed for Hatteras Island. We do not know for certain, but it seems reasonable to believe that Manteo was still alive and king of the Croatoans at this time. Thus, and having been bestowed with a title from Raleigh, he would probably have felt duty bound to arrange for their safety on the island. Archaeological discoveries also strongly suggest where on Hatteras they lived, that being the same location as Lane's military outpost of 1585. Hatteras Island was also the site of a significant harvest of shellfish, as the author's study of 2011 revealed. Therefore, while the Outer Banks region was suffering from a significant drought, food, however meagre, was probably still available in sufficient quantity on the island to sustain the combined populations.

How long they remained there may be indicated by the recent archaeological investigations, which have revealed a complete dearth of European finds for a period of at least fifty years between circa 1600 and 1650, and only a tiny but important collection of materials that pre-dates this period. The colonists' stay on the island may therefore have been short lived, a reason for which may have been uncovered during these investigations. What we observed was the encroachment of a substantial line of sand dunes over the archaeology from the early seventeenth century period. The assumption is that the island suffered a catastrophic hurricane or series of hurricanes, which devastated the colonist and native settlements, crops, and the all-important shellfish harvest.

At the time of their departure, and assuming the colonists still believed that an English rescue mission might relieve them, they could have left another message that found upon an ancient Live Oak known as the "CORA" tree for the inscribed letters upon it.

So where did the Hatteras Island colony go? Logically, they headed for the relative safety of the mainland. At this point, I would agree that it might be fanciful to think that they settled near or with the Coree tribe but in the absence of anything more tenuous, I would side with this hypothesis. I also believe that by now, perhaps a generation later, intermarriage and assimilation would have started to take place, a view also shared by Quinn.[5]

Then, following a period of relative stability, I believe there could have been a further split within the remaining group. Some may have stayed with the Coree, subsequently integrating into that tribe, and moving with them through their own fortunes and misfortunes to become members of the Catawba, albeit that I think we are dealing with a very small number of colonists taking this route; while the remainder headed back to Hatteras Island after it had recovered from the probable storm damage.

If some did return to Hatteras Island, this, in effect, may infer that Lawson's Indians who talked of their ancestor's ability to "speak from a book," could really have been telling the truth. Unfortunately, there is a somewhat hazy gap between his report and the deeds relating to William Elks in 1756, but if asked, I would be inclined to believe that some of the Hatteras Islanders who today claim to be descendants of the lost colony should be taken seriously.

So there you have it, the results of my seven years, unsponsored, and perhaps uncultured research into a story I think has become fertile ground for many a retelling, some well-founded, and others perhaps more fanciful. Nevertheless, it is a fact that if we find just one descendant of a lost colonist or a descendant of Grenville's men, alive today, that revelation will rewrite the history of America. It should also provide the necessary catalyst to guarantee recognition for Sir Richard Grenville, for without him, I doubt the story of the lost colony of Roanoke would have ever been written.

Chapter Notes

Chapter One

1. George Peckham, *A True Report of the Late Discoveries and Possession, Taken in the Right of the Crown of England, of the Newfound Lands: by that Valiant and Worthy Gentleman, Sir Humphrey Gilbert Knight, 1583*. Richard Hakluyt, *The Principal Navigations, Voyages, Traffiques and Discoveries of the English Nation: Made By Sea or Overland, to the Remote and Farthest Distant Quarters of the Earth, At Any Time Within the Compasse of These 1600 Yeres: Divided Into Three Severall Volumes According to the Positions of the Regions Whereunto They Were Directed ...* Imprinted at London: By George Bishop, Ralph Newberie and Robert Barker. 1600, 165–181.

2. Hakluyt, Richard, Leonard Woods, and Charles Deane. *A Discourse Concerning Western Planting*. Cambridge, MA: Press of J. Wilson, 1877.

Chapter Two

1. Thomasine Cole's great grandfather, John Cole, had a brother, Stephen, who was married to Joan White. Joan White's father, John White had a brother. Painter John White is descended from this line. Royal College of Arms ms E15 (Visitation of Cornwall 1573–4), folio 43/44.

2. There are two known copies. One held by the National Portrait Gallery, London (reference: NPG1612), and one owned by Sir Hugh and Lady Angela Stucley of Hartland Abbey. The latter is on long-term loan to Bideford Town Council and presently hangs in their Town Hall.

3. Inquisition Post Mortem; Greenfield, Richard, knight: Cornwall; 4 Edward VI [1550];

National Archives ref: C142/90/12 Transcription by David Carter.

4. David Carter (editor) and Andy Powell (contributor), Grenville Research, unpublished, www.nimrodresearch.co.uk/grenville/

5. National Archives, England, Patent Rolls, 5 Elizabeth 1, C66/989

6. P.W. Hasler (editor), *The History of Parliament: the House of Commons 1558–1603* (London: Her Majesty's Stationery Office, 1981).

7. Oswyn Murray collection of Wills, Vol.13, located on microfilm in Salt Lake City Family History Library.

8. John Watkins, "An Essay Towards a History of Bideford, in the County of Devon" (Exeter: Printed by E. Grigg, 1792), 19–27. (The original Charter hangs in the Burton Art Gallery, Bideford.)

9. *Ibid.*

10. *Ibid.*

11. State Papers Domestic, Elizabeth I, 95, 63–65

12. British Library, Lansdowne Manuscripts, MSS100/f4

13. John Stow, "Bridge warde without [including Southwark]," in *A Survey of London*. Reprinted from the Text of 1603, ed. C. L. Kingsford (Oxford: Clarendon, 1908), 52–69, www.british-history.ac.uk/no-series/survey-of-london-stow/1603/pp52–69

14. Church Rates, Bideford 1672 North Devon Record Office ref: NDRO-2379A/Z11.

15. Ibid.

Chapter Three

1. Later versions give the specific departure port as Plymouth.

2. Amadas and Barlowe met Raleigh in London, probably at his home, Durham

House. Whether they travelled overland to receive those instructions and collect their ships, thus explaining the curious comment "at our leaving of the river of Thames," or whether they sailed there and back, is unclear.

3. "diurnall"—a cross between a journal and a diary

4. A fawning and awkward few sentences, essentially pleading satisfaction of the outcome of their voyage from Raleigh

5. "disbagging"—possibly meaning "disbocking" from the Spanish word "desbocar"— to be caught up or swept along (as in a strong wind or current).

6. This "firm land" must have been Cape Lookout. Cape Fear, slightly farther south and less prominent, was part of Spanish territory at this time. Amadas and Barlowe would have known to stay some distance offshore to allay Spanish interest.

7. Once discovering the coast, Amadas and Barlowe continued to sail parallel to it but evidently remained some distance offshore as they missed several of the more low-lying inlets in the "120 miles" they travelled before finally spotting one. If [6] is correct then this would bring them to the area just north of Bodie Island, though the location of a former inlet which must have closed long before John Lawson wrote about the area in 1701.

8. "Harquebushot"—an arquebus (also known as a "harkbut") was an early smooth bore matchlock. The distance of an arquebus shot was based on its effective killing distance. This was approximately the same distance at which a good archer could kill someone with an arrow, or about one hundred yards. Thus, they anchored roughly three hundred yards inside the inlet to the inner sea.

9. "land next adjoining"—taken to mean what is now Bodie Island, which at the time they arrived was part of the north end of Hatteras Island and not part of the south end of the Currituck peninsula, as it is today.

10. A note in the margin reads "July 13. Possessions taken"

11. The grapes described here can only be the local scuppernong grapes, which are still cultivated today. They produce a very sweet wine.

12. "leagues"—a league measured on land was roughly three miles; however, if discussed in nautical terms, as the author of this account, being a mariner, may have done, then a league would have measured around three and a half miles. Thus, when Barlowe

states the island they were exploring was "twentie leagues long" we can interpret this as the island being sixty or seventy miles in length. This confirms they were exploring the "land next adjoining" Hatteras Island, specifically the northern tip around Bodie Island, which was part of Hatteras Island at that time. However, the 1600 edition of Hakluyt has the words "twenty leagues" replaced with "twenty miles" and the comment "The isle of Wokokon" inserted in the margin. This amendment by Hakluyt cannot be correct because "Wokokon" (modern day Ocracoke) was, and remains, only about ten miles in length. In addition, the description given by Barlowe would still stand up to scrutiny as a description of Hatteras Island today.

13. The discharge of the harquebus (arquebus) did not arouse an immediate response from any natives. This fact and later notes in the account confirm that Amadas and Barlowe were exploring unpopulated land. This adds to the hypothesis that they may have been on or near Bodie or Pea Island, neither of which have any recorded evidence of Native American habitation in the Precolonial era.

14. In England, waterfowl migration is usually determined by the winter season. In summer the coastal mudflats are almost empty, hence their obvious surprise at the sight before them.

15. Russia.

16. The area to the south of the Caspian Sea

17. The Azores.

18. Lebanon.

19. "Lentisk"—meaning the mastic tree *Pistacia lentiscus*, for which its close cousin the pistachio tree was probably mistaken.

20. The 1600 edition states that the narrator was Captain Arthur Barlowe. In this, the 1589 version, no one is credited. However, this sentence effectively confirms Captain Arthur Barlowe was indeed the author of this account.

21. "boweshoote"—a "bowshot" is about one hundred yards, the same distance as a harquebushot.

22. The name Virginia for the country was in honor of the Virgin Queen Elizabeth I, and was not one influenced by the similarity of the native name "Wingina." Of note is that Thomas Harriot later determined that the name "Wingandacoa" translated as "You have nice clothes"!

23. In the 1600 edition there is a margin

note that qualifies this as "white coral and pearls."

24. This implies that the Croatoan Indians presented Raleigh with a pearl bracelet; however, no evidence of it exists today.

25. "of the bigness"—meaning "of the size."

26. "aburne"—auburn

27. "durst"—dared.

28. The context used here suggests that Amadas and Barlowe's account was written after their return to England. The two men they refer to being brought home with them were Native Americans Manteo and Wanchese.

29. Manteo and Wanchese.

30. Ship's nails found in context with other Native American finds during archaeological excavations on Hatteras Island between 2009 and 2011 had clearly been fashioned into fishhooks. This confirms Barlowe's observation of the Native's practice of fashioning ship's nails into "their best instruments."

31. "great bore of pearls in gage"—bore is an old measurement for a barrel; the pearls being termed "in gauge" meant that they were at least of a diameter considered to give them a marketable value. In short, a valuable offer by the King's brother.

32. "underwoods"—low-growing shrubs in a wood or understory.

33. "Occam"—interpreted as meaning Pamlico Sound.

34. The distance from Roanoke to Amadas and Barlowe's ships is therefore about twenty-one to twenty-four miles. In relation to n6 this would have to equate to the modern day Oregon Inlet area, as Ocracoke ("Wokokon") is at least sixty miles distant from Roanoke. Barlowe's words therefore serve as confirmation that Hakluyt's correction of 1600 was mistaken.

35. The Indian village on Roanoke was therefore clearly near the water's edge, close enough to observe passing ships.

36. "billoe"—more correctly "billow"—a large swell, as of the sea. (Source: OED)

37. This is probably an English assumption. The heat of high summer would have caused the grapes (known today as scuppernong, a particularly sweet grape with a high sugar content) to take on a taste like wine within a day of being crushed for their juice, due to nothing more than their natural fermentation.

38. "earthen pots, very large, white, and sweete"—the use of the word "sweet" is probably implied here to mean appealing or proficient, functional in design.

39. "Pemeoke"—later referred to as "Pomeiooc."

40. Meaning it would take more than a day to walk to around Schycoake.

41. "Nomopana"—today known as the Chowan River.

42. If these mariners were Spanish, as is most likely, then their intended destination would have been Spanish Florida, possibly Port Royal. The island they were "cast away" (probably died upon) was obviously south of Wococan (Ocracoke) and therefore most likely Portsmouth Island.

43. "tooth of a fish"—possibly that of a shark?

44. "marvellously wasted"—an interesting description of something that probably equated to genocide.

45. "Neus"—the River Neuse today.

46. It is evidence from the stories related to the English by the Croatoan Indians that the coastal region of North Carolina had been the subject of intertribal warfare for some time prior to the arrival of the English. It was clearly not lost on the Native Americans either that the English had significant firepower and would be a formidable ally in these wars.

47. "Croonoake"—a typographical error by Hakluyt? Barlowe had already identified the island as Roanoke earlier in this narrative.

48. Perhaps to be interpreted as a rather awkward way of saying that only the Gentleman listed below should be trusted as having seen the land with their own eyes?

49. This Grenville was the brother of George Grenville, a close relative of Sir Richard Grenville through his grandfather. He also served with Sir Francis Drake on his West Indian voyage that relieved Lane's colony in 1586.

50. This is the Simon Ferdinando who three years later was to lead the fleet carrying the settlers to Roanoke Island.

51. Transcribed from Richard Hakluyt, *The Principall Nauigations, Voiages and Discoueries of the English Nation: Made By Sea or Ouer Land, to the Most Remote and Farthest Distant Quarters of the Earth At Any Time Within the Compasse of These 1500. Yeeres: Deuided Into Three Seuerall Parts, According to the Positions of the Regions Wherunto They Were Directed. ... Whereunto Is Added the Last Most Renowmed English Nauigation, Round About the Whole Globe of the Earth. By Richard Hakluyt Master of Artes, and Student Sometime of Christ-church in Oxford.* Imprinted at London: By George Bishop and

Ralph Newberie, deputies to Christopher Barker, printer to the Queenes most excellent Maiestie, 1589. 728–733

Chapter Four

1. Karen Ordahl-Kupperman states that Grenville "had no experience of sea voyages and especially not of the problems with trans-Atlantic ventures." Karen Ordahl-Kupperman, *Roanoke, the Abandoned Colony* (Totowa, NJ: Rowman & Allanheld, 1984), 16–17. While this is a reasonable assumption, very few in England at the time had these desired qualities. However, in the Domestic Correspondence of Elizabeth I will be found a Petition to the Queen dated March 22, 1574, "to allow of an enterprise for discovery of sundry rich and unknown lands, fatally reserved for England and for the honor of Your Majty" which is endorsed "Sir Humfrey Gilbert, Sir Geo. Peckham, MR. CARLILE, and Sir Ric. Greenvile, and others, voiages." (Great Britain. Public Record Office, William Noel Sainsbury, J. W. Sir Fortescue, Cecil Headlam, and Arthur Percival Newton. Calendar of State Papers, Colonial Series. London, 1860 1). Grenville's father, as we have also learned, was Captain of the *Mary Rose*, and his grandfather had held a Privateering License issued by Lord Seymour. In addition, Grenville himself had planned a round-the-world voyage and was fast developing his hometown of Bideford into a seaport. Thus, while there is no prior record of Grenville's skill on the high seas, he must have possessed a maritime knowledge of sufficient respect to be given command of this voyage.

2. This has to be a typographical error as the ships arrived in the Canaries on April 14, apparently thirty-three days before they left Plymouth. It should read "March."

3. "Candishe"—Cavendish.

4. "Lancacota"—Lanzarote.

5. "Forte Ventura"—Fuerteventura.

6. "10th day following"—meaning May 10.

7. "Cotesa" is an island that lies just off Puerto Rico.

8. This is a typographical error. It should read "12" (the twelfth of May).

9. "Bay of Muskito"—a location known today as "Bahia Tallaboa," near the town of Guayanilla, on the south coast of Puerto Rico.

10. A "fawlcon," or more likely a falconet were a type of cannon of around four feet in length with a two-inch bore, the best of which had an effective distance of up to a mile.

11. "Greenvill"—one of many spellings of Sir Richard Grenville's surname.

12. "fet"—meaning "fetched." From www.shakespeareswords.com.

13. In the Coleccion Navarette (Seville, Spain), there is a letter from the Abbot of Jamaica, Marques de Villalobos, to the King of Spain, from which we may deduce that Master Cavendish probably first landed on Jamaica before joining Grenville. At Jamaica, Villalobos reports that the Spanish found twenty sick men. The letter goes on to state that they captured and interrogated one "Don Armedes Eduarte" (Edward Amadas), a probable relative of Philip Amadas, and one of only two survivors from this group. Amadas evidently relayed the English plan to build a fort on what the Spanish considered to be their land, and later to populate it with settlers. He also names Grenville as being in command of the fleet, and the Captain of his group as John Coplestone. The Spanish incarcerated Edward Amadas and sent him to Seville with the Abbot's letter. The fate of Edward Amadas is unknown. Archivo General de Indias, and Irene Aloha Wright. *Further English Voyages to Spanish America, 1583–1594: Documents From the Archives of the Indies At Seville Illustrating English Voyages to the Caribbean, the Spanish Main, Florida, and Virginia* (London: Printed for the Hakluyt Society,1951), 174–176.

14. The Coleccion Navarette also contains a letter recording the Spanish version of this incident. Written by Diego Menendez de Valdes, the governor of Puerto Rico, and addressed to the House of Trade, Havana. It tells us he sent thirty-five arquebusiers (mounted riflemen) and forty soldiers to view what Grenville was up to at the fort. It goes on to say that, the English declared that they had Spanish prisoners and intended to sell them in Florida. The report concludes with the words "This is unlikely." There is also a postscript to the letter stating that Grenville tried to ransom two Spanish ships in return for horses, cattle and supplies, an offer the Governor refused (*ibid.*, 9–10).

15. In the same records referenced in notes 13 and 14 there is another letter, this one from Don Diego de Alcega to the House of Trade in Havana, that claims the English carved a message into a tree before they left. The message, translated into Spanish by a Flemish

trader, reputedly stated "On May 11th we reached this place with the Tiger and on the 19th the Elizabeth came up and we are about to leave on the 23rd in good health, glory be to God. 1585" (*ibid.*, 11–12).

16. Typographical error: should read "24."

17. "Roxo Bay"—Cabo Rojo, Puerto Rico.

18. "mauger"—more likely "maugre"—meaning "in spite of." From www.shakespeareswords.com.

19. "plate"—meaning "pewter."

20. "kyne"—old English (archaic) word for cows, collectively. (Source: OED)

21. This is strong evidence that Grenville's *Tyger* almost certainly had Spanish mustangs on board when it ran aground on Ocracoke in the Outer Banks. Although virtually unprovable, it seems highly likely that their descendants are the Ocracoke "Banker" horses of today. Certainly, DNA testing has confirmed these horses as having Spanish origins. (Dr. Ernest G Cuthran, 1992)

22. According to A. L. Rowse, the Coleccion Navarette contains the report of Don Fernando de Altamirano, Captain of the Spanish frigate captured by the English on May 24. In it, Altamirano states that the English told him they were exploring the West Indies with a view to asking Spain to consider joint rule, their authority for being there supposedly granted to them by "a great English lord" (Raleigh) and their admiral being one "Richarte de Campo Verde" (Grenville). Altamirano finished by noting that the two Indians on board were richly dressed, spoke good English, and were lovers of music. A. L. Rowse, *Sir Richard Grenville of the Revenge* (London: Jonathan Cape, 1940), 211–214.

23. "Saint John de Ullua"—a Spanish fort by the port of Veracruz, Mexico. In 1568, a sizeable Spanish fleet set upon Sir John Hawkins, who, along with Sir Francis Drake, barely escaped with his life in the ensuing battle.

24. "John Oxnam"—John Oxenham was an English privateer who crossed the Isthmus of Panama to plunder Spanish shipping in the Pacific Ocean. The Spanish captured and took him to Panama City, and later Lima, Peru, where they finally executed him for piracy in 1580.

25. "Halter for his hire"—effectively meaning a noose around his neck.

26. These locations remain unidentified. From the course given, these are probably locations in the Bahamas.

27. *Ibid.*

28. Grenville's ship did not sink. Although the grounding damaged it, Grenville had it repaired and it later rejoined the fleet. On this, Quinn states that the inlet on which the ship ran aground was between Ocracoke Island and Portsmouth Island. This cannot be correct. It is more likely to have been the inlet slightly to the north of the present day inlet between Hatteras Island and Ocracoke Island. David B Quinn, *Set Fair for Roanoke: Voyages and Colonies, 1584–1606* (Chapel Hill: Published for America's Four Hundredth Anniversary Committee by the University of North Carolina Press, 1985), 63. The pilot "Fernando" is almost certainly the same Simon Ferdinando responsible for piloting the 1587 colonist's voyage and recorded in the State Papers Colonial Series as "Simon Ferdinando, Sec. Walsingham's man…." Great Britain. Public Record Office. William Noel Sainsbury, J. W. Sir Fortescue, Cecil Headlam, and Arthur Percival Newton. Calendar of State Papers, Colonial Series. London, 1860, 1–2. www.british-history.ac.uk/cal-state-papers/colonial/america-west-indies/vol1/pp1–2.

29. Captain Reymond was in charge of the *Red Lyon*. How he became separated from the fleet is not detailed in Hakluyt's narrative but it is reasonable to assume this took place during the storm off Portugal. Evidently, he had made his way to Croatoan knowing that this was the intended destination of the fleet.

30. "Paquype"—Lake Mattamuskeet, a large shallow lake near the east coast of North Carolina.

31. The word "fledde" appears transcribed as "sledde" in other editions of Hakluyt's work, but in this edition, the word is "fledde." Because of this confusion, latter-day authors and historians have frequently interpreted this to mean that the villagers had been slain rather than, as is far more likely, having run away (or fled) from the settlement on sighting Lane's militia.

32. Grenville met Granganimeo (Grangino) and Manteo on board his flagship *Tyger*.

33. An astonishing eyewitness account, written by Enrique Lopez, a passenger on board the Spanish ship (the *Santa Maria de san Vincente*), is transcribed at the end of this chapter.

34. "landes ende"—the most southwesterly point of the English mainland.

35. "Falmouth"—Principal port on the south coast of Cornwall, approximately midway between Land's End and Plymouth.

36. Records of Plymouth City confirm that Sir Walter Raleigh was among those "worshipful friends." (Plymouth Muniments, Widey Court Book 1584/1585 state that Hawkins was paid £4 and Martin White £8. 11s. 4d, for his entertainment.)

37. One of the objectives of the voyage was to establish the relative wealth of minerals found in the New World. Raleigh employed Bohemians for their skills in this field. These are probably them.

38. Given the meticulous recording of names, these are probably cabin boys, who were often orphans or possibly indentured West Africans and thus probably never had a known surname.

39. *Ibid.*

40. *Ibid.*

41. Records of Plymouth City confirm that Doughan Gannes was among those "worshipful friends."

42. This is surely "Haunce the surgeon" recorded as drowning in a boat which capsized during an attempted landing in the voyage of 1590. In his book *Set Fair for Roanoke* Quinn states that Haunce Walters was probably a metallurgist but later contradicts this (92, 96).

43. Records of Plymouth City confirm that Thomas Skevelabs was among those "worshipful friends."

44. Transcribed from Richard Hakluyt, *The Principall Nauigations, Voiages and Discoueries of the English Nation: Made By Sea or Ouer Land, to the Most Remote and Farthest Distant Quarters of the Earth At Any Time Within the Compasse of These 1500. Yeeres: Deuided Into Three Seuerall Parts, According to the Positions of the Regions Wherunto They Were Directed. ... Whereunto Is Added the Last Most Renowmed English Nauigation, Round About the Whole Globe of the Earth. By Richard Hakluyt Master of Artes, and Student Sometime of Christ-church in Oxford.* Imprinted at London: By George Bishop and Ralph Newberie, deputies to Christopher Barker, printer to the Queenes most excellent Maiestie, 1589, 733–737.

45. The inlets of the Outer Banks are notoriously fickle, the opening and closing of inlets occurring with almost every major hurricane. Only Ocracoke ("Ococan") has ever remained stable.

46. Great Britain. Public Record Office. William Noel Sainsbury, J. W. Sir Fortescue, Cecil Headlam, and Arthur Percival Newton. Calendar of State Papers, Colonial Series. London, 1860, 2–3.

47. "Gynneye"—Guinea wheat or Indian corn.

48. Great Britain. Public Record Office. William Noel Sainsbury, J. W. Sir Fortescue, Cecil Headlam, and Arthur Percival Newton. Calendar of State Papers, Colonial Series. London, 1860, 3–4.

49. Santo Domingo is on the south coast of what we know today as the Dominican Republic.

50. The Tierra Firma fleet operated from mainland Spain.

51. The New Spain fleet originated from Mexico.

52. "lie in a cross sea"—in this interpretation, meaning to turn the ship into the wind, placing the bow directly into the oncoming waves.

53. Spanish cannons of this period where kept loaded but could only be fired once since the Spanish did not have the recoil system of the English, which allowed the cannon to be retracted and reloaded for a further volley. They were also subject to fracturing muzzles and backfires, thus critically weakening their ability to provide a defense. This, the element of surprise, and the ease with which English ships could outmaneuver the Spanish Galleons of the period, is almost certainly the reason why Grenville could take a ship more than twice his size.

54. "arrobas"—an old Spanish weight equivalent to about 25 pounds.

55. Taking an average from various sources, a ducat had an estimated worth of about eight UK shillings in 1585. Using the UK National Archives inflation calculator as a guide, this equates to approximately £60 in today's terms. Thus, Grenville's total haul of 160,000 ducats (according to Enrique Lopez) would have been worth £9.6 million Sterling / $14 million U.S. at 2010 values, a sum considerably higher than Sir Francis Drake's haul at St Augustine.

56. "deponent"—the person making the statement (Enrique Lopez).

57. Grenville did not release all of the Spanish passengers and crew at the island of Flores; he had removed twenty and taken them aboard his flagship, the *Tyger*.

58. A "Galleasse" was a design of ship by Matthew Baker, Master Shipwright to Elizabeth I. The Galleasse was the first ship considered capable of firing a broadside without risk of capsizing. From Lopez's description,

and by comparing it to the image of the Galleasse *Swallowe* in the 1546 "Anthony Rolls"; it is highly probable that the image of the ship lying close to Ocracoke on John White's map of 1585, is indeed, Grenville's *Tyger*. (The Anthony Roll of Henry VIII's Navy: Pepys Library 2991 and British Library MS 22047.)

59. This can only be the same Simon Fernando (or Ferdinando) of the 1587 lost colony voyage.

60. A reference to the *Tyger* beaching on the shores of Ocracoke.

61. The reason why Grenville dispatched John Arundell from Roanoke on August 5, 1585.

62. Archivo General de Indias, and Irene Aloha Wright, *Further English Voyages to Spanish America, 1583–1594: Documents From the Archives of the Indies At Seville Illustrating English Voyages to the Caribbean, the Spanish Main, Florida, and Virginia* (London: Printed for the Hakluyt Society, 1951), 12–15.

63. Great Britain. Public Record Office. William Noel Sainsbury, J. W. Sir Fortescue, Cecil Headlam, and Arthur Percival Newton. Calendar of State Papers, Colonial Series. London, 1860, 4.

64. Archivo General de Indias, and Irene Aloha Wright, *Further English Voyages to Spanish America, 1583–1594: Documents From the Archives of the Indies At Seville Illustrating English Voyages to the Caribbean, the Spanish Main, Florida, and Virginia* (London: Printed for the Hakluyt Society, 1951), 237–241.

65. The date given by Diaz does not tie up with the journey of the *Santa Maria de San Vincente*. We have to assume therefore that Diaz was held captive onboard the *Tyger*.

66. The "bar of Barnstaple" is a dangerous sand bank, which, more than 400 years later, still lays across the entrance to the estuary through which ships gain access to the Port of Bideford.

67. Somerset Record Office (England) DD/SF/2/103/8, unpaged.

Chapter Five

1. "Pemisapan"—A Native Indian King who plotted against the English.

2. Ralph Lane's calculation places Secotan near the present-day town of Belhaven on the Pungo River.

3. "thorowe"—probably meaning "thorough."

4. "without kenning of land"—meaning "without any sight of land." A term still used colloquially in the west of England today.

5. "furniture"—meaning their weapons.

6. Meaning Lane was unable to explore the area around Secotan or the Pamlico Sound due to his pinesse having too deep a draft. He chose instead to leave this area until his hoped-for supplies arrived in the spring.

7. "flawe"—meaning "gust" or "squall." Thus, this sentence is stating that there was little opportunity of finding a safe haven in bad weather. This description, and Lane's competent compass directions, confirms that he can only be referring to the Currituck Sound. The distance recorded, 130 miles, would take Lane up to the Chesapeake Bay area, possibly as far as the James River.

8. This statement would have provided a persuasive argument for Sir Walter Raleigh's decision to settle the 1587 colony in Chesapeake Bay rather than Roanoke.

9. This makes it clear that somewhere in the James River or Chesapeake Bay area another English encampment that pre-dates the 1607 Jamestown site may be awaiting discovery—assuming that the Jamestown site was not built over the Lane encampment.

10. The site of Choanoke is widely regarded as being Edenton, but if Lane's calculations are correct then Edenton is some fifty miles short of the site visited by him. The nearest settlement today would in fact be Winton, less than twenty miles from the Virginia border.

11. About eight hundred feet.

12. This is the location of the "Avoca" site of today, a location which John White marked on his map of 1585 but which he then covered over, almost certainly because it was later dismissed as a possible location for the English settlement.

13. Meaning he was disabled.

14. Difficult to determine where this island was. If one travels three days by canoe up either the Chowan or Nottoway rivers and then heads northeast, as per Menatonon's directions, this would take you to the Chesapeake Bay area. There are several islands in the bay, which would then be candidates for the home of the "certaine kings" discussed.

15. There are no known accounts of English contact with Native Americans in the Chesapeake Bay area prior to this account. It is possible, therefore, that these "white men" were in fact Spanish.

16. "sconse"—small military fort, or redoubt.

17. "harboroughs"—deduced as meaning "harbors."

18. The Morotico River could be the Roanoke River, emptying as it does into the Chowan River.

19. About a thousand feet

20. "a bale water"—most likely interpreted as "a baleful water" meaning "malignant" or "dangerous," as in a fast-flowing water like the ebbing tide seen at London Bridge, England.

21. Menatonon's description involving a sea is confused and difficult to identify. Is he re-telling a myth?

22. "crenepoes"—a word mistakenly believed to refer to another tribe. A margin note in the 1600 version, which states "their women," resolves the true meaning.

23. "weirs"—fish traps.

24. "mastives"—mastiffs, a breed of dog.

25. Given that the Native Indians were able to melt the metal, it had to be something that had a relatively low melting point. In consideration of the description too, the metal described was probably iron pyrites (fool's gold).

26. "skeure"—logically this word is, or means, "secure."

27. "Easter eve"—the Saturday before Easter Sunday. In 1586, this "Easter eve" would have fallen on April 2.

28. "Perfited"—meaning "perfected"—to have achieved the objective in this sense.

29. "Master Yougham"—probably Doughan Gannes, one of the German metallurgists that accompanied the voyage.

30. Transcribed from Richard Hakluyt, *The Principall Nauigations, Voiages and Discoueries of the English Nation: Made By Sea or Ouer Land, to the Most Remote and Farthest Distant Quarters of the Earth At Any Time Within the Compasse of These 1500. Yeeres: Deuided Into Three Seuerall Parts, According to the Positions of the Regions Wherunto They Were Directed. ... Whereunto Is Added the Last Most Renowmed English Nauigation, Round About the Whole Globe of the Earth. By Richard Hakluyt Master of Artes, and Student Sometime of Christ-church in Oxford.* Imprinted at London: By George Bishop and Ralph Newberie, deputies to Christopher Barker, printer to the Queenes most excellent Maiestie, 1589, 737–742.

Chapter Six

1. The voyage recounted in the previous chapter.

2. "bruite"—a rumor (OED).

3. This may be the first observation of the impact of European diseases introduced to Native American society.

4. "Weroanza of England"—meaning Queen Elizabeth I.

5. "Cassada"—"arrow arum" or "tuckahoe" (*Peltandra virginica*)—a plant with an unpalatable root which the native Indians boiled for a long period in order to make it edible.

6. "Chyna"—uncertain definition, possibly "chine"—a joint of meat (OED). Deduced from Lane's comment: "... if the savages should not helpe us with Cassada, and Chyna, and that our weares (fish weirs) should fayle us...."

7. "Moneths minde"—a service or feast held in honor of a dead person, one month after their death. The practice has fallen into disuse in England.

8. Confirmation of the existence of a fort on Roanoke, and that Lane and his officers had separate lodgings, possibly living with or by the native Indians at their village (almost certainly the same village where Granganimeo's wife had previously shown them hospitality). This is a fascinating point as it clearly suggests Lane did not fear the Native Americans. Indeed, why should he? Manteo knew the villagers and Granganimeo, while Lane would no doubt have learned from Philip Amadas about his encounter the previous year where he had been "entertained with all love, and kindnes, and with as much bountie, after their manner, as they could possibly devise." (See chapter on the voyage of Amadas and Barlowe.)

9. "Ottorasko"—Hatorask (Bodie Island).

10. "...my lord Admirals Island"—this can only be a reference to Lord Howard of Effingham, who was Lord High Admiral of England at the time.

11. "imprest"—in this context, something received from a government for services rendered.

12. "bylboes"—An iron bar with sliding shackles, used to shackle prisoners.

13. "canuisado"—possibly from the Spanish "cansado," meaning an irritation, something tiresome. In this context, Lane probably intended to thwart the Indians' plans by re-

moving the canoes to prevent them from raising the alarm.

14. "Canoas"—canoes.

15. "allarum"—alarm, fright, panic.

16. "Frish boy with my Petronell"—meaning "servant with my large-caliber gun."

17. Edward Nugent ("Nugen" in the names listed by Hakluyt in chapter three) cut off "the king" Pemisapan's head.

18. "Contentation"—meaning "satisfaction" (*Collins English Dictionary*).

19. Sir Francis Drake.

20. "calievers"—"calivers," a smaller version of the arquebus.

21. "experimented"—meaning "experienced."

22. "gings"—meaning a gang (of people), or Company of men. Source: www.shakespeareswords.com.

23. "tarry"—in this context meaning "stay" or linger with. Source: www.shakespeareswords.com.

24. It is clear from this statement and Lane's earlier reference to August that he did not intend to overwinter a second year on Roanoke, meaning, therefore, that in any event he planned to leave in three months' time regardless.

25. "the doings in England for Flaunders"—Lane must have learned from Drake that England was at this time supporting the Dutch in their war against the Spanish occupation, Flanders then being part of The Netherlands.

26. Transcribed from Richard Hakluyt, *The Principall Nauigations, Voiages and Discoueries of the English Nation: Made By Sea or Ouer Land, to the Most Remote and Farthest Distant Quarters of the Earth At Any Time Within the Compasse of These 1500. Yeeres: Deuided Into Three Seuerall Parts, According to the Positions of the Regions Wherunto They Were Directed. ... Whereunto Is Added the Last Most Renowmed English Nauigation, Round About the Whole Globe of the Earth. By Richard Hakluyt Master of Artes, and Student Sometime of Christ-church in Oxford.* Imprinted at London: By George Bishop and Ralph Newberie, deputies to Christopher Barker, printer to the Queenes most excellent Maiestie, 1589, 742–747.

27. Lane landed on Roanoke with 107 men but according to Captain Bigges' report left with 103, while the ship's log of the *Primrose* states: "(we) browghte thence all those men with us except iij (3) who had gone further into the countrie, and the winde grew [so that] wee coulde not staie foor them." Francis Drake, and Mary Frear Keeler, *Sir Francis Drake's West Indian Voyage 1585–1586* (London: Hakluyt Society, 1981), 209.

28. Pedro Diaz states in his deposition of 1588 that the island was inhabited by Indians who were at war with those of the mainland, for which reason they admitted the English, of whom the mainland Indians killed some four, and Francis Drake took the rest away because he found them dispersed and greatly in need of food supplies. The suggestion is that the three that went into the "countrie," probably to return Okisko to his home, were presumed to have been killed by the mainland Indians, while the remaining soul was found hanged the following year by Grenville, his death probably a punishment meted out by Lane for a crime unknown.

29. Walter Bigges, Lieutenant Croftes, and Thomas Gates, *A Summarie and True Discourse of Sir Frances Drakes West Indian Voyage*, 1596, pages unnumbered.

Chapter Seven

1. Somerset Record Office reference: DD/SF/2/103/8 unpaged. Note: The local inhabitants of Bideford and Barnstaple still knew Roanoke Island as "Wyngandecora" despite Thomas Harriot having by now established the island's correct name. We might also note that the two week delay Grenville suffered between this mishap and his final sailing equate to about the same length of time by which he missed Drake's relief of Lane's colony at Roanoke Island.

2. Archivo General de Indias, and Irene Aloha Wright, *Further English Voyages to Spanish America, 1583–1594: Documents From the Archives of the Indies At Seville Illustrating English Voyages to the Caribbean, the Spanish Main, Florida, and Virginia* (London: Printed for the Hakluyt Society, 1951) 237–241. As a footnote to this record, "400" men might seem a rather substantial number of personnel for what was ostensibly a voyage of re-supply. The answer may lie in a badly damaged record in the archives of the High Court of the Admiralty for 1586 that confers a right upon Grenville to establish his own base on the eastern seaboard of America. The document also confirms that his fellow Commissioners from the town council, Aldred Stockombe and

Richard Willott, were involved in the project. (The National Archives, H.C.A. 1586–25/2, pkt.5.)

3. This detailed account of Lane's withdrawal must have been recounted to Hakluyt by a member of Lane's colony, who that was, is unknown. However, from Hakluyt's condemnation of the actions Lane took against the Native Americans, it is unlikely to have come from Lane himself. Hypothetically, this information could have come from John White.

4. At the time of writing, no records giving any detail whatsoever of this ship, or its captain, have been uncovered. It is possible that it was part of Grenville's fleet, which made an aborted attempt to sail from Bideford on April 16.

5. "Grindfield"—another spelling of Grenville

6. Grenville expected to find the ship waiting for him at Roanoke, perhaps further evidence that it too had sailed from Bideford as part of Grenville's original fleet.

7. Suggesting Grenville explored the Outer Banks region in some detail in search of the colony.

8. Transcribed from Richard Hakluyt, *The Principall Nauigations, Voiages and Discoueries of the English Nation: Made By Sea or Ouer Land, to the Most Remote and Farthest Distant Quarters of the Earth At Any Time Within the Compasse of These 1500. Yeeres: Deuided Into Three Seuerall Parts, According to the Positions of the Regions Wherunto They Were Directed. ... Whereunto Is Added the Last Most Renowmed English Nauigation, Round About the Whole Globe of the Earth. By Richard Hakluyt Master of Artes, and Student Sometime of Christ-church in Oxford.* Imprinted at London: By George Bishop and Ralph Newberie, deputies to Christopher Barker, printer to the Queenes most excellent Maiestie, 1589, 747–748.

9. These two prizes, dispatched for the port of Bideford, could be the same two ships that sailed for Roanoke in the ill-fated voyage of 1588. Archivo General de Indias, and Irene Aloha Wright, *Further English Voyages to Spanish America, 1583–1594: Documents From the Archives of the Indies At Seville Illustrating English Voyages to the Caribbean, the Spanish Main, Florida, and Virginia* (London: Printed for the Hakluyt Society, 1951), 237–241

10. *Ibid.* The Spanish generally referred to the whole of the explored American territory as Florida.

11. *Ibid.* Diaz is offering his description of Roanoke Island.

12. This Indian can be none other than "Rawly," the Native American Indian who was baptized in Bideford and later died there.

13. "…in the water"—it is widely thought that this is Diaz's description of Fort Raleigh. However, Grenville did not allow Diaz to go ashore, therefore he could at best only be reporting what he had gleaned from Grenville's men, or what he could see. Given that Grenville's ship was of too great a draft to reach Roanoke, it is therefore possible that Diaz was describing Port Ferdinando on modern Bodie Island and presumed it to be Fort Raleigh. This hypothesis is supported by a comment in Luis de Gerónimo de Oré's *The Martyrs of Florida.* In it, he records that Pedro Diaz, when furnishing the Spanish with information on the Roanoke Island colony and responding to the question of why he did not actually see the fort, stated "he was not able to see, since it was ten leagues from the port by the arm above the shore of the northern entrance," the "arm" being Outer Banks shoreline around Bodie Island.

14. Diaz was present to witness the number of men Grenville left behind. Therefore either some credibility must be given to Diaz's figure of eighteen, as opposed to the fifteen quoted elsewhere, or this is a simple transcription error.

15. In this statement, Diaz gives us the only known references to any of the names of Grenville's men left behind to defend Virginia in 1586.

16. This circuitous route via Newfoundland, not recounted in Hakluyt, suggests that Grenville was desperate to find food and respite. He probably viewed Newfoundland, having already been "possessed" by England, as the nearest safe haven by which he could achieve that end.

17. Archivo General de Indias, and Irene Aloha Wright, *Further English Voyages to Spanish America, 1583–1594: Documents From the Archives of the Indies At Seville Illustrating English Voyages to the Caribbean, the Spanish Main, Florida, and Virginia* (London: Printed for the Hakluyt Society, 1951), 237–241.

18. "Simancas: February 1588, 16–29," in *Calendar of State Papers, Spain* (Simancas), Volume 4, 1587–1603, ed. Martin A.S. Hume (London: Her Majesty's Stationery Office, 1899).

Chapter Eight

1. Archivo General de Indias, and Irene Aloha Wright, *Further English Voyages to Spanish America, 1583-1594: Documents From the Archives of the Indies At Seville Illustrating English Voyages to the Caribbean, the Spanish Main, Florida, and Virginia* (London: Printed for the Hakluyt Society, 1951), 237–241.

2. Richard Hakluyt, Leonard Woods, and Charles Deane, *A Discourse Concerning Western Planting* (Cambridge, MA: Press of J. Wilson, 1877).

3. "Simon Fernandez ... the person who induced them to settle there." Archivo General de Indias, and Irene Aloha Wright, *Further English Voyages to Spanish America, 1583-1594: Documents From the Archives of the Indies At Seville Illustrating English Voyages to the Caribbean, the Spanish Main, Florida, and Virginia* (London: Printed for the Hakluyt Society, 1951), 237–241

4. Further information on the project is available online at www.ucl.ac.uk/news/news-articles/0601/06011801

5. Great Britain. Public Record Office, and Mary Anne Everett Green. *Calendar of State Papers, Domestic Series, of the Reigns of Elizabeth and James I: Addenda, 1580-1625, Preserved in Her Majesty's Public Record Office* (London: Longman and Trübner, 1872), 176–177.

6. Transcribed Richard Hakluyt, *The Principall Nauigations, Voiages and Discoueries of the English Nation: Made By Sea or Ouer Land, to the Most Remote and Farthest Distant Quarters of the Earth At Any Time Within the Compasse of These 1500. Yeeres: Deuided Into Three Seuerall Parts, According to the Positions of the Regions Wherunto They Were Directed. ... Whereunto Is Added the Last Most Renowmed English Nauigation, Round About the Whole Globe of the Earth. By Richard Hakluyt Master of Artes, and Student Sometime of Christchurch in Oxford.* Imprinted at London: By George Bishop and Ralph Newberie, deputies to Christopher Barker, printer to the Queenes most excellent Maiestie, 1589, 770–771.

7. James P. P. Horn, *A Kingdom Strange: The Brief and Tragic History of the Lost Colony of Roanoke* (New York: Basic Books, 2010), 126.

8. Grant of Arms to the Cittie of Ralegh, College of Arms MS Vincent, vol. 157, folio 397, Determined from a copy made after 1660 by John Vincent, Queens College, Oxford; MS137, No. 120, P1.

9. Report to the National Park Service of America in a letter dated 23rd June 1987, titled "John White of Roanoke" (from the archives held at NPS Fort Raleigh); also, Royal College of Arms ms E15 (Visitation of Cornwall 1573–4), folio 43/44, and Private correspondence Dr. Kim Sloan / Clive Cheesman, Richmond Herald, Royal College of Arms.

10. National Archives, Prerogative Court of Canterbury PROB 11/68/363.

11. PCC Probate 6, Administration Act Books 1559-1858 (entry for May 22, 1606).

12. Peter Cunningham, and J. O. Halliwell-Phillipps. *Revels At Court: Being Extracts From the Revels Accounts of the Reigns of Queen Elizabeth and James I* (London: Printed for the Shakespeare Society, 1853).

13. PCC PROB 11/69 June 25, 1586.

14. Archivo General de Indias, and Irene Aloha Wright, *Further English Voyages to Spanish America, 1583-1594: Documents From the Archives of the Indies At Seville Illustrating English Voyages to the Caribbean, the Spanish Main, Florida, and Virginia* (London: Printed for the Hakluyt Society, 1951), 237–241.

Chapter Nine

1. Hakluyt wrote at the beginning of his transcript that Raleigh was sailing with 150 Colonists.

2. The Isle of Wight lies a few miles offshore from Portsmouth.

3. The "Bay of Portingall" (Portugal) does not exist. In Shakespeare's play *As You Like It* (act 4 scene 1), Rosalind, speaking to Celia of her love for Orlando, says, "But it cannot be sounded: my affection hath an unknown bottom, like the bay of Portugal." The suggestion therefore is that the English used the term to mock the Portuguese for their pretentious claim to the Atlantic Ocean.

4. "Santa Cruz"—Saint Croix, U.S. Virgin Islands.

5. There were only two women on the voyage with children, therefore the unfortunate victims were either Joyce Archard and her son Thomas, or Elizabeth Viccars and her son Ambrose.

6. Two fruits could be attributed to this description but since one of them is deadly, it is likely the colonists tried to eat unripe black sapote fruit, which can yield these symptoms.

7. "Torteses"—probably meaning sea turtles.

8. Given the area's oil deposits, it is possible that the water the colonists drank was contaminated with crude oil derivatives seeping through from the substrate below. This would explain the symptoms reported.

9. "Guiacum"—or more correctly "guaiacum," is the lignum vitae tree, probably known to the English via the Spanish as a source of treatment for syphilis, a condition widespread in Europe at the time. (Source: OED)

10. "S. Johns"—Meaning Puerto Rico. The island was originally named by Christopher Columbus in honor of Saint John the Baptist.

11. "Musketas Bay"—Mosquito Bay.

12. There is a fascinating fragment of Darby Glande's (or Glaven) life following his stranding. It is contained in Fray Luis Geronimo de Ore's book *Relacion de los Martires que ha habido en Florida*, written in 1604. It records that after his capture, Glande became a Spanish galley slave before being transferred to St Augustine in 1595. He was a soldier at St. Augustine from 1595 until at least 1600. (Taken from Geiger Maynard, *Franciscan Studies* No.18, Joseph F. Wagner Inc., July 1936, 49)

13. "Plantonos"—plantains

14. This reference to some of the planters having previous knowledge of the island confirms that several of them must have travelled either as part of the military colony of 1585, or possibly as members of Grenville's 1586 relief voyage. St. Germans is recorded in the margin of the original text as being "A pleasant and fruitful Country, lying on the west end of S. Johns Island where grows plenty of Oranges, Lemons, Plantains and Pines."

15. "Two cables length"—a cable's length was traditionally the length of an anchor chain (or rope), equivalent to about six hundred feet. Thus the ships came within about twelve hundred feet of the shore.

16. John White clearly knew that Grenville had left these men on Roanoke and so must have met with Grenville sometime between 26 December 1586 (Grenville's return from his voyage that year) and 26 April 1587, when John White departed on this voyage.

17. This is confirmation that Roanoke was not the intended location for Raleigh's "Cittie of Ralegh."

18. "Rased downe"—meaning that the palisade of the fort had been razed (burned) to the ground but the houses remained intact.

19. This comment infers that Hatteras Island was not a seasonal habitation as has been suggested.

20. This statement indicates there were thirteen survivors from Grenville's original fifteen left on Roanoke in 1586.

21. "Pompions"—meaning pumpkins or squashes

22. "Master Stafford"—Captain Edward Stafford, who had previously travelled to Roanoke with Grenville in 1585 and remained as part of Ralph Lane's Military Colony.

23. "Elenora"—recorded as "Elinor" in the Parish records for her birth and later marriage.

24. "Virginia"—the christening took place on Sunday August 23, 1587.

25. This makes it clear that John White must have canvassed some of the colonists to join him on this voyage to settle America.

26. The colonists had obviously been discussing relocation. Given the knowledge they had gained of the area, thanks largely to Lane's voyages of exploration on which some of the colonists travelled in 1585, they would have known that Chesapeake Bay, the original intended location, was around 100 miles distant. Fifty miles would have only taken them as far north as present-day Currituck, close to the border with Virginia, or towards Avoca, a small area to the northwest.

27. This apparent accusation of theft suggests that at least some of the colonists may not have been entirely trustworthy. Alternatively, White could have been mistaken. It is possible that the Native Americans friendly to Wanchese were responsible for the pilfering of White's possessions.

28. "Both the shippes"—there is no further reference in any documentation relating to Roanoke of Master Edward Stafford or the pinnace he commanded. If they, too, stayed at Roanoke, the remains of that ship lie undiscovered, and Edward Stafford and his crew also became lost colonists.

29. "...Coruo (Corvo) and sawe Flores"—islands in the Azores.

30. "Hampton"—some sources state that this is Littlehampton, a small port on the Sussex coast, but they are mistaken. "Hampton" is more correctly identified as the modern day port and town of Southampton. Littlehampton and Southampton were once both known as Hampton but the former changed its name to Littlehampton in 1492, signifying its much smaller size. "Hampton" rather ironically also

renamed itself, to Southampton, barely a century later.

31. "Dingen cushe"—White first landed at Smewicke (Smerwick) and declared "Dingen Cushe" was "five myles distant." Therefore, it seems certain that "Dingen Cushe" refers to the harbor or port town of Dingle, Ireland.

32. "lands end"—the most southwesterly point of the British Isles.

33. "Severne"—this is a reference to the River Severn, which empties into the modern-day Bristol Channel. In the sixteenth century this substantial channel was still referred to as the Severn Estuary. Since White's ship "doubled," we can deduce that instead of heading northeast for this channel, the ship returned south and head along the English Channel.

34. "Martasew"—a corruption of "Marghasyew," the Cornish name for the village of Marazion, near Penzance on the south coast of Cornwall.

35. This account was transcribed from Richard Hakluyt, *The Principall Nauigations, Voiages and Discoueries of the English Nation*, 1589, 764–771.

36. Who "Towaye" was is unknown. It is unlikely to have been "Wanchese" as he appears to have stayed on Roanoke in 1585 to lead the Indians against the English. Another candidate is "Rawly," the Indian captured by Grenville in 1586 and finally buried in Bideford. However, Parish Records confirm his death at Bideford in 1589. It seems therefore that "Towaye" must have been another Croatoan Indian, possibly acting as Manteo's servant.

Chapter Ten

1. Diaz defines these colonists as amounting only to "seven men and four women." Archivo General de Indias, and Irene Aloha Wright, *Further English Voyages to Spanish America, 1583–1594*, 237–241.

2. "In the Countrey"—meaning in the country of Virginia.

3. John Pine (Engraver), "The Tapestry Hangings of the House of Lords, representing the several engagements between the English and Spanish fleets in the ever memorable year MDLXXXVIII" (1588), John Pine, London 1739, 9–11

4. "the English commander made ready two small vessels ... for the said settlement with supplies for them of biscuit, meat and vegetables, with which cargo he sent these vessels out in command of Captain Amadas with Pedro Diaz as pilot." Archivo General de Indias, and Irene Aloha Wright, *Further English Voyages to Spanish America, 1583–1594*, 237–241; in the Blanchminster Charity records, a John Henders was asked (and given one shilling for his troubles) "to run to Bideford with post letters to Sir Richard Greynvile that came from sessions." Stratton, and Richard William Goulding. *Records of the Charity Known As Blanchminster's Charity, With Intr. and Notes Compiled By R.W. Goulding*. Louth &c, 1898, 73. Held at the Cornwall Records Office: P 216/25/268/2

5. "Cornewal"—Cornwall

6. The "isle of Lundy" lies twenty miles off the coast from Bideford. At this date, Grenville owned the island. Its strategic position guarding the entrance to the Bristol Channel would not have been lost on him; perhaps the unusual layover at Lundy was to allow messages to be passed to the island commanders to prepare for the defense of the Channel.

7. The Scottish and Breton ships represented enemies to England at the time.

8. "clap us aboord"—meaning to use grappling irons by which to board the ship.

9. "Flushing bound for Barbarie"—Flushing is a seaport of The Netherlands (now called Vlissingen); "Barbarie" meaning the coast of Africa from Morocco to Libya, an area notoriously linked with the slave trade. We can therefore deduce that this Dutch ship was probably a slave trader.

10. "Gave us a Piece"—meaning fired a shot. The English response of "two pieces" suggests this was a mutual exchange to note a truce.

11. "Cape Finister"—the most westerly point of France.

12. "to the weather of us"—meaning "to be behind."

13. "to the wind of us"—meaning "to be in front."

14. "ken"—used in this context, meaning "to see."

15. The *Roe* realizing she was fighting alone left the quarry to re-join the *Brave*.

16. "Rochel"—(La) Rochelle is a port of France on the Bay of Biscay.

17. "amayne"—meaning "in a forceful manner."

18. "Pestred with cabbens"—meaning uncertain. The inference is that the author of the

account (John White) thought the ship was so full of cabins that it made it hard to fight effectively with a sword.

19. "Isle de Mayo"—part of the Cape Verde islands.

20. Archivo General de Indias, and Irene Aloha Wright, *Further English Voyages to Spanish America, 1583–1594*, 237–241

21. Meaning that the ship stayed as far offshore as possible in the hope of avoiding being spotted.

22. "Harting point"—Hartland Point, a promontory some fifteen miles west of Bideford.

23. "Chavell Key"—Clovelly Quay, a small village and harbor some ten miles from Bideford.

24. Transcribed from Richard Hakluyt, *The Principall Nauigations, Voiages and Discoueries of the English Nation*, 1589, 771–773.

Chapter Eleven

1. "Shallop"—a small open boat usually fitted out with oars and one or two masts.

2. "Ile of Mogador"—a small island in the harbor of Essaouira, Morocco. (Essaouira was formerly called Mogador.)

3. "Virgines"—Virgin Islands.

4. "Pedro a Mollato"—More correctly "mulatto"; meaning he was of mixed race. He was a member of the crew of the *Hopewell*.

5. "Cape Tyburon"—the westernmost point of modern day Haiti.

6. "Cape St Anthony"—the westernmost point of Cuba.

7. "Cannafistula"—from the Spanish word for a cassia tree, the bark of which had medicinal value.

8. "the Martires"—today known as the Florida Keys.

9. "disbocked"—possibly from the Spanish word "desbocar"—to be caught up or swept along (in this case as in a strong wind).

10. 35 degrees latitude would bring the ships to the northern tip of Portsmouth Island, which lies to the west of Ocracoke (Wokokon). This therefore is either a description of their landing on Portsmouth Island or possibly the southern tip of Ocracoke.

11. The latitude quoted places this breach just north of modern-day Rodanthe on the island of Hatteras. The detailed soundings taken prior to passing over the breach are de-

scribing the false cape also known today as "Whimble Shoals."

12. "Kindrikers Mountes"—"kindrick" is the English translation of the Celtic word for a high hill; possibly also from the Welsh word "Cynwrig," which means the same thing. Quinn determines the location as the sand dunes that may have existed by Wimble Shoals, an area of dangerous shallows lying offshore near the town of Rodanthe. While, John Lawson confuses matters by referencing a ridge he calls "Kindricks" on his map of 1701, along the southern shore of the Chowan River, by its entrance to the Albemarle Sound. The author believes that the correct location is Jockey's Ridge State Park, an area of sand dunes near the modern-day town of Nags Head. The dunes at this location, according to scientists, are over 7,000 years old and therefore would certainly have been present at the time of White's voyage.

13. "Hance the Surgion"—the same Haunce Walters of the 1585 voyage.

14. It is possible that the fire seen was no more than a natural wildfire.

15. 1586 is an error. The date should read 1587.

16. "50 miles into the main"—A comment debated by many lost colony theorists who believe that the colonists planned to move inland to a site previously surveyed by Ralph Lane in 1585, and not to Croatoan (Hatteras) Island as evidence suggests.

17. "Cortynes"—defensive slots for looking or firing through.

18. Surely confirmation that Edward Stafford and his pinesse remained at Roanoke in 1587?

19. "two yeeres past" would suggest the year 1588. In that year Amadas was captain of the *Roe*. However, the account of that year states that the *Brave* and the *Roe* arrived back at Bideford without having relieved the colony. Therefore the correct interpretation is that Amadas was a member of the 1587 voyage even though his name is not recorded as a captain of any of the vessels, or referred to in any of White's narrative from that voyage. John White therefore means three years past.

20. This last sentence is confirmation from John White that he was convinced the message "CROATOAN" left by his colonists was confirmation of their relocation to the modern day island of Hatteras.

21. Perhaps Bodie Island?

22. "accompted of"—"accounted for." www.shakespeareswords.com.

23. "atry"—nautical term "to lie a-try" meaning "to point the bow of the ship into the wind."

24. Not to be confused with the *Mary Rose*, flagship of King Henry VIII's fleet, which sunk so catastrophically in 1545 with Sir Richard Grenville's father on board, but another ship named in its honor by Queen Elizabeth I.

25. "Gratiosa"—Graciosa, an island in the Azores.

26. These opening words confirm that this letter was included with John White's account of the 1590 voyage when delivered to Hakluyt three years after the event.

27. This John Wattes could be Sir John Watts, who was master of the Clothworkers' Company in 1594 and knighted in 1603 before finally becoming Lord Mayor of London in 1606-7. He died in 1616 (*Stow's Survey of London*: volume 8: Shoreditch 5–14).

28. From this discourse, it is evident that the voyage was intended to take more colonists to Roanoke, as well as supplies. Yet, in reality it appears to have been used as a cover for what, in essence, were the piratical activities of its financial backers.

29. "forwardly"—early, prematurely Source: www.shakespeareswords.com.

30. Transcribed from Richard Hakluyt, *The Principal Navigations, Voyages, Traffiques and Discoveries of the English Nation: Made By Sea or Overland, to the Remote and Farthest Distant Quarters of the Earth, At Any Time Within the Compasse of These 1600 Yeres: Divided Into Three Severall Volumes According to the Positions of the Regions Whereunto They Were Directed* ... Imprinted at London: By George Bishop, Ralph Newberie and Robert Barker, 1600, 287–295

Chapter Twelve

1. David B. Quinn, *Set Fair for Roanoke: Voyages and Colonies, 1584-1606* (Chapel Hill: Published for America's Four Hundredth Anniversary Committee by the University of North Carolina Press, 1985), 441.

2. Archivo General de Indias, and Irene Aloha Wright, *Further English Voyages to Spanish America, 1583-1594*, 9.

Chapter Thirteen

1. Account taken from the following: A.L. Rowse, *Sir Richard Grenville of the Revenge*:

An Elizabethan Hero (London: Jonathan Cape, 1937); Roger Granville, *The History of the Granville Family: Traced Back to Rollo, First Duke of Normandy. With Pedigrees, Etc.* Exeter: W. Pollard & Co., 1895; Edmund Goldsmid,. *The Last Fight of the Revenge: And the Death of Sir Richard Grenville. (A.D. 1591) Related by Sir Walter Raleigh, Sir Richard Hawkins, Jan Huygen Van Linschoten, Lord Bacon, And Sir W. Monson. Together With the Most Honorable Tragedie of Sir Richard Grinuile, Knight.* By Gervase Markham (1595). Edinburgh: Priv. print, 1886; Cesáreo Fernández Duro (1898). "Armada Española desde la unión de los reinos de Castilla y Aragón." Published in English and Spanish by Nabu Press, 2011.

2. Wallace W.A. "The Durham Thomas Harriot Seminar Occasional Paper No. 2

3. National Library of Ireland; Collection List 129 Lismore Castle Papers, MS 22,068— Manuscript estate map of Sir Walter Raleigh's estate at Mogeely, Co. Cork 1598.

4. National Library of Ireland; Collection List 129 Lismore Castle Papers MS 43,270

5. National Library of Ireland; Collection List 129 Lismore Castle Papers, MS43,304/3— Acquittances for rents, debts, and miscellaneous financial transactions between Sir Richard Boyle and various persons, comprising acquittances from John White to Sir Richard Boyle. 31st Jan & 7th Mar 1606/7.

6. W. Maziere Brady, *Clerical and Parochial Records of Cork, Cloyne, and Ross: Taken From Diocesan and Parish Registries, Mss. in the Principal Libraries and Public Offices of Oxford, Dublin, and London, and From Private or Family Papers.* London: Longman, Green, Longman, Roberts, and Green, 1864. 48

7. Luis Jerónimo de Oré, and Maynard J. Geiger. *The Martyrs of Florida (1513–1616).* New York: J.F. Wagner. 1936, 47–49.

8. David B. Quinn, *Set Fair for Roanoke: Voyages and Colonies, 1584-1606* (Chapel Hill: Published for America's Four Hundredth Anniversary Committee by the University of North Carolina Press, 1985), 275.

9. Luis Jerónimo de Oré, and Maynard J. Geiger. *The Martyrs of Florida (1513-1616).* New York: J.F. Wagner. 1936, 62.

10. Samuel Purchas, and Early English Books Online, *Purchas His Pilgrimes: In Fiue Bookes. The First, Contayning the Voyages and Peregrinations Made By Ancient Kings, Patriarkes, Apostles, Philosophers, and Others, to*

and Thorow the Remoter Parts of the Knowne World: Enquiries Also of Languages and Religions, Especially of the Moderne Diuersified Professions of Christianitie. The Second, a Description of All the Circum-nauigations of the Globe. The Third, Nauigations and Voyages of English-men, Alongst the Coasts of Africa ... The Fourth, English Voyages Beyond the East Indies, to the Ilands of Iapan, China, Cauchinchina, the Philippinæ With Others ... The Fifth, Nauigations, Voyages, Traffiques, Discoueries, of the English Nation in the Easterne Parts of the World ... The First Part.* London: Printed by William Stansby for Henrie Fetherstone, and are to be sold at his shop in Pauls Church-yard at the signe of the Rose, 1625, 1646–1647

11. Virginia Company of London. *The Records of the Virginia Company of London: the Court Book, From the Manuscript in the Library of Congress.* Washington, D. C.: Government Printing Office, 1906, 37.

12. Fullam, Brandon. "The Slaughter at Roanoke" Parts 1, 2, 3. Research paper, revised 2014.

13. William Strachey, and Richard Henry Major. *The Historie of Travaile Into Virginia Britannia: Expressing the Cosmographie and Comodities of the Country, Togither With the Manners and Customes of the People.* London: Printed for the Hakluyt Society, 1899, 83.

Chapter Fourteen

1. John Lawson, et al. *A New Voyage to Carolina: Containing the Exact Description and Natural History of That Country; Together With the Present State Thereof; and a Journal of a Thousand Miles, Travel'd Thro' Several Nations of Indians, Giving a Particular Account of Their Customs, Manners, Etc.* London: Printed, 1709. 62

2. A story related to the author, not authenticated. Reputedly, the letter is contained in the North Carolina Colonial Archive.

3. Roberta Estes, et al., "Melungeons: a Multi-Ethnic Population," *Journal of Genetic Genealogy*, April 2012.

4. David B Quinn, *Set Fair for Roanoke: Voyages and Colonies, 1584–1606* (Chapel Hill: Published for America's Four Hundredth Anniversary Committee by the University of North Carolina Press, 1985), 255, 286. N.b.: Others have perpetuated this misconception.

5. Prerogative Court of Canterbury,

Index to Acts of Administrations, 1596–1608, June 1597, 213.

6. Confirmation of the Eno merger into the Catawba nation is discussed in Steven G. Baker, "The Historic Catawba Peoples: Exploratory Perspectives in Ethnohistory and Archaeology." Prepared for Duke Power Company and other sponsors of Institutional Grant J-100. Office of Research, University of South Carolina, 1975.

Chapter Fifteen

1. John Lawson, et al. *A New Voyage to Carolina: Containing the Exact Description and Natural History of That Country; Together With the Present State Thereof; and a Journal of a Thousand Miles, Travel'd Thro" Several Nations of Indians, Giving a Particular Account of Their Customs, Manners, Etc.* (London, 1709), 62.

2. Quoted by Charles W. Porter, "Fort Raleigh National Historic Site, North Carolina," *North Carolina Historical Review* (1952), vol. 20, no. 1.

3. Bruce, Edward C; "Lounging in the footsteps of the pioneers" *Harpers New Monthly Magazine* vol. 20, no. 120, p733–735.

4. *Ibid.*

5. Harrington, J. C.; "Search for the Cittie of Ralegh: archaeological excavations at Fort Raleigh National Historic site, North Carolina. National Park Service 1962.

6. Hume, Ivor Noel; "Fort Raleigh National Historical Site, 1991 Archaeological Investigation, Phase II Interim report." Submitted to SEAC December 1991.

7. Examination of patches on a map of the E coast of America by John White ("La Virginea Pars"; 1906,0509.1.3) Department of Conservation and Scientific Research (British Museum) CSR Analytical Request No. AR2012–21

8. Direct observation and research by the author.

Chapter Sixteen

1. Ch. Kingsley, *Westward Ho! Or, The Voyages and Adventures of Sir Anyas Leigh, Knight, of Burrough, in the County of Devon, in the Reign of Her Most Glorious Majesty Queen Elizabeth: Rendered Into Modern English.* London, 2016.

Chapter Seventeen

1. Great Britain. Public Record Office., William Noel Sainsbury, J. W. Sir Fortescue, Cecil Headlam, and Arthur Percival Newton. Calendar of State Papers, Colonial Series. London, 1860, 3–4

2. Edward Arber, Walter Raleigh, Gervase Markham, and Jan Huygen van Linschoten. *The Last Fight of the Revenge at Sea: Under the Command of Sir Richard Grenville On the 10– 11th of Sept., 1591*. London, 1871.

3. Edmund Goldsmid, *The Last Fight of the Revenge: And the Death of Sir Richard Grenville. (A.D. 1591) Related by Sir Walter Raleigh, Sir Richard Hawkins, Jan Huygen Van Linschoten, Lord Bacon, And Sir W. Monson. Together With the Most Honorable Tragedie of Sir Richard Grinuile, Knight. By Gervase Markham* (1595). Edinburgh: Priv. print, 1886.

4. Richard Hawkins, and C. R. Drinkwater Bethune, *The Observations of Sir Richard Hawkins, Knight in His Voyage Into the South Sea in the Year 1593: Reprinted From the Edition of 1622* (London: Printed for the Hakluyt Society, 1847) 20.

5. David B. Quinn, *Set Fair for Roanoke: Voyages and Colonies, 1584–1606* (Chapel Hill: Published for America's Four Hundredth Anniversary Committee by the University of North Carolina Press, 1985), 351.

Bibliography

Archivo General de Indias, and Irene Aloha Wright. *Further English Voyages to Spanish America, 1583–1594: Documents From the Archives of the Indies At Seville Illustrating English Voyages to the Caribbean, the Spanish Main, Florida, and Virginia.* London: Printed for the Hakluyt Society, 1951.

Drake, Francis, and Mary Frear Keeler. *Sir Francis Drake's West Indian Voyage 1585–1586.* London: Hakluyt Society, 1981.

Frankenberg, Dirk. *The Nature of the Outer Banks: Environmental Processes, Field Sites, and Development Issues, Corolla to Ocracoke.* Chapel Hill: University of North Carolina Press, 1995.

Granville, Roger. *The History of the Granville Family: Traced Back to Rollo, First Duke of Normandy. With Pedigrees, Etc.* Exeter: W. Pollard & Co., 1895.

Hakluyt, Richard. *The Principal Navigations, Voyages, Traffiques and Discoveries of the English Nation: Made By Sea or Overland, to the Remote and Farthest Distant Quarters of the Earth, At Any Time Within the Compasse of These 1600 Yeres: Divided Into Three Severall Volumes According to the Positions of the Regions Whereunto They Were Directed ...* Imprinted at London: By George Bishop, Ralph Newberie and Robert Barker, 1600.

_____. *The Principall Nauigations, Voiages and Discoueries of the English Nation: Made By Sea or Ouer Land, to the Most Remote and Farthest Distant Quarters of the Earth At Any Time Within the Compasse of These 1500. Yeeres: Deuided Into Three Seuerall Parts, According to the Positions of the Regions Wherunto They Were Directed. ... Whereunto Is Added the Last Most Renowmed English Nauigation, Round About the Whole Globe of the Earth. By Richard Hakluyt Master of Artes, and Student Sometime of Christchurch in Oxford.* Imprinted at London: By George Bishop and Ralph Newberie, deputies to Christopher Barker, printer to the Queenes most excellent Maiestie, 1589.

_____, Leonard Woods, and Charles Deane. *A Discourse Concerning Western Planting.* Cambridge, MA: Press of J. Wilson, 1877.

Hawkins, Richard, and C. R. Drinkwater Bethune. *The Observations of Sir Richard Hawkins, Knight in His Voyage Into the South Sea in the Year 1593: Reprinted From the Edition of 1622.* London: Printed for the Hakluyt Society, 1847 (1st Series).

Horn, James P. P. *A Kingdom Strange: The Brief and Tragic History of the Lost Colony of Roanoke.* New York: Basic Books, 2010.

Kupperman, Karen Ordahl. *Roanoke, the Abandoned Colony.* Totowa, NJ: Rowman & Allanheld, 1984.

Lawson, John, et al. *A New Voyage to Carolina: Containing the Exact Description and Natural History of That Country; Together With the Present State Thereof; and a Journal of a Thousand Miles, Travel'd Thro' Several Nations of Indians, Giving a Particular Account of Their Customs, Manners, Etc.* London: N.p., 1709.

Oberg, Michael Leroy. *The Head in Edward Nugent's Hand: Roanoke's Forgotten Indians.* Philadelphia: University of Pennsylvania Press, 2008.

de Oré, Luis Jerónimo, and Maynard J. Geiger. *The Martyrs of Florida (1513–1616)*. New York: J.F. Wagner, 1936.

Purchas, Samuel, and Early English Books Online. *Purchas His Pilgrimes: In Fiue Bookes. The First, Contayning the Voyages and Peregrinations Made By Ancient Kings, Patriarkes, Apostles, Philosophers, and Others, to and Thorow the Remoter Parts of the Knowne World: Enquiries Also of Languages and Religions, Especially of the Moderne Diuersified Professions of Christianitie. The Second, a Description of All the Circum-nauigations of the Globe. The Third, Nauigations and Voyages of English-men, Alongst the Coasts of Africa ... The Fourth, English Voyages Beyond the East Indies, to the Ilands of Iapan, China, Cauchinchina, the Philippinæ With Others ... The Fifth, Nauigations, Voyages, Traffiques, Discoueries, of the English Nation in the Easterne Parts of the World ... The First Part*. London: Printed by William Stansby for Henrie Fetherstone, and are to be sold at his shop in Pauls Churchyard at the signe of the Rose, 1625.

Quinn, David Beers. *The Roanoke Voyages, 1584–1590: Documents to Illustrate the English Voyages to North America Under the Patent Granted to Walter Raleigh in 1584*. London: Hakluyt Society, 1955

_____. *Set Fair for Roanoke: Voyages and Colonies, 1584–1606*. Chapel Hill: Published for America's Four Hundredth Anniversary Committee by the University of North Carolina Press, 1985.

Rowse, A.L. *Sir Richard Grenville of the Revenge: An Elizabethan Hero*. London: Jonathan Cape, 1937.

Sloan, Dr. Kim. *A New World, England's First View of America*. London: The British Museum Press, 2007.

Stick, David. *The Outer Banks of North Carolina, 1584–1958*. Chapel Hill: University of North Carolina Press.

Strachey, William, and Richard Henry Major. *The Historie of Travaile Into Virginia Britannia: Expressing the Cosmographie and Comodities of the Country, Togither With the Manners and Customes of the People*. London: Printed for the Hakluyt Society, 1899.

White, John, P. H. Hulton, and the British Museum. *America, 1585: The Complete Drawings of John White*. Chapel Hill: University of North Carolina Press, 1984.

Index

Numbers in *bold italics* refer to pages with photographs.